Too Happy A Face

Andrew Ross was born in Bishop Auckland in County Durham. He moved to Australia with his parents as a child and later graduated from the University of Western Sydney where he obtained a Bachelor of Arts Degree in History.

Andrew went on to become an established media researcher and his study of film and television has earned him credits in *Halliwell's Filmgoer's Companion* (1997) and *Halliwell's Who's Who in the Movies* (1999 and 2001). He is the author of *Carry On Actors – The Complete Who's Who of the Carry On Film Series* (2011) and has also compiled a number of quiz books.

Andrew returned to England in 2003. Recently he has been a guest on more than a dozen radio programmes, including BBC Radio Five Live (*The Nicky Campbell Show*, with Fenella Fielding), and featured in the Channel 5 television documentary *The Greatest Ever Carry On Films*.

Too Happy A Face

The authorised biography of

Joan Sims

Andrew Ross

Foreword by Sherrie Hewson
Introduction by Eleanor Fazan OBE

fantom
publishing

First published in hardback 2014 by Fantom Films
Reprinted in paperback 2017
fantomfilms.co.uk

A catalogue record for this book is available from the British Library.

Hardback ISBN: 978-1-78196-121-6
Paperback ISBN: 978-1-78196-269-5

Typeset by Phil Reynolds Media Services, Leamington Spa
Printed and bound by CPI Group (UK) Ltd, Croydon, CR0 4YY

All photographs not specifically credited are courtesy of the estate of
the late Joan Sims.

For Pat Clayfield, with my deepest thanks

Contents

Acknowledgements

I WOULD LIKE TO THANK the following actors, agents, authors, individuals and agencies for their responses and help:

Stephen Atkinson (Rex Features), Samantha Blake (BBC Written Archives), Barry Burnett, Norma Farnes, John Foster (archivist), Richard Hatton Management (Mrs Elizabeth Hatton), Gillian Hewitt, Georgy Jamieson, Sue Jennings (PA to Dame Judi Dench), Bo Keller (Mahoney Bannon Associates), Ged Kivlehan, Laindon & District Community Archive, Virginia McKenna CBE, Mahoney Gretton Associates (MGA), Andy Merriman, Simon Rook (BBC Archives), Oliver Stockman (Sands Films), Becky Stevenson (PA to Dame Cleo Laine), James Thornton (RADA Archives), Westminster City Council.

Special thanks

I am greatly indebted to the following individuals for taking the time to share with me their memories of Joan Sims:

Renée Asherson, Gyles Brandreth, Ray Brooks, Judy Buxton, Darren Carey (The Joan Sims Appreciation Society), Paul Chapman, Pat Clayfield, George Cole OBE, Bruce Copp, Sir Tom Courtenay, Alan Curtis, Dame Judi Dench, Paola Dionisotti, Angela Douglas, Yvonne Doyle, Eleanor Fazan OBE, Fenella Fielding, Nicholas Ferguson, Tim Goodchild, the late Richard Griffiths OBE, Joe Grossi, Anita Harris, Julie Harris, Elizabeth Hatton, Sherrie Hewson, Dr Arnold Kalina, Anna Karen, the late Sam Kelly, David Kernan, the late Bob Larbey, the late Dilys Laye, Ernest Maxin, the late Frank Middlemass, Joan Le Mesurier, the late Jimmy Logan OBE, Don McCorkindale, Gillies MacKinnon, Sean Magee, Ron Moody, Margaret Nolan, Christine Ozanne, Geoffrey Palmer OBE, Nicholas Parsons OBE, Leslie Phillips CBE, Stephanie Powers, John Quayle, Lord Rix (Brian Rix), the late Peter Rogers, Thelma Ruby, the late Sir Donald Sinden, Audrey Skinner, the late Elizabeth Spriggs, Sheila

ix

Acknowledgements

Steafel, Una Stubbs, Sylvia Syms OBE, Angela Thorne, Gudrun Ure, June Whitfield CBE, Barbara Windsor MBE, Victoria Wood CBE.

This book would have been impossible to write without the invaluable assistance of those closest to Joan, namely her cousin Yvonne Doyle and her lifelong friends Eleanor Fazan and Pat Clayfield. I am grateful to all three ladies – to Pat for her immense enthusiasm and hospitality (without her insight I would not have attempted to write a biography of Joan), to Yvonne for her kindness and for authorising the book (which means more to me than I can ever say) and to Eleanor for her memories, encouragement and superb introduction.

I owe thanks, once again, to my dear friend Fenella Fielding not only for her generous recollections of Joan but also for putting me in touch with other contemporaries.

I am very grateful to Barbara Windsor for taking time out of her busy schedule to talk to me about her old 'china' and to Scott Mitchell (Barbara's husband and manager) for helping to arrange this. Likewise, I would like to thank Barbara for granting formal permission to quote from her autobiography.

Many of Joan's other friends and colleagues also took the time to speak with me at length among whom I am particularly obliged to Bruce Copp, Sir Tom Courtenay, Nicholas Ferguson, Joan Le Mesurier and Geoffrey Palmer for their varied and insightful reminiscences.

Special thanks go to Sherrie Hewson who agreed without hesitation to write the foreword to my book. I could not have asked for a more sincere and heartfelt contribution.

Finally, I would like to thank my family and friends, and especially my parents, for their continued support which is much appreciated.

Preface

JOAN SIMS FIRST CAME TO MY ATTENTION when I was a child. I still clearly remember watching her brilliant performance as Lady Fox Custard in the BBC television series, *Simon and the Witch*. Aptly, at around the same time, the *Carry On* series of films began to be released on VHS for home viewing. *Carry On Abroad* and *Carry On Camping* became the first in my collection and have remained favourites – thanks mainly to Joan's starring performances. By the time I reached my teens I was an ardent fan of Joan Sims and have remained so ever since.

I first wrote to Joan at the end of 1996 and was delighted to receive in reply my first ever autograph – a personally signed photograph – and a copy of her résumé of work. It is fair to say this first piece of correspondence provided the inspiration for me to write to other *Carry On* actors, ultimately leading to my first book, *Carry On Actors – The Complete Who's Who of the Carry On Film Series* (2011).

Over the years, both in England and Australia, I avidly looked out for Joan's television appearances and became a devoted fan of the 'Queen of the *Carry Ons*'. Few of her appearances escaped my attention, each savoured until her last ever role as Betty in *The Last of the Blonde Bombshells*.

I wrote to Joan again in August 2000 after reading her autobiography and sent her a photograph taken during the filming of *Farrington of the F.O.* I duly received a reply, thanking me for writing and for buying her book and the photograph was returned, signed by Joan with her best wishes.

When Joan Sims died in 2001 I was truly saddened. She had been a part of my life, albeit through her film and television performances, for many years. In more recent years, as I have researched and written this book, Joan has been a part of my daily life.

It was Joan's co-star, the charming leading actor Geoffrey Palmer, who said to me in discussion, 'You've got a difficult book to write, haven't you?' His sentiments were echoed by director Nicholas Ferguson who thought Joan to be 'a complicated person to write about'. Both gentlemen were of course referring to the complex nature of Joan's personality – the fine line between her on-screen and off-screen personas and finding the right 'balance' in summing up one of Britain's best-known stars. Her biography could never be a glitzy Hollywood story; indeed one of her friends and colleagues felt almost unable to contribute to this biography since Joan's loneliness and 'heavy drinking' made for 'too sad a story'. Joan certainly had her fair share of demons and during her lifetime was very honest about them. Equally, she had much happiness in her life – and brought laughter to millions of people around the world. The laughter of course carries on and I for one continue to delight in her performances.

On a practical level Joan was an extremely shy and private person and despite an acting career spanning some fifty years she hardly ever gave interviews. Equally, unlike many of her contemporaries, she was not a great letter-writer and the diaries she kept were deemed 'too personal' ever to be seen and subsequently destroyed after her death. Joan admitted in her autobiography that she had not chronicled her career and it seems that much of the theatre memorabilia she had amassed relating to her early work was 'culled' during her move from Hurlingham Road in 1980. Therefore relatively little material is in existence to help build up an accurate picture of the actress and the person.

I am therefore grateful to Joan's estate for allowing me full access to the archive material she left behind, including letters, newspaper clippings and photographs. With a distinct lack of primary evidence I have relied heavily upon Joan's surviving friends and colleagues for their thoughts and memories of the lady I have admired for so long, and have attempted to include as many as possible. While many of Joan's personal anecdotes are contained in her autobiography, I hope that *Too Happy A Face* will provide added insight into her life and career and the strength of spirit which allowed this great actress to delight audiences for so long.

Andrew Ross, 2014

Foreword

I HAVE MANY PEOPLE TO THANK IN MY CAREER, none more than the truly wonderful Joan Sims. She was a joy to be with and an exceptional talent to watch.

My first job from RADA was in *Carry On Behind*. Not only was I working with Joan, I was actually living in her house at the time. The days were taken up with filming at the iconic Pinewood Studios and the evenings were either a Carry On Soirée at Joan's, with all the amazing actors from the film, or me and Joanie having supper whilst she regaled me with joyous anecdotes.

The photos around the house were of a lifetime of wonderful work. So beautiful, so delightful, and I was lucky enough to be part of her world for a short time.

The definition of a legacy is 'a gift handed down from the past'. That says it all about Joan. That is how I will always remember her. I hope all young actors will watch her and learn their trade – learn 'how to do it' from this amazing, generous, talented star.

Sherrie Hewson, 2014

Introduction

JOAN SIMS WAS GREATLY ADMIRED as a witty and lovable comedienne. Her sharp and often hilarious insight into the behaviour of other people was something she could use in the many characters she played much to the joy of her adoring public.

Joan was also adored by her parents. Her father was a station-master and Joan told me that her earliest performances had been on a grassy bank at the side of the railway line where she would wave and dance about for the passing trains. I remember when spending a weekend with Joan and her parents how surprised I was to be handed a huge pile of scrapbooks entirely about Joan. We were both in our early twenties! Whether her parents' adoration of her led to a need for public acclaim I have no idea. But despite her bouncy girl-next-door personality, and her apparent dismissal of anything too serious, there was no doubt that Joan was a considerable artist with all the ups and downs that brings in its wake, including the isolation.

In her later years she found being recognised in the street, or in shops, impossible to handle. She would simply have everything delivered and order a private chauffeur should she need to go to work.

It is a very happy thing that Andrew Ross has decided to winkle her out and bring her back to life on the page. Like everyone else Joan Sims was a creature of her time – a time before 'celebs' when it was a simple question of: Can you do it? Or not? Joan with her amazing instinct would hit the jackpot every single time.

Eleanor Fazan OBE, 2014

1

The Stationmaster's Daughter

'A funny girl'

TO MANY PEOPLE THE HOME COUNTY OF ESSEX is now synonymous with bleached blonde hair, fake tans, white stilettos and reality television programmes. Clichés and stereotypes aside, it is worth remembering that this historic part of England is also well known for beautiful scenery (immortalised in John Constable's famous painting 'The Hay Wain') and over 14,000 listed buildings. Over eighty years ago being an 'Essex girl' undoubtedly had very different connotations to those that may be conjured up today. One of the county's most famous 'girls' was born into a distinctly middle-class family at the stationmaster's house at Laindon at 3.20pm on Friday 9th May 1930. In 2005 a blue plaque was unveiled at the location to commemorate the life of Irene Joan Marion Sims – more commonly known as Joan Sims – one of Britain's best-known and best-loved actresses.

Laindon at the time of Joan's childhood was a relatively small community with the railway station providing a vital link to London for thousands of commuters. At the heart of the station presiding over the day to day running of the platform was Joan's father, John Henry Sims, a proud and disciplined stationmaster.

It would surely have given Joan's father (known to some as John, to others as 'Harry' and to many as Mr Sims) immense pride to know that his daughter was commemorated with a plaque at their former home on the railway line. Born in Grays, in the summer of 1888, the son of Robert Henry Sims (1862-1928), a lighterman, and his wife Maud Mary (1866-1928), he was described by his only daughter as 'good-looking, tall and erect, with deep blue eyes'.[1] By the time he

1

reached his twenties John was an employee of the Midland Railways Company and he is listed in the 1911 census as a Railway Clerk living in the boarding house of Isabel and Mary Ann Smith.[2] His time with the railways was interrupted by active service in World War I during which time he rose to the rank of Sergeant in the 2/1st City of London and saw active service in Malta and in the trenches. Like many men of his generation who were lucky enough to survive the Great War, he returned home with shell-shock and never discussed the horrors he must inevitably have witnessed.

By the time of Joan's birth her father was once again employed by Midland Railways and had risen to the eminent position of Stationmaster. His military background evidently impacted on his everyday life, ensuring he took his role as stationmaster, and his appearance, very seriously. Well respected by his employees, he was rarely seen without a pair of kid gloves. Generally speaking John was considered an amiable character. His niece, Yvonne Doyle, remembers her Uncle Harry as 'a good old boy'[3] and he was a doting father to Joan.

John's wife, almost a decade his junior, was an altogether different character. Born Gladys Marie Ladbrook on 16th January 1896 at Pleasant Cottages, Great Wakering, she was the daughter of Ernest Henry Ladbrook (1866-1937) and his wife Martha (née Corder, 1867-1942). Comparatively speaking Gladys was from humble stock. Her father was a gardener and house painter, and throughout her life she remained conscious and 'sensitive' about being from 'country folk'.[4] At the age of sixteen Gladys was working as a servant at Margery House, Kingswood, Reigate, for Herbert De Renter, a fifty-nine-year-old managing director, and his wife Edith.[5] Pretty in her youth, with dark hair and hazel-brown eyes, by the time of Joan's birth Gladys had been elevated to the position of stationmaster's wife. Suddenly propelled into the bracket of a middle-class housewife she became something of a snob – a characteristic that would increase notably with age.

Weighing in at a very healthy nine pounds, Joan was John and Gladys's only child, born almost eight years after the couple's marriage when Gladys was thirty-four years old and John almost forty-two. Now fragile, torn and faded, there exists among Joan's effects a record of her 'baby milestones', showing that the fair-haired, hazel-eyed baby first went out when she was three days old, cut her first tooth on 11th January 1931 and first stood on 23rd June 1931. Joan's first word is recorded as 'Mamma'.

Among Joan's three godparents was her maternal aunt, Florence Ada Smith (and her husband Cecil Edgar Smith), always known within the family as 'Floss'. Born in 1890, and physically very similar to her younger sister Gladys, Florence had no children of her own but was adored by her nieces and nephews whom she treated as if they were her own offspring. Although similar in looks to Gladys, the sisters were very different in temperament and personality.

Aside from Aunt 'Floss' and Uncle Cecil, Joan's extended family was relatively small. Joan's maternal grandparents both died during her childhood and she would make no reference to her grandfather or her grandmother, remembered by Joan's cousin as 'a little old lady with a bun on her head', in her autobiography.[6] An early note written by Joan shows that she did spend time with her 'Gran' during a visit to see her Aunt Edith, always known within the family as 'Dick', and baby cousin, Yvonne.[7]

> April 22nd
> Dunrovin, Barling, Essex
> Dear Mummy and Daddy,
>   I hope you are well.
>   I am having such a lovely time here. Yvonne is getting so fat Auntie Dick says. Auntie Dick will be up on Wednesday with Yvonne.
>   Love from Miss Morgan, Gran, Auntie Dick, Joan and Yvonne.[8]

In addition to 'Aunt Floss', Gladys's youngest sister, Edith (born in April 1913), was a familiar figure to Joan since she served in the sweet and tobacco kiosk at Laindon Station. Edith married Malcolm John Mumford and went on to have two children, Yvonne and Michael. Despite being a small family the Ladbrook cousins were not especially close. Yvonne remembers occasionally staying with her aunt and uncle at the Stationmaster's House but a large age gap between her and Joan meant that Joan was already at drama school in London before Yvonne had reached her tenth birthday.

Nearer in age to Joan were the four children of her maternal uncle, George Stanley Ladbrook (1893-1967). Joan was perhaps closest to Audrey Ladbrook, just a year her senior, but the family lived in London and the distance between the pair was hardly ideal in forming a close family relationship.

Whilst the family may not have been especially close, Joan's mother was immensely proud of their connections to Royalty and this pride was mirrored by Joan herself. The link was reasonably significant; Joan's Uncle Stanley was chauffeur to the Prince of Wales (later King Edward VIII), a role he occupied for eighteen years. Apart from their daughter, Audrey, George and his wife Sarah (1895-1971) also had three sons, Joan's cousins, Noel, Geoffrey and Patrick.[9] Following King Edward's dramatic abdication in December 1936, George accompanied his employer into exile to Austria. The Ladbrook family later made newspaper headlines when the Duke of Windsor (who was godfather to all three of the Ladbrook boys) subsequently allowed George to return home from Austria to spend Christmas with his wife and children. 'Home' for the family was in fact Buckingham Palace where they lived in a six-roomed flat 'on the first floor of one of the quietest parts of the palace'.[10] Sadly the family's fortunes quickly changed when George found his employment terminated shortly after his return to England. By 1938 he was earning a living as a doorman at a London restaurant. Despite this, for Joan there was always great pride in the fact that her uncle had been a loyal servant of the Royal Family for almost two decades. His position within the Royal Household enabled him to allow his niece to visit Marlborough House in her early childhood where she was able to see Queen Mary sitting in the summer house. On 12th May 1937 Joan was again at Marlborough House, with her four cousins, and watched the Coronation procession of King George VI and Queen Elizabeth from one of the balconies. Over sixty years later Joan recalled that her excitement on the occasion resulted in her wetting her knickers and subsequently slipping them off and hiding them under a bath in the Royal residence!

Joan's childhood was an isolated one. Adored by her parents, she was nevertheless brought up strictly. As a proud stationmaster John Sims disapproved of his daughter using the platform and surrounding areas as a playground. A wooden cane hung on the back of the kitchen door of the Station House as a constant reminder of the possible punishment that could be inflicted should Joan misbehave. She later recalled that the instrument was never used and at the age of about nine she smashed it into three pieces and threw it on the fire. As an only child, without any close family or even neighbours at hand, Joan was forced to entertain herself – a task she performed admirably. In her fifties Joan would recall:

> I used to dress up from a very small age I remember and could often
> be found on the railway station, sitting there in some eiderdown or
> something![11]

Joan's passion for dressing up and performing in front of the
railway passengers (whom she regarded as a 'built-in' audience)
quickly led to her amassing a wardrobe of costumes since she was
industrious enough to ask passengers for their unwanted garments:

> I used to scrounge clothes and shoes [from the passengers]. I used to
> eye their feet and I thought, 'That lady's got small feet, I'll catch her
> tomorrow,' and I'd say, 'If you've got any old shoes going would you
> leave them care of the stationmaster?' My father used to get these
> various bits of clothing popping up and he used to get furious with
> me.[12]

From the beginning of her life Joan was 'a funny girl'[13] who was
at her happiest entertaining the crowds at Laindon railway station.
She had an appreciative audience and plenty of characters to 'study'
– not only in the passengers she encountered on a daily basis but also
among the station's employees. Her parents, and in particular her
father, tried their best to discourage Joan's antics (she was often
summoned back indoors by her father bellowing 'Joan – doors!') to
little avail. The need to entertain and be lost in the magic of make-
believe was seemingly in Joan's blood from the very start.

The isolation Joan suffered during her childhood was compounded by the fact that she was not allowed to attend the local
primary school and was thus unable to form friendships with other
local children. Instead she was educated at a private school, St John's
School, Billericay, a decision made by Gladys as Joan would recall in
later years:

> I think I was sent to another school because of my mother's inverted
> snobbery. She wanted the best for me, which was understandable but
> wrong because it made me even more of an outsider.[14]

Her time at St John's was not helped by the headmaster and his
disciplinarian ways. Joan loathed him, and one particular example of
his harshness was never forgotten by his young pupil. Having being
dared to kiss Colin Blanks, a boy in her class with whom she had
fallen 'hopelessly in love', the spirited little girl duly obliged – only to

be caught by her teacher and sent to the headmaster's office. While Joan escaped with a 'severe ticking-off' the unfortunate little boy received 'six of the best' from the headmaster. Happily Colin gallantly admitted that a kiss from Joan had been worth it! The incident remained firmly embedded in Joan's memory for decades. A happier memory of her primary-school days occurred when Joan made the local press at the age of just eight. While still attending St John's School, Joan was recorded as standing out among the elocutionists and doing 'particularly well' during the school's Annual Speech Day and Concert. It was an initial taste of fame and the article reporting the occasion was duly preserved by her parents – the first of many.

Once Joan's acting career began John and Gladys Sims took great pains to record their daughter's achievements in a series of scrapbooks that stemmed back to the 1940s. Joan's eventual success as a professional actress was a huge source of pleasure to both her parents and especially to her father. As their daughter became the sole focus of their lives her fame as an actress almost overwhelmed them – leaving little room for anything else. From her earliest days Joan had been aware that her parents' marriage was not an especially happy one. She would recall that the couple were never physically demonstrative or affectionate – with either each other or their only child. Likewise the family would never holiday together, possibly because John hated the disruption of travelling (Joan would later suspect this had much to do with the shell shock he experienced during the Great War) and preferred to relax in his garden or by listening to the radio.

At times Gladys could also be a fragile character and was subject to bouts of depression, particularly during Joan's childhood. Periodically she would holiday alone, usually staying with her elder sister at her home, Orchard House, in Great Wakering. This 'magical place', with its fruit trees, animals and tranquillity, also provided a safe haven, away from the tensions of her own home, for Joan who was a frequent visitor (Joan was with her aunt and uncle when war was announced in September 1939). It was at a very early age that Joan became privy to the cause of her mother's bouts of depression when she was informed of Gladys's 'dark secret'.

Before she met John Henry Sims, Gladys had been deeply in love. Her boyfriend, whom she fully expected to marry, was from what was considered a better background than Gladys and when it was suggested that she meet his parents, Gladys, acutely aware of her own humble origins, got 'cold feet' and backed out of the arrangement. The relationship subsequently ended – with Gladys's boyfriend assuming that she was no longer interested in him.

Gladys then went on to marry John, on 11th December 1922, although she admitted to her young and impressionable daughter that she practically had to be forced to go to the registry office. Tragically, just weeks after the nuptials had taken place, Gladys's former boyfriend got in touch – unaware of the rebound wedding which had taken place in the interim period. He declared his love for Gladys and proposed, only to be told he was too late.

Years after the event Gladys still had a photograph of her boyfriend hidden at the back of a desk drawer. She had clearly never forgotten her first love and the pitifully sad irony of her situation.

The impact of this revelation upon a nine-year-old Joan was massive and would forever change the way in which she viewed her parents' marriage. Suffice to say it explained the tension and lack of affection between John and Gladys but it would also have an effect on Joan's own ability to find lasting happiness. She would grow up to detest arguments or upset and had an idealised vision of what married life should be like. Settling for a 'second best' relationship, as her mother had done, would never suffice for Joan.

Physical affection was something Joan envied in other families especially since it was most definitely not part of life at the Stationmaster's House. As an adult when she discussed the issue with Gladys over the telephone it was met with guarded disapproval. When Joan next visited her parents she was met at the door by Gladys and the comment: 'Well, I suppose I'd better give my daughter a hug.' Joan was then greeted with a 'forced' embrace from Gladys as she recalled in her autobiography:

> She felt completely frigid, her arms stiff and unyielding like the branches of a tree. It was as if she was recoiling from me, and before I could stop myself I found myself saying: 'If that's the best you can do, don't bother in the future.'[15]

Sadly, Joan's comments seemingly left Gladys as cold as her feeble attempt to bond with her daughter.

*

Additional tuition was needed for Joan to gain a place at Brentwood County High School for Girls. Many of the teachers at the school would form lasting impressions upon her, several even being used to base her later screen characters on, but it was her elocution teacher, Miss Wilson, who not only helped Joan drop her Essex accent but also provided her with some much needed confidence. Joan later admitted that she struggled to concentrate at school, particularly whenever she had to read something. Elocution lessons were the only time when she didn't feel a 'failure' and she longed to find something at which she could 'excel'.

By the time Joan joined Brentwood County High School the Second World War was already well under way. Despite the railway being a prime target for German bombers, Joan was thankful that she did not have to be evacuated – unlike three of her cousins, Audrey, Geoff and Patrick who were sent to Minehead. She became used to regular trips to the station bomb shelter as German planes flew overhead, using the railway lines to guide them to London. Like many other families, if there wasn't time to reach the shelter, Joan would find refuge under the stairs of the family home. It was because of her immediate proximity to the railway line that Joan would encounter an anti-aircraft gun, which scared 'the living daylights' out of her when she first heard it fire after an enemy bomber. Another vivid memory was the sight of her father marching up and down the platform shouting '*Raus!*' (German for 'get out') to German prisoners of war as they were being transported to nearby camps.

The horrors of war truly hit home for Joan when word came that her twenty-one-year-old cousin Noel Ladbrook (who was a Flight Sergeant in the Royal Air Force and was serving with Coastal Command) had been killed when the plane he was flying hit a snow storm and crashed into a hill. Joan was just fourteen years old at the time of her cousin's death on 26th November 1944. It was a loss she would never forget.

Joan's own wartime effort involved what she regarded as her first 'official' acting role (as a wounded casualty) for the St John Ambulance brigade who held regular practice sessions at the station. Her solitude was also slightly alleviated at the time when she became leader of the Blue Tit Patrol (part of the local girl guides).

By the time she joined the Langdon Players (part of the local Youth Centre group) in her teens Joan was already something of a seasoned performer, having of course spent years entertaining passengers at the railway station. Hardly surprising, then, that she would later admit she took to amateur dramatics 'like a duck to water'.[16]

Joan's artistic talents were partly inherited from her mother, a fine singer and accomplished pianist, who encouraged her daughter to take piano lessons at an early age.[17] Described by her daughter as an efficient 'tough cookie' Gladys was also 'brilliant' at crochet and enjoyed knitting, pottery and gardening. Those close to the family confirm that Joan's comedic talents, on the other hand, were a trait inherited most definitely from her father.

Joan's first taste of 'professional' success came in 1947 when she appeared with the Players in the South East Essex Drama Festival. Here she was given the opportunity to display her talents to the general public on a wider scale and her performance as Emma, a mill girl, in *Lonesome Like* earned her the Palm of the Day for Best Individual Performance of the Festival. The programme from the event was something Joan proudly retained among her possessions. Around the same time she played Sarah Pugh in *The Corn is Green* for 'Southend's Own Repertory Company'. It was a short run but another step on the acting ladder.

Although she was good at English, Art and Domestic Science, Joan's lack of aptitude for Science and Maths resulted in her failing her School Certificate (despite two attempts). Joan was the first to admit that she was not an 'academic star'. In spite of her early success in the theatre John and Gladys tried their very best to persuade their daughter to avoid a career as an actress. John hoped that Joan would train for a job on the railways and a career as an interior designer of hotels was also suggested. Gladys was keen for Joan to take on a clerical role – even taking her to London to view a large 'typing pool' in an insurance office. Years later Joan would admit that she was 'never really cut out for a nine-till-five office job'.[18]

Only when Joan's burning 'passion' for the stage became clear did her parents become 'sympathetic and supportive' of their daughter. With the assistance of Miss Wilson and Mr Hill (warden of the Youth Centre) the Essex Education Committee agreed to finance Joan if she was successful in gaining a place at either the Royal Academy of Dramatic Art (RADA), the Central School of Speech and Drama or the Young Vic. Joan had set her heart on studying acting at RADA and duly auditioned in front of a panel of half a dozen, performing two different readings: one an extract from *Winnie the Pooh* (by A. A. Milne) and the other from Shaw's *Saint Joan*.

Amongst the panel of interviewees was actress Athene Seyler[19] who in later years admitted to Joan that she was not a fan of A. A. Milne's work. Joan was aware that her choice of material had not impressed her audience and she duly received a letter saying she had not been successful in gaining entry to the Academy. A lifeline was, however, offered when it was suggested that Joan spend time at PARADA, the preliminary academy, and audition for RADA again the following term. Joan seized the opportunity, despite being filled with doubts about her true ability to pursue a career as an actress, and enrolled at PARADA at the beginning of 1947.

Commuting every day from Laindon to Highgate in London, Joan relished her time at PARADA where she received lessons in elocution, diction, ballet, mime and even fencing. Lifelong friendships were formed at the time and Joan felt 'liberated' to be among like-minded individuals. Her confidence increased and, despite her dread of auditions – a fear which would never leave her – she felt positive that her second audition for RADA would be successful.[20] Alas, on Christmas Eve 1947 Joan received word back from RADA with devastating news. Not only did the letter confirm that she had failed her second audition but it went on to say that she was 'quite unsuitable for the profession'. Joan would never forget this rejection, later admitting: 'It broke my heart.'[21]

Although her parents had initially been reluctant for Joan to become an actress, it was Harry's intervention that would secure Joan another chance at gaining entry to the Academy after he wrote to Sir Kenneth Barnes (Principal of RADA) asking if his daughter could be given another opportunity to audition. To support his request Harry even enclosed local newspaper reviews confirming Joan's dramatic ability. Sir Kenneth's reply offered Joan the opportunity to return to PARADA for another term. A third audition for RADA duly followed which was again unsuccessful. However, when it was suggested that Joan stay on at PARADA for a third term she realised that her talent had been spotted. A fourth audition finally secured Joan's long-awaited place at RADA.

*

Once accepted into RADA – her first day at the Academy was 6th October 1948 – Joan proved to be a diligent student. She took her craft very seriously as shown in the detailed handwritten notes on stagecraft and pronunciation she kept in a hard-backed black notebook which survives to this day. Her reports during her time at the Academy were undoubtedly honest but generally encouraging. Although Miss Wilson had tried her best to modulate Joan's native Essex accent, she was warned that her 'vowels are still rather weak' and that Joan's accent was 'not very good at present'. Joan certainly heeded the comments since it was later reported by her diction tutor that she 'studies keenly and her range of vocal tones, especially the low notes, has greatly improved'.[22] In time Joan went on to become well known within the profession for her ability to master any accent.

As far as her acting ability was concerned Joan was considered, from the outset, to be a 'clever comedienne' but advised in no uncertain terms that her voice needed 'work... Otherwise she will be doomed to character parts'. Ironically it was her ability to master character roles that appealed to Sir Kenneth Barnes, the Academy's long-standing Principal Director, who commented that she was a 'talented character actress'.[23]

Joan's contemporaries at RADA included future greats of British acting such as Dame Dorothy Tutin, Rachel Roberts, Barbara Jefford and James Grout. Jimmy Perry, who went on to become the creator of legendary television series such as *Dad's Army*, was also among Joan's peers. In his 2002 autobiography Perry recalled Joan as a 'bubbly girl' and a 'delight' to work with during their days as students.[24] Other key figures met during this time and during her time at PARADA included Myles Rudge (the well-known songwriter), character actor Ronnie Stevens, David Morrell (Joan's first 'serious' boyfriend) and the comedy actor Derek Royle. Sir Sean Connery's first wife, the Australian-born actress and author Diane Cilento, was also with Joan during her first year at RADA and was remembered as 'so sweet and quite shy'.[25]

During her time at PARADA Joan also met Patricia Mary Hornsby, a pretty, petite, green-eyed budding actress just six days her senior. Like Joan, Patricia (known herein by her married name, Pat Clayfield) was an only child and had connections with the railway.

Despite such initial similarities Pat's background was very different from that of Joan's. Brought up partly in Consett, County Durham, and educated at boarding school in Hastings, Pat's grandfather was general manager of London Northern Eastern Railways – an eminent position – and was also a considerable landowner.

Like Joan, Pat moved on to RADA in due course. The pair quickly became the best of friends – and would remain so for the next fifty years. Their antics together, while still teenagers, were many and varied and their day spent swimming in the Thames with Derek Royle and Brian Matthew remains firmly embedded in Pat's mind: 'It was such a glorious day... we swam in our pants and bra. It shocked my granny when she saw the photos!'[26]

Whilst at RADA Joan acted in numerous plays from *The Shrew* to *And So to Bed* (see Appendix A for a full list of Joan's RADA performances). She played Maudie in *Peace In Our Time* with a cast of over thirty student actors, including Philip Latham, and made a 'particularly charming' Catherine Howard in a 1950 RADA matinee performance of *The Life and Loves of Henry VIII*.[27] One particular performance at RADA remembered by Pat Clayfield was that of Queen Margaret in *Richard III* in which she thought Joan 'absolutely brilliant'. This dramatic performance would be recorded and praised by Pat in a letter at the time to her mother, Molly Hornsby. Years later, when Joan was visiting Pat's parents during their time in South Africa, Molly would read the letter back to Joan who thought it ironic that she was receiving heartfelt praise for her acting work as she was on her hands and knees scrubbing a floor![28]

A letter on behalf of Sir Kenneth Barnes shows that Joan was chosen to be a 'Lucky Programme' seller at the RADA reunion dance at the Lyceum Theatre on 15th May 1950. The letter outlined that the duty would require all of Joan's 'energy, best attention and glamour'.[29] As a 'reward' for her services Joan was given a complimentary ticket to the dance.

Among Joan's effects is one of her qualifying tests from the Royal Academy of Dramatic Art showing that at 10.45am on Monday 26th July she was required to 'learn and speak in character' from one of the following nine passages:

1). St John – Chapter IV, Verses 5-14 inclusive
2). *As You Like It*, by William Shakespeare, Act III, Scene 2

3). *Romeo and Juliet*, by William Shakespeare, Act II, Scene 2

4). *Mary Stewart*, by John Drinkwater, Act 1

5). The Host of Heaven (from *The Coming Christ*) by John Masefield

6). *The Rivals*, by Richard Brinsley Sheridan, Act 1, Scene 2

7). *Caesar and Cleopatra*, by Bernard Shaw, Act 1

8). *The Taming of the Shrew*, by William Shakespeare, Act IV, Scene 3

9). *Alice In Wonderland*, by Lewis Carroll, Chapter VII

Joan graduated from RADA with a Diploma on 4th April 1950.[30] Along with other graduates she took part in a 'showcase' production at Her Majesty's Theatre displaying her skills to not only the general public but also prospective agents. Joan later admitted that she was 'not considered posh enough for a serious role' (that of Abraham Lincoln's wife in this case) and was thought of even at this early stage in her career as 'a bit too musical comedy'.[31] Joan's final RADA report featured glowing remarks from Sir Kenneth Barnes:

> A talented and thoroughly cooperative and keen student who has completed her Diploma course with distinction. She is fully equipped for useful work in a good Repertory Company as she is versatile and effective as a young actress. She was always a most promising student and we are sorry to lose her.[32]

Before leaving the Academy Joan was thrilled to be awarded the £10 Mabel Temperley Prize for Grace and Charm of Movement by leading actress Margaret Leighton. The ceremony allowed Joan the perfect opportunity to show off her comic skills and she later revealed that she deliberately missed her footing at the top of the stairs leading to the stage, causing her to go through a comic 'trip-down-the-stairs' routine to the delight of her peers! The antic seemed to set the tone for a career spent making people laugh.[33]

From the very start of her professional career Joan's talent was being noticed by all the right people. Her performance in the showcase production brought her to the attention of Dorothy Mather (of Film Rights Limited) who immediately wrote to Joan, in a letter dated 4th April 1950, requesting they meet as soon as possible.[34] Peter Eade, a young theatrical agent who had recently set up his own business, had also noticed Joan at RADA having seen her during her fourth term at the Academy in Noël Coward's *Peace In Our Time*.

Joan admitted that her shyness and fears of being left alone with a theatrical agent led to her destroying (and ignoring) Peter's subsequent letter inviting her to his office to discuss her future career. It was only after being persuaded by her RADA contemporary Bill Becker that Joan agreed to meet with Peter (she was duly accompanied by Bill for the occasion).

Upon meeting Peter, Joan's fears were immediately dispelled. He became her first agent and would remain a mainstay of her life for the next thirty years.[35] A charming and good-looking man, described by one source as 'not gay but a neuter',[36] Peter became Joan's mentor and an extremely valued friend – taking care of all her concerns, both professional and personal. Throughout his life Peter kept his client list deliberately small and select. It says much about him that many of his clients, including Ronnie Barker and Kenneth Williams, stayed with him until his death.

2

Theatre Days

'The nerves get worse – they don't get better'

FOR MANY ACTORS OF JOAN'S GENERATION working in the constantly changing world of repertory theatre, particularly at the beginning of their careers, provided them with the chance to perfect the skills learnt at drama school and build up experience, contacts and confidence. Touring theatrical companies are now relatively rare but during the early 1950s they were positively thriving and repertory theatre was at its peak. The pace of life was hectic to say the least with actors performing a role whilst learning lines for their next. On top of this was a constant change of venue which invariably meant long journeys by train and staying in less than salubrious boarding houses.

For two years Joan lived in the 'demanding' world of rep, travelling the country, living in various digs and coping with the anxiety of homesickness, first-night nerves and the ever present attention of various memorable landladies. In her autobiography she would recall in detail the characters met during this time and the far from glamorous locations in which she worked – from Chorlton-cum-Hardy where she starred in the title role of *Sarah Simple* to Luton where she would celebrate her twenty-first birthday with fellow cast members, a cake, silver-key card and a bottle of champagne.

Following nine weeks in Chorlton-cum-Hardy in 1950 Joan returned to the south of the country where various assignments would soon follow. It was during these early days that Joan worked with Pat Clayfield (under her professional name of Patricia Hornsby) at the 'Q' Theatre with Donald Sinden ('before he was well known') and 'various Dames'. The two friends played suffragettes and it was

15

the only time that Pat got top billing over Joan. Pat would later recall that she had the programme framed and when she and Joan lived together it was on display in their bathroom.[37]

Joan's return to London was not to be long-lived since at the end of 1951 she was cast in the role of Principal Girl in *The Happy Ha'penny*, a new pantomime at the Glasgow Citizen's Theatre. Joan delighted in the company of her fellow artists (including Stanley Baxter, with whom she would later work on television) and during her time in pantomime learned one of the most valuable lessons of her career – never to drink alcohol before a performance.

With her comic talents recognised from the earliest stage of her acting career Joan was a natural choice to appear in theatrical revue. *The Bells of St Martin's – An Intimate Revue* starred Douglas Byng and Hattie Jacques and opened at St Martin's Theatre in the late summer of 1952. Joan featured significantly in the production, along with various other actors including Roma Milne, and her segments in the revue were 'Pity About Kitty' (with Hattie and Roma), 'Working Model' (solo), 'Piccadilly Incident' (the company), 'Christmas in Kensington' (solo), 'Charity Begins at Home' (with Hattie and Richard Waring) and 'Belles of St Martin's' (the company). The revue not only gave Joan further stage experience but was also significant in her personal life since it brought her into contact with Hattie Jacques, already an established comedienne on stage and screen, with whom she later became best friends.

Hattie, eight years Joan's senior, had made her stage debut at the Players' Theatre in 1944 and would become a familiar figure there over the next fifteen years. She also became a well-known voice on radio, particularly as Sophie Tuckshop, the greedy schoolgirl in *ITMA* (*It's That Man Again*), and by the time she met Joan she had already appeared in a handful of films including a memorable role as Daisy in *Trottie True* opposite Jean Kent and Bill Owen. Well known for her generosity as a hostess and for 'bringing joy to a lot of people's lives' Hattie's home at 67 Eardley Crescent, Earls Court, became a haven for many of her friends and in time Joan would become 'an essential guest', especially at Christmas time.[38]

The madcap world of comedy revue with its fast pace of humour, sketches, songs and ad-libbing appealed to Joan's nature and the backstage excitement ensured each act was fresh and invigorating. One of Joan's finest performances came in *Just Lately* in which she played Miss Potting Hill, a holiday beauty-queen contestant. Suitably attired in a bathing costume, high heels and fishnet stockings, it was one of the first times Joan's justly famous legs were displayed in a performance to spectacular effect. As well as being reunited with friends from RADA (notably Ronnie Stevens who directed the production) Joan would also become acquainted with future co-stars including Kenneth Connor (who went on to appear in seventeen *Carry On* films).

The pace and scope of Joan's career was now increasing rapidly and her next professional success came in another revue, *Intimacy at Eight*, at the New Lindsey Theatre Club in Notting Hill, alongside Leslie Crowther, Eunice Gayson, Ron Moody and a very young Dilys Laye, who would become another lifelong friend.[39]

Photographs in *The Sketch* from *Intimacy at Eight* show Joan's versatility, even at this early stage in her career. In one shot she is scantily clad, again revealing her shapely legs, and playing an accordion. Another photograph shows Joan in costume as a 'toothless' gran complete with flowered hat alongside an upbeat Dilys Laye, Ronnie Stevens and Geoffrey Hibbert. As the thwarted station-announcer Joan was credited with 'stopping the show',[40] while *The Stage* considered her role as the 'sultry station announcer' a 'highlight' of the play.[41]

The success of *Intimacy* resulted in it being rejigged, with new material added and some material removed, and renamed as *High Spirits*. Suitably refreshed the company then toured with the production for five weeks before it opened at the London Hippodrome, Leicester Square, where Joan made her West End debut in May 1953.

By this time Joan had already met Eleanor Fazan, an elegant and eloquent dancer who has enjoyed a successful career as a choreographer working on stage, screen and television productions for which she received the Order of the British Empire in 2013. Known within the profession as 'Fiz', Eleanor, who was born in Kenya in 1930, would become one of Joan's closest friends over the next five decades. Eleanor recalls Joan in those early days as a 'lovely, adorable dolly to work with – an actress who was wonderfully observant and perceptive which fed her talent to amuse'.[42] It was thanks to Fiz that Joan was able to leave the rented accommodation in which she was living in St John's Wood and move into a luxury flat on the Bayswater Road overlooking Hyde Park. The residence belonged to Sir Charles Vyner-Brooke (the last white Rajah of Sarawak) who happened to be a family acquaintance of Fiz's. Fiz had been offered the use of his wife's flat for Joan, who was only too pleased to escape her current living arrangements.

Following 125 performances of *High Spirits* at the Hippodrome Joan went on to appear in a new revue, *More Intimacy at Eight*, which went on to become the hugely successful *Intimacy at 8.30* and ran for 552 performances from April 1954 until September 1955.

Almost sixty years after the revue Ron Moody, in his nineties one of the last survivors of the production, remembers Joan with affection: 'She was a great, good natured clown and enormous fun to be with.'[43] Actress Thelma Ruby, who began her career in 1944 with ENSA, first met Joan in 1953 when she featured in *High Spirits*. She recalled Joan as 'always a bright, affectionate, funny, darling girl' and was thrilled to be able to take over from her in *Intimacy at 8.30* on Sunday nights, when Joan had a scheduled radio broadcast. Ron Moody would later say 'Sunday night is Ruby night!'[44] Joan and Thelma would later appear together in *Night of 100 Stars* (1956) and remarkably would re-encounter one another in 1999 on the set of *The Last of the Blonde Bombshells*.

Fenella Fielding admitted to being 'very new' when she understudied both Joan Sims and Joan Heal after the revue had been running for nearly two years. Her vivid memories of those far-off days are worth recording in full:

> I came into it as an understudy and I had to understudy both Joans – Joan Sims and Joan Heal. I decided to learn Joan Sims first. I began rehearsing on a Thursday afternoon, quite casual, just me and the stage-manager. No call Friday, no call Saturday because of the matinee. My next call was for Monday at 2. They rang up to say quite casually, 'I suppose you know you're on tonight!' I said, 'Which one am I on for?' and they said, 'Joan Heal' – who was really the leading lady. I rushed to the theatre and got there for 2pm and between two and eight-thirty I had to learn all her stuff... and I had to have fittings for all the costumes and I had to go out and buy myself a pair of fishnet elastic tights and also a pair of shoes to wear in the show.
>
> What was more difficult than learning all the lines was knowing where to come on from because of course it wasn't even a play, it was a revue. I also had to ring up my mother and get her to come up from Edgeware and bring my strapless [bra].
>
> They were all marvellous, they all helped me and they all sort of shoved me on at the right moments. I remember at one point before

we went on someone in the cast (I'm not going to say who!) asked me if I'd like an 'upper'… I said, 'No thank you! I'm quite charged up as it is…' And there we were. I went on and everybody helped me and it really went terribly well and I have to say that Joan Sims was just like an angel because there's nothing more stomach-churning than an understudy having to go on – not just for the understudy but for the company. They'd been running for nearly two years but I was very, very lucky because I went down terribly well and I didn't have to go on the next night because I'm sure if I had I would have been awful! Joan Sims was just lovely to me and I have to say that Joan Heal came back immediately – there was no more being off for her!

It was very hot in that theatre – the Criterion – in that hot summer because it was underground and there were lots of restaurants surrounding it with their kitchens. The dressing rooms were well underground and boiling hot and the actors used to sit around there with very little on and I have to say that Joan, when she wasn't being fat, looked absolutely beautiful in the nude in her dressing room between the shows.[45]

The runaway success of *Intimacy at 8.30* attracted a host of famous names to the Criterion to watch the revue, including Noël Coward and Gene Kelly (then a major star following the release of *Singin' in the Rain*). On the back of the revue a major professional and personal highlight of 1954 for Joan was her appearance in the Royal Command Variety Performance and being presented to the young Queen Elizabeth II at the end of the production. For this grandest of occasions Joan took part in a sketch with leading names of the day: Jack Buchanan, Frankie Howerd, Peter Sellers and Donald Wolfit.

As a result of her triumphant performances in *High Spirits* and *Intimacy at 8.30* Joan secured her position as a star actress. By now the round-faced, pleasantly plump, mousy-haired Essex girl who had worked so hard to secure her place at drama school had transformed into a professional actress; blonde-haired, stunningly pretty, curvaceous and sophisticated. Having struggled to achieve this early success the desire to continue acting and maintain her stardom became instilled in Joan. Her career became the driving force in her life and would remain so until the end.

*

Having enjoyed the comforts of a luxury flat overlooking London's best-known park, Joan's next move inevitably meant a straitening of circumstances. Thankfully her new living arrangements ultimately proved to be one of the happiest periods in her life. Having departed Bayswater Road Joan went on to move into a top-floor annexe furnished flat at Jermyn Street, close to Piccadilly and next door to the Cavendish Hotel. Here she would share a bedroom – and countless laughs – with Pat Clayfield.

Joan's friendship with Pat had already been cemented during their time together at drama school. Living together at Jermyn Street allowed them to indulge in many girlish antics – from playing matron and nurse when changing their bed sheets ('We always did hospital corners,' recalls Pat) to 'living dangerously' and dining out at an Italian restaurant on spaghetti Bolognese and coffee after Pat received the princely sum of £5 from her grandfather for a birthday present. Despite being relatively strapped for cash another occasion saw the two friends splash out to test their culinary skills as Pat recalls:

> We wanted to start doing some really good cooking so one day I came up with the idea we'd do pig's head. So we went to this butcher and we bought a pig's head and got the book out and I rang my grandmother. It was all cleaned, the eyes were out and it was perfectly washed. We stuffed it, did all we needed to and put it in the oven. We watched it go perfectly crispy and lovely and we planned to eat it that evening. I hate to tell you that when we looked at it we loved it so much we couldn't put a knife in it! We couldn't eat it. It was pathetic! So Miles Eason who lived in the flat beneath us (and at that time was the murderer in *The Mousetrap*) said it was fantastic – he was entertaining so it was given to him. We used to do lots of silly things like that.

Since there were numerous other friends and colleagues at the time named Pat, Patricia or Trish, Joan decided she would call Pat 'Jerry' – a nickname which would stick, on and off, over the years. Joan in turn became known to Pat as 'Timmy' or 'Timkins'. Such was the affectionate relationship between the two ladies.[46]

While her living arrangements were more than harmonious, by now Joan was starting to experience the difficulties of being a public figure as she began to be recognised during the course of her everyday life. It was the start of a lifetime spent in the public eye, a trapping of fame with which Joan was never especially comfortable. As Eleanor Fazan remembers, 'Being recognised and pointed out by people she didn't know, was painful to her.'[47] Pat Clayfield was with Joan in the early 1950s when she was approached by fans requesting her autograph and remembers her timid response:

> She was always very down to earth but froze up at times when approached by members of the public. During her time in *Intimacy at 8.30* I remember two people came rushing up to her in the street and said 'Miss Sims you're so wonderful' and asked for her autograph... I had to prompt her to take the pen. She was very nervous and signed their book but it didn't look like her autograph! She later said, 'What have I done to deserve that?' She was just so humble.[48]

Likewise, Joan also had to deal with members of the press although from her very earliest days she became expert at declining interviews. Even when living at Jermyn Street it was invariably left to Pat to answer the telephone and inform the caller that Miss Sims was unavailable (Joan would usually be in the background wickedly sending up her friend while she was trying to be 'ladylike and polite').[49]

It was during her time in rep that Joan realised she was already being typecast as a comic actress. Private correspondence as early as 1954 shows that she was already considered to be 'developing along revue lines' rather than as a 'straight' actress and she was told at one audition by the director Anthony Asquith[50] that she had 'far too happy a face' to be considered for serious roles. While Mr Asquith is to thank for the title of this book his opinion was almost damning for Joan. In retrospect his words largely rang true and Joan considered her looks to be a mixed blessing. The happy face allowed her to work with some of the greatest comic actors of the era whilst still in her twenties and ultimately would put her in good stead for the legendary career she would have in film and television comedy. On the other hand she was painfully aware very early in her career of the dangers of being pigeonholed.

By the late summer of 1952 Joan's father had retired from his position as stationmaster at Laindon with a capital superannuation payment of £826.10 and an annuity of £275.10.[51] Upon his retirement John had to give up the Stationmaster's House where the family had lived for over twenty years. With the assistance of their daughter Mr and Mrs Sims were able to retire to a pleasant semi-detached property in Thurston Avenue, Southend-on-Sea, where they would spend their remaining years together. The property was just a couple of miles away from Cliff Avenue, where John had lived at the time of his marriage to Gladys.

During their days at RADA Pat Clayfield had often stayed with Joan and her parents at the Stationmaster's House in Laindon and during the early 1950s she got to know John and Gladys Sims well. Pat remains convinced that Joan's theatrical talents were inherited from the old stationmaster whom Pat adored:

> She got all her acting talent, I'm sure, from her father... he used to make us laugh so much... I remember one day watching the London Philharmonic Orchestra on their black-and-white television and Mr Sims asking me which one of the orchestra members wasn't playing. I sat watching intently and at the end I said, 'I don't know Mr Sims. Which one was it?' to which he replied, 'Don't be so silly Pat – they are all playing!' He was such fun![52]

Eleanor Fazan was another of Joan's friends who became well acquainted with Mr and Mrs Sims. Ever the snob, Gladys 'was enormously impressed by Fiz's aristocratic connections'.[53] She was perhaps one of the few chums Gladys actually approved of since virtually none of Joan's friends or colleagues seemed to meet with Mrs Sims' demandingly high expectations. Gladys's attitude towards Pat Clayfield for instance was distinctly cool in the early days – at least until the latter met Pat's mother and realised that socially speaking the Hornsbys were far superior to the Sims family. Thereafter Gladys's attitude towards Pat was friendly – so much so that while Pat always referred to John Sims as 'Mr Sims', his wife became known to her as 'Mummy Sims' (a title Pat uses to this day when remembering Joan's mother). The relationship was cemented some time afterwards when Gladys was paying an extended visit to her daughter's home. This particular occasion saw Pat persuade her boyfriend at the time to take Gladys for a drive in his brand-new car – a red Volvo with bucket seats. After Gladys had spent some time admiring the car, Pat knew that she would be thrilled to be a passenger in the vehicle and the extended drive in the two-seater allowed Joan a much deserved break from her mother.

As well as becoming a star in the theatre Joan's career had also branched out in television and radio and her first work on the small screen in 1952 was as the voices of Oscar Onion, Millicent Mushroom and Barbara Beetroot in the children's puppet programme *Vegetable*

Village, directed by Vivian Milroy. The fact that Joan was heard but not seen in her television debut was an ironic start to her small-screen career. As a result she always considered her first 'real' television work to be her appearance as secretary Marjorie Dawson in 'Hot Money', an episode of the series *Colonel March of Scotland Yard* (the series was later edited and released as *Colonel March Investigates*, a B-grade feature film, in 1952). The role remained a memorable one for Joan since it allowed her to work alongside one of her great idols, the legendary British-born Hollywood star, Boris Karloff (1887-1969), best known on screen as Frankenstein's monster. Prior to working with Karloff Joan was in awe and slight fear of him, having seen so many of his eerie screen portrayals in her youth. Her fears were completely dismissed as soon as she began work with him and she recalled Karloff as 'very docile and sweet, more inclined to talk about gardening than wander around the countryside terror-ising the natives'.[54]

Joan's work on radio also began in 1952 and in the early stages of her career would, at times, provide a welcome relief from the relentless repetition of stage work, particularly during her time in *Intimacy at 8.30* when working underground night after night in the intense heat of the Criterion Theatre began to depress her. By the middle of the decade she was appearing regularly in *The Floggits*, alongside Elsie and Doris Waters (the famous female comedy act who were real-life sisters), Kenneth Connor, Ronnie Barker and a young Anthony Newley. Her most substantial work on radio came in 1960/61 when she starred in fifty-two episodes of *Something to Shout About*. With scripts written by Myles Rudge and Ronnie Wolfe, the series starred Michael Medwin as Michael Lightfoot, an account executive, Eleanor Summerfield (as efficient television executive Maggie Tufnell) and Joan as Mavis Willis, a shorthand typist who could neither type or spell! Plans to bring the series to television screens, with Joan reprising the character of Mavis, were discussed by BBC executives but sadly did not transpire.

Fenella Fielding played Michael Medwin's secretary in *Something to Shout About*, and in 2012 remembered not only the series but also Joan's career on radio in general:

> I worked with her on radio with Michael Medwin, Warren Mitchell (who wasn't well known then) and Eleanor Summerfield in a series

which was terribly popular called *Something to Shout About* – set in an advertising agency. I think we did about three series. Joan was brilliant. She could play anything in film and the theatre that she looked like but on the radio she could do anything she could do the voice of – so that meant she could play pretty girls which she never did when you could see her – except in *Carry On Don't Lose Your Head*. I think she did look rather marvellous in that.[55]

Meanwhile work in the theatre continued to flow in and it was during her run of *Man Alive!* in the spring of 1956 that Joan became friends with Lord Westwood[56] who came to see her when the play reached Newcastle. Having visited Joan and Pat at Jermyn Street (and catching them unawares since they were both wearing short Chinese-style pyjamas at the time) he greeted Joan with the comment 'How nice to see you dressed' when he entered her dressing room at Newcastle's Theatre Royal. The incident, as Pat recalls, resulted in the two flatmates wearing kaftans thereafter instead of pyjamas in case of further unexpected guests![57] An even more high-profile friendship would form later in the same year with the handsome, dark-haired Hollywood film star Tyrone Power.

Joan's brief and very innocent romantic interlude with Tyrone Power was one of the greatest moments of her life. They met when Joan was cast to appear in *Night of a Hundred Stars*, a midnight matinee at the London Palladium in which Joan featured as a chorus girl, along with over half a dozen other leading actresses including Dulcie Gray, Anna Massey, Peggy Cummins, Jean Kent and Brenda Bruce.

Joan was besotted with Tyrone (or 'Ty' as he insisted the girls call him) who had been one of her all-time favourite screen idols since her childhood. Along with several other members of the chorus Joan was invited to a dinner party at the house Tyrone was renting in London. The thrill of the occasion was matched only by the fact that he insisted on dropping her off at home in his 1935 Rolls-Royce (with personalised number plate, TP1). Upon returning to Jermyn Street, Joan jokingly commented that she would love to return Tyrone's dinner invitation but only had bacon and eggs to offer him. Responding that he loved bacon and eggs Tyrone bade Joan goodnight and allowed her to return to the flat to regale Pat with all the news from her evening spent dining with a Hollywood star.

Little did Joan realise that her comment regarding bacon and eggs would stay with Tyrone and she duly received a telephone call from his manager, Bill Gallagher, asking if a date could be set up. To Joan and Pat's amazement they did indeed entertain Tyrone (and Bill) in their modest London flat where they dined on Caesar salad (as suggested by their neighbour Miles Eason) and bacon and eggs, cooked by Joan and her American beau.

Almost sixty years after the event, Pat would remember that she and Joan 'couldn't get over the thrill of meeting Tyrone Power'.[58] They were even more amazed when he took a pinafore off Pat, cut the rind off the bacon and insisted on helping Joan with the cooking. The occasion proved to be a long evening – with Tyrone and Bill dancing, talking and laughing with Joan and Pat into the small hours.

Pat Clayfield witnessed first hand Joan's friendship with Power, recalling that he was so well mannered and gentlemanly and always brought Joan home at a reasonable hour. To Pat it was 'quite obvious that he adored Joan'.[59]

Joan and Pat often joked about how 'Mummy Sims' would have reacted if Joan's romance with Tyrone had culminated in marriage and Joan being whisked off to America; 'We never did come to a conclusion on that,' remembers Pat.[60] Many of Joan's friends and colleagues, including Barbara Windsor, Sherrie Hewson and Geoffrey Palmer, clearly remember Joan talking about her time with Power and it is obvious that she was captivated by the dark-haired American film star, whom she would remember with affection until the very end of her life.

Joan's short relationship with Power ended when he returned to America. A few weeks later he sent Joan a card from his home saying he had enjoyed their time together but did not wish to become romantically involved. Although Tyrone had let Joan down gently she was not the only British actress to attract his attention. He went on to have a relationship with Thelma Ruby (which she later wrote about in her autobiography, *Double or Nothing*) as she reiterated to the author in 2014:

> Joanie and I met Tyrone at the same time, and afterwards were both invited for dinner to his London home. After that I was lucky enough to have a romance with him, which was a very glamorous time of my life!![61]

Within a short time of his return to America, Power married his third wife, Deborah Ann Minardos.[62] She was pregnant with their first child (a son born in January 1959) when Power died from a heart attack on the set of his latest film (*Solomon and Sheba*) on 15th November 1958 aged just forty-four.

A touching reminder of this happy time was kept by Joan: a Christmas card, delivered by hand to Joan at the Aldwych Theatre. Found among Joan's possessions at the time of her death it is embossed with the name 'Tyrone Power' in bold black type over which he simply inscribed 'Love Tyrone'. The card was accompanied by a compliments slip on which Power wrote: 'Don't just do something – stand there!'[63]

Not long after her friendship with Tyrone (and a brief spell where she hoped *Intimacy at 8.30* would transfer to America) Joan's time living in Jermyn Street came to an end. In retrospect Joan admitted this brief space of time in the mid 1950s was certainly one of the happiest periods of her life. She was young, slim, pretty, naturally cheerful and full of fun. She had the company of a dear friend, who was almost like a sister, and her career was taking off in a big way. Her social life was full and active and she had the thrill of boyfriends and admirers. For Joan, as the end of the 1950s approached, it seemed almost as if the world was her oyster.

*

Breath of Spring opened at the Cambridge Theatre on 26th March 1958. The cast was headed by the redoubtable and long-lived Athene Seyler as Dame Beatrice Appleby, and also included Michael Shepley (1907-61), Mary Merrall (1890-1973), Elspeth Duxbury (1909-67), Hazel Hughes (1913-74) and David Chivers. Among the veteran actors Joan was the youngest member of the cast, her nearest contemporary in age being Antony Baird, a rugged actor who had already appeared in several films and television productions, with whom she would become romantically involved (see Chapter 4).

After an absence from the theatre of two years Joan's next work on stage was in *The Lord Chamberlain Regrets...!* a musical revue written and devised by Peter Myers and Ronald Cass which opened at the Theatre Royal, Newcastle, on 12th June 1961. Joan was the star of the show, with billing above the title, along with character actor Ronnie Stevens and the effervescent musical star, Millicent Martin.

The Lord Chamberlain Regrets...! ended after twenty-one performances at the Saville Theatre on 24th February 1962. Thereafter Joan's appearances in the theatre became increasingly rare as she became more and more known as a film and television actress. It would be a further two years before her next work in the theatre in a new musical entitled *Instant Marriage*, written by Bob Grant[64] and with music by Laurie Holloway (perhaps best known as the resident pianist on the Michael Parkinson show for many years). The storyline saw Joan as Lavinia, Bob Grant's sister, 'an innocent girl from the north... coming south, getting involved with a marriage bureau and inadvertently becoming a stripper'[65]. While some critics thought the musical to be like a *Carry On* film with songs, once again Joan received favourable reviews for her performance:

> Joan Sims, as Lavinia, is more interesting and amusing when transformed into a lush beauty than as the plump spinster.[66]

Among the cast was Don McCorkindale,[67] then a young supporting actor, who remembers Joan with deep affection and gratitude:

> A really generous actor who was always ready with advice and encouragement for the younger members of the cast and offered in the most uncondescending way. I never felt as though I was a supporting artist but a valued member of the cast. The year I spent in *Instant Marriage* was a happy one, made possible by Joan.[68]

Joan later admitted to being thrilled at having the chance to sing in a musical and to be given the opportunity to have the backing of a full orchestra. It was during her run in *Instant Marriage* that Joan was introduced to Fred Trueman (1931-2006), the Yorkshire-born cricket player generally recognised as one of the fastest bowlers in cricket history. The pair 'hit it off immediately' and not only did Fred come and see the show, along with many of his teammates, but he also visited Joan in her dressing room, bringing with him a large bouquet of flowers. The encounter was fondly recalled by Joan almost forty years later in her autobiography. Alas, as if by a bizarre stroke of fate, during Fred's visit to her dressing room Joan would receive a telephone call from her mother. Thrilled at the presence of 'a gorgeous black-haired hunk'[69] Joan naturally told her mother of his visit whilst Fred was there. Her embarrassment at Gladys's reaction, as she berated her daughter for allowing a married man into her dressing room, must have been quite overwhelming. Pat Clayfield recalled that Gladys was 'outrageous and rude' and extremely annoyed at Joan's behaviour, however innocent it may have been.[70] Even if Fred had been an eligible bachelor it is doubtful whether he would have met with approval from Gladys who was apparently totally unimpressed by his world-class sporting skills or reputation. Joan's joy in the innocent attention of a male admirer would be scuppered by her over-protective mother. It was not the first time Gladys had interfered in the romantic side of Joan's life and it would certainly not be the last.

Reviews of the musical *Instant Marriage* were decidedly mixed. One critic deemed that Joan was 'completely wasted in the show' and thought the show 'corny' with 'poor music'.[71] R. B. Marriott writing for *The Stage* thought the production put British musicals back 'ten, twenty or thirty years'.[72] Joan's attempt at a striptease in the second half of the play was considered a highlight of the show.

Joan left *Instant Marriage* after 366 performances on 19th June 1965 and was replaced by character comedienne Patsy Rowlands, who would later work with Joan in the *Carry On* series.[73] Her departure from the play was perfectly timed to allow Joan to have a four-week 'break' before she returned to Pinewood Studios to start filming *Carry On Cowboy* in July 1965.

In her autobiography Joan's recollections of her next appearance in the theatre are almost non-existent and centre solely on her memories of her co-star Nicholas Parsons deliberately breaking up a scene to remove a scrap of paper from the stage which he thought may have distracted the audience! The play was *Uproar in the House* – a farce at the Whitehall Theatre – in which she played Melanie Sinclair from 19th October 1967.

Nicholas, who had worked with Joan in *Carry On Regardless* six years previously, admits he enjoyed a 'natural rapport' with his co-star. Joan's oft-said slogan that she was 'a stationmaster's daughter so never went off the tracks and always knew her lines' is one of Nicholas's fondest memories of her.[74] Equally amusing to Nicholas was Joan's love of spring onions – which she had taken to eating during her six-month appearance in the play – a passion he recalled in his autobiography and to the author:

I have a sensitive nose and rarely like kissing anyone, even professionally, if they have eaten strong-smelling food. Joan had an
ingenious solution to the problem: whenever she ate spring onions
before a performance she would always save two, which she would
then arrange to have laid out before the mirror on my make-up
tray.[75]

Whist Nicholas recalled the gesture as 'sweet and thoughtful' he
was not always keen to oblige Joan – especially before a matinee
performance![76]

As well as Nicholas Parsons the production also featured Peter
Butterworth (Joan's frequent *Carry On* co-star) and a future *Carry
On* performer in the form of Patricia Franklin. Then in her mid
twenties, Patricia remains extremely grateful to Joan for acting as her
guide and mentor during the play's run. Joan was evidently suitably
impressed with Patricia's acting skills and following their time
together in the theatre recommended to Peter Rogers that the young
actress should become a member of the *Carry On* team – a suggestion
he duly followed up on.[77] The play also reunited Joan with Brian Rix
(Lord Rix) with whom she had first worked on television almost a
decade earlier and in the 1956 film, *Dry Rot*. Lord Rix would recall
Joan as 'a very funny actress'[78] while she credited him with being the
only person ever to be able to persuade her to give up smoking
cigarettes. It was during their time together filming *Beside the Seaside*
(a 1959 BBC filming of the popular stage farce) that Lord Rix took
umbrage to kissing Joan because of the smell of smoke and tried hard
to persuade most of the other cast members to give up the habit.
Happily Joan did manage to break the habit, albeit only for six
months.[79]

Joan received good notices for her role in the production but was
clearly not challenged artistically by the farce: 'Joan Sims is
completely credible as "the wife", quickly establishing herself as the
pivot around which the confusion revolves. She is fun, but does not
have a real opportunity to fully extend herself.'[80] She was replaced
by her former co-star Eunice Gayson,[81] after almost two hundred
appearances in the play, on 17th April 1968 when filming commitments beckoned.

*

Since Joan's theatre credits after this point number just a handful of appearances it is worthwhile detailing them in this chapter, rather than placing them in chronological order.

The chance to work in another musical and the opportunity to co-star with Ronnie Barker, whom she admired greatly and who would become one of her great friends, saw Joan return to the stage at the end of 1971 in *Good Time Johnny*, a musical version of *The Merry Wives of Windsor*.

The costume designer on the play was Tim Goodchild who recalled Joan as 'very charming and a lovely lady to work with'.[82] His lavish creations suited Joan's figure perfectly and she was always at her happiest – and arguably looked her best – in period finery, something many of her friends, including Nicholas Ferguson, agree upon: 'Her style was more like an eighteenth-century lady – a sort of cuddly lady in frills. She was so opposite to the modern slim shape but it still was attractive.'[83]

Paul Chapman, one of her colleagues in the play, remembered 'being surprised and impressed with her singing and dancing abilities… which I don't think she was often called on to display'.[84] Three decades later Chapman was briefly reunited with Joan on the set of the BBC sitcom, *As Time Goes By*. The relatively short eight-week run saw Joan 'indisposed' for two performances of the play, in which her character of Queenie was played by Valerie Griffiths.[85] Likewise, Ronnie Barker also experienced his share of health problems during the show's run at Birmingham Rep Theatre and he was forced to withdraw from the production to undergo an operation on his vocal cords. Joan's hopes that the show would transfer to the West End were dashed when the play folded after less than eight weeks.

Queen Elizabeth II's silver jubilee celebrations were the key focus of 1977. For Joan the year was significant since it was the first year since 1965 when she did not work on a *Carry On* film. Instead Joan returned to the stage after an absence of more than five years to star in *In Order of Appearance* (A Musical Re-View) compiled by Wally K. Daly and Keith Michell.

The play was described as 'a look at Royalty' and among Joan's colleagues in the production were Paul Moffatt, Oz Clarke (the future wine critic, writer and broadcaster), Norman Vaughan, Paul Jones, Tony Robinson (who would achieve fame on television in the

Blackadder series in the 1980s and later as the host of *Time Team*) and Elizabeth Seal. For Joan a highlight of the event was meeting Princess Alexandra who was a guest at the Festival on 12ᵗʰ June, and being able to watch screen legend Ingrid Bergman (a friend of Kenneth Williams) who was also appearing in the Festival in a revival of N. C. Hunter's *Waters of the Moon*.

The Stage was delighted by Joan's return to theatre work, regarding her presence on stage as 'always welcome' and her performance as 'highly amusing'.[86] With material by Ronnie Barker, Sir John Betjeman, Spike Milligan, Tim Rice and Aubrey Woods[87] the production was undoubtedly a lavish one, with Joan taking on various roles including playing (Queen) Boadicea, Queen Anne and the widowed Queen Victoria.

During her time at Chichester Joan would make a rare public appearance at Ivanhoe's annual cricket match where she 'hit the first ball hard and truly'.[88] After a memorable day's cricket Joan would later attend a party to celebrate the occasion. It was a fleeting chance for fans to encounter Joan and one of only a handful of public events she would attend.

Almost a decade would pass before Joan would again choose to tread the boards. Stage work and the need to be word perfect was something Joan never relished.

In 1987 she would recall her time in Chorlton-cum-Hardy when she was given the lead in *Sarah Simple* – a role she considered at the time to be an 'enormous part'. This starring appearance remained firmly embedded in her memory and she confessed to being 'practically suicidal' with fear that she wouldn't know her lines. On this subject she went on to say: 'The nerves get worse – they don't get better.'[89]

Several years before her 1987 television interview – where she admitted to stage fright or at least the fear of forgetting her lines – she had been the subject of whispered criticism regarding her long absence from work in the theatre. Indeed it was suggested that she had lost her nerve and could no longer face the pressure of acting before a live audience. Such criticism, despite Joan's admission of stage fright, was fairly unfounded. Acting before a live audience was something she had had to cope with since her earliest days on stage and television and the latter would remain a fixture until the end of her working life. Like many of her colleagues and contemporaries (most notably Kenneth Williams) Joan simply found work in the theatre, with its long and unsociable hours, to be too demanding and too repetitive, particularly as she got older. As early as 1975 she admitted: 'Most managements are loath to give you a short run. They usually want you to stay in it for a year, but after about three months I must be honest and say I've had enough.' [90]

An additional factor to her lack of work in the theatre in the second half of Joan's career must also have been financial – since she could earn much more money from work on television where the pace was brisk and the performances never stagnant. Thankfully a steady stream of work on the small screen during the 1970s and 1980s meant that she was not forced to rely on long runs in the theatre or seasonal appearances in pantomime for financial support.

Nevertheless, almost in retaliation against the suggestions of her increasing stage fright, Joan took on the role of Fairy Sweetcorn in a pantomime production of *Jack and the Beanstalk* at Richmond Theatre at the end of 1984. It allowed her to silence any critics who may have doubted her nerve and also reunited her with an old *Carry On* chum, Kenneth Connor, making his final stage appearances and thus concluding a career in the theatre dating back to 1936. The cast also included Jimmy Edwards and Suzanne Danielle, who had starred in *Carry On Emmannuelle* six years previously. The role brought favourable reviews and she was 'all cuddly, twinkles and twirls' according to *The Stage*. Pat Clayfield was thrilled to see Joan on stage again and remembered the mere sight of Joan caused the audience to erupt.

> She came in as the Fairy and everyone roared with laughter as soon as they saw her… she remained absolutely serious and stayed quiet until the audience had calmed down before carrying on with her performance.[91]

Despite such success it was to be Joan's penultimate appearance in the theatre.

The chance of an all-expenses-paid trip to the Far and Middle East proved to be the major attraction for her final work on stage in Derek Nimmo's *Bedroom Farce* in 1988. Co-starring as Delia, the wife of Ernest (played by the prolific character actor Peter Jones[92]) the play also featured Barry Evans,[93] the star of the popular television series *Mind Your Language*, Richard Denning and Judi Maynard. It was well received with reviews confirming that 'the dialogue never failed to generate spontaneous guffaws from the audience till the curtain fell'.[94]

During her time on tour she would again admit that work in the theatre was not her personal preference: 'No actor should really say this, but I don't like the long stage runs. I find it very difficult to keep each performance fresh and besides I like getting up early in the morning.'[95]

3

The Big Screen Beckons

'They're not to know it's a piss-hole, Joanie!'

JOAN'S SUCCESS IN THEATRE REVUE meant that in 1952 she was not only performing in *The Bells of St Martin's* but also featuring in another revue, *Just Lately* (at the tiny Irving Theatre), at the same time. On top of this she was also understudying Gabrielle Bloom and Betty Marsden in yet another revue, *Ten Fifteen*. Joan's ability to succeed in this madcap world proved to be her saving grace in securing her career as a prolific film actress.

While work in the theatre was now flowing in, Joan hankered to be a big-screen actress. She had grown up watching sirens of the silver screen such as Rita Hayworth and Betty Grable and her child-hood dreams of following in their footsteps had never really left her. Joan's desire to break into films at the time was soon fulfilled, but almost inevitably was not a straightforward exercise. Meeting casting director John Redway for an audition was a terrifying experience for her. Sitting through the audition (which involved walking up and down the room in her 'best Rank Charm School manner') Joan realised that nerves had got the better of her and she had not performed well. Several days later Peter Eade was duly informed that his client did not have enough 'passion' in her performance, so much so that John Redway expressed his doubts about Joan's suitability for film work.

Within weeks of her disastrous audition, John Redway's initial thoughts on Joan's potential had been dispelled after seeing her perform on stage in *Just Lately* and she was duly offered the part of Beryl in *Will Any Gentleman?* directed by Michael Anderson. Based on the play by Vernon Sylvaine, and starring George Cole as a young bank clerk hypnotised into becoming a 'ladies' man', the film was the first time Joan featured in a production which included Sid James (the South-African-born actor who would later become a good friend and frequent co-star) and also featured future *Doctor Who* stars William Hartnell and Jon Pertwee and *Carry On* stalwart Peter Butterworth. It was not strictly Joan's first film appearance (see Chapter 2) but earned her the princely sum of £25 which she subsequently spent on her passion at the time – domestic goods (purchased from Selfridges). The occasion was not the first (or last) time Joan's extravagance would get the better of her when it came to money.

Joan's next film role saw her in the tiny role of the Fairy Queen in *Meet Mr Lucifer*, directed by the writer and actor Arnold Ridley – best known in later years as Private Godfrey in *Dad's Army*.[96] Several cameo roles subsequently followed (including a fleeting appearance with decent billing in the Sir Norman Wisdom comedy *Trouble in Store*) before Joan was cast as Nurse Rigor Mortis in *Doctor in the House*. The film was produced by Betty Box (wife of *Carry On* producer Peter Rogers), who at the time was one of the most powerful women in the film industry, and directed by Ralph Thomas – the elder brother of *Carry On* director, Gerald Thomas. Joan's one scene as the sexually repressed, apple-munching Nurse Rigor Mortis, with Dirk Bogarde as Dr Simon Sparrow, was significant since it allowed her to go on to appear in three more 'Doctor' films and through this role she also came to the attention of Peter Rogers, with whom her later career was inextricably linked.

From this point onwards Joan's film career simply took off, and over the course of the next five years she acted in more than twenty feature films, often in cameo roles. *The Belles of St Trinian's* is among the best known (and best loved) of Joan's early screen appearances. Starring Alastair Sim in the dual roles of headmistress Miss Fritton and her brother Clarence, the film also featured a fine selection of British character actresses including Joyce Grenfell, Irene Handl, Hermione Baddeley, Renée Houston and Beryl Reid. Joan, at her slimmest and sporting a flowing blonde wig, was cast as biology teacher Miss Dawn – it was a decorative role and somewhat more sizeable than those in which she had previously been cast.

Stilettoed, tearful and ultra-blonde Joan made another cameo appearance as Mrs Tebbitt in *The Sea Shall Not Have Them* before the success of *Doctor in the House* resulted in her being cast in its follow-up, *Doctor at Sea*. Joan's appearance as the plain, bespectacled Wendy Thomas could not have been further removed from the glamorous, statuesque beauty she had played a year earlier in *The Belles of St Trinian's*. The transformation was taken in her stride and displayed her striking versatility as an actress despite her youth.

Although Joan was conscious at this early stage in her career that she was often cast as clumsy maids, she later admitted to accepting any decent role in a film that came her way. Her appearance in *Dry Rot*, directed by Maurice Elvey and starring Brian Rix, Peggy Mount, Ronald Shiner and Sid James, saw her playing a cardigan-wearing chambermaid who was the love-interest of Brian Rix (as Fred Phipps). The role demonstrated her lack of vanity and willingness to play character parts even in her mid twenties.

By 1957 when she featured in *Carry On Admiral* (which had no connection with the *Carry On* films in which Joan would later star) Joan was an established film actress. The production, directed by Val Guest, saw Joan's curvaceous figure and shapely legs being used to full advantage in publicity photographs when she modelled Janet Dickinson swimsuits to help promote the film. Joan's legs would remain one of her best physical features throughout her life and a source of wonder to many of her friends and colleagues. In the mid 1960s, for example, Barbara Windsor would question why Joan hadn't played 'more sexy roles' because of her shapely legs and looking at Joan in films such as *Doctor in Love* it is easy to see that the praise was well justified.

Playing Phoebe in the Norman Wisdom classic comedy *Just My Luck* allowed Joan to show that she had perfected the ability to change her high-pitched tones from mock-refined Cockney to those of a shrill harridan. Joan and Norman's encounter in the cinema (where she demands a kiss if he is to secure payment of £1 from her) saw her receive good billing underneath several big names including Margaret Rutherford and Leslie Phillips. To her slight dismay Joan was rarely seen at her more glamorous on screen for very long, and she was soon back to playing a character role as Peggy Mount's nervous daughter in *The Naked Truth*, a classic comedy starring Terry-Thomas and Peter Sellers. One of Joan's scenes involved being submerged in the Thames at night as she attempted to assist her mother from being blackmailed. After being in and out of freezing cold water during the shoot Joan became very stiff and returned home in great pain. Pat Clayfield remembers that the production company sent a masseur to relieve Joan's muscular tension (the occasion allowed Pat to pick up some handy tips which she has used, on and off, ever since). Thanks to regular television repeats *The Naked Truth* remains one of Joan's best-known early film roles and despite her dowdy appearance in the film she revelled at being able to work alongside some of the country's best-known comedy actors. When filming was completed Joan was equally pleased to accompany the film's director, Mario Zampi, and his wife Kitty on a three-week holiday to Italy. Mario subsequently became a good friend to Joan up until his death at the age of fifty-nine in 1963.

This happy and intensely busy period of Joan's life saw her social life expand. There were numerous parties to attend at Peter Eade's flat in Duke of York Street and although Joan remained essentially shy there were occasions, as recalled by Pat Clayfield, when she was able to relax and be completely carefree:

At times she wasn't bothered about other people around her – would happily dance on her own at parties and wouldn't think about anyone else or the effect she may have on them – maybe she got herself into another part?[97]

Eleanor Fazan would also witness Joan at her best, especially when music was added to the equation: 'She could turn her hand to anything and would happily dance to the gramophone. She certainly knew what she was doing (as a dancer).'[98]

Although she could find it very difficult to start a conversation with strangers, privately, and when comfortable, Joan was wonderful company. 'She was a great mimic and very good at "taking people off",' remembers Pat Clayfield; 'the little monster would take me off as well!'[99] This party trick was also recalled by Eleanor Fazan who reiterates that Joan was 'very good at sending up other star actresses, behind closed doors'.[100]

David Kernan, who made his name in musical theatre alongside the likes of Jean Simmons and Julia McKenzie and who would later feature in *Carry On Abroad*, clearly remembers Joan's vitality:

My first meeting was at my agent's flat in Knightsbridge… It was my birthday and he invited Joan for supper… we're talking here 1968! After a considerable amount of bubbles and the red stuff I cheekily asked her to sing me a song on my birthday. She gave a splendid impersonation of Judy Garland singing *The Man that Got Away!*[101]

Part of a typed letter, dated 18th March 1958 and sent to Peter Eade at his address in Cork Street, was found amongst Joan's personal papers. It serves to emphasise the zany light-heartedness of the time and is worth recording in full:

WHITELIPT & TREMBLING
'You require a top-flight star?'
'We have got the best by far'

Kindly note new address:
ST. JAMES'S THEATRE, SW1
(To leeward of demolition hut)

NEW YORK OFFICE:
M.C.A. Building
Lower Ground Floor
Boiler Room

PARIS OFFICE:
Café aux Deux Magots
(Blanche Bouche et Tremblant can usually be found at pavement table nearest to the abattoir)

ALL COMS:
The Hall Porter
Atheneum
Pall Mall
(Messages are promptly delivered as the partners at present are lending a hand in the kitchens)

Dear Pete,
Re: the Platinum/Golden/Red/Mouse/Jet/Highlighted/Bald/Joan Sims (delete whichever are inapplicable)
Once more it is my duty, nay pleasure, to contact you re this capital little performer. Two of our associates – who must remain nameless for reasons of high theatrical policy – are desirous of engaging her to depict as leading woman in their new review, 'For Ulcers Only'. Were the circumstances not, as Mr Whitelipt vivaciously says, 'Dicey', I am sure that the West End standard of the patter would convince you that this is an engagement your formidable artiste should accept. But dicey being the 'mot juste' I have a suggestion to make. For the first time in living memory the

agency, nay personal management, has talent on its books that is currently resting. This is due to the end of term of 'School' coming rather sooner than we hoped. Now, as you know, we are an organisation of unimpeachable integrity who bear no grudge towards the Kosher Lady with the Beads (Michael Codron[102]). But under the circs. [sic] aforesaid talent would, subject to mutually satisfactory terms being arranged, band together and create all hell in the gallery of the Cambridge next Wednesday. Do give this idea your mature consideration.

Enclosed please find the dots of 'For Ulcers Only'. Miss Sims role is as follows:

DAWN FANTASY – District Nurse
STAR QUANTITY – Ada
SIC TRANSIT GLORIA – Front cloth single
THREE MEN IN THE SAME BOAT – Dr Summerskill
THE SHOW MUST GO ON… AND ON – Linda
HALLS OF ILL FAME – Kitty

The author of the one-page letter is unknown since only one section has survived. It is possible it was the work of Kenneth Williams.

Along with the string of appearances on the big screen, ranging from cameo roles to key supporting parts, Joan was also taking on an increasing amount of work on television as the medium slowly became a household commodity in many homes around the country.

In Philip King's farce *On Monday Next* (part of the BBC's Sunday Night Theatre series) Joan co-starred with Leo Franklyn (1897-1975) and Cyril Chamberlain.[103] It clearly showed her talent to a wider audience and *The Stage* would comment that 'Miss Sims hasn't been exploited nearly enough on the small screen'.[104]

Another television performance saw Joan feature in ABC Television's star-studded 1960 adaptation of *Alice Through the Looking Box*, as a chambermaid alongside Irene Handl. Other cast members included Bernard Braden, Barbara Kelly, Jeannie Carson (as Alice), Spike Milligan (as the White Rabbit), Harry Secombe (as Humpty Dumpty), Bernard Bresslaw (as the Doormouse), Bob Monkhouse (as the Cheshire Cat), Michael Medwin (as Knave of Hearts), Ron Moody (the Mad Hatter) and Dora Bryan as the Red Queen. The Christmastime special, directed by Michael Mills and recorded in two parts, saw a 'modern' Alice entering 'the fantastic world of television'.[105] Despite its stellar cast, a copy of the production does not appear to have survived, to the disappointment of fans of British comedy.

As the 1950s drew to a close Joan was firmly established as a key feature in many Rank productions and she revelled in being a specialist in cameo roles. Her talent, versatility and professionalism helped build up a good reputation among casting directors and booking agents and it was no great surprise that she was called upon again in 1960 to feature in another Ralph Thomas film, *Doctor in Love*, playing a shapely stripper alongside Liz Fraser, with whom she would become friends. It was one of Joan's more glamorous roles and two years later she was again called upon to play another stripper (the wonderfully named Gale Tornado) in *A Pair of Briefs* in which she provided an upbeat cameo role alongside Bill Kerr, Amanda Barrie and Judy Carne. In between there were other memorable performances including that of Blodwen (another maid!) in *Upstairs and Downstairs*, dual roles in *Please Turn Over* (a *Carry On* type affair with another all-star cast in which she played a French maid and cigarette-smoking cleaning lady), *Mr Topaze* (directed by Peter Sellers) and the Michael Redgrave comedy *No, My Darling Daughter*.

Nurse on Wheels was just one of several screen comedies starring Joan which were effectively *Carry On* films in all but name.[106] She was thrilled to be cast in the lead role of the Gerald Thomas/Peter Rogers 1963 production but subsequently quietly heartbroken when the role was recast because she was deemed too plump to take on the glamorous female lead. While Juliet Mills was cast to effectively replace Joan, as a consolation prize she was given her pick of any other female role in the film and eventually settled upon playing the part of the vicar's daughter, Deborah Walcott. Amazingly Peter Rogers even increased Joan's appearance fee and she had the added bonus of being reunited with Athene Seyler (of whom Joan was very fond), making her final feature-film appearance. Despite such compensations, the damage to Joan's morale and self-confidence had been done. She took the rejection badly.

In addition to regular work in all areas of the profession, as seemed to be the fashion at the time Joan also took to the recording studios in her thirties, following in the footsteps of numerous colleagues who had novelty hits in the charts including Bernard Cribbins ('Right Said Fred', number 1 in the charts, 1962), Barbara Windsor ('Sparrows Can't Sing') and even Bernard Bresslaw ('Mad Passionate Love').

Joan was undoubtedly a talented singer and her comedy timing meant she was an 'obvious candidate to record a silly song or two'.[107] Composer Ted Dicks was the man behind the runaway success of Bernard Cribbins's novelty songs and teamed up with Myles Rudge to work with Joan. Her first LP, featuring 'Hurry Up Gran' and 'Oh Not Again Ken' was released in 1963 and followed shortly afterwards by 'Spring Song' and 'Men'. Joan realised that the recordings were never destined for greatness but enjoyed her time working with Sir George Martin who produced the records and returned to the studio again in 1967 to record a third (and final) single featuring 'Sweet Lovely Whatsisname' (a homage to Engelbert Humperdinck) and 'The Lass With the Delicate Hair'. Sadly the LPs failed to make much of an impact, to the dismay of Joan's friends; 'I'm surprised they never did better – it was a great pity,' laments Pat Clayfield.[108] Joan was later heard singing on the 1970 LP *The Sleeping Beauty* (in which she sang as the Wicked Fairy), in *Carry On Stuffing* (on television in 1972) and finally in a 1997 episode of *As Time Goes By* when she could be heard briefly blasting out several lines from 'Tie a Yellow Ribbon'.

By the mid 1960s Joan had been a professional actress for more than a decade. Although still only in her mid thirties she had achieved stardom in a society and profession very much dominated by men. While Joan would never consider herself a pioneer within the industry, her career certainly provided inspiration for a host of young actresses who would attempt to follow in her considerable footsteps. Interestingly by this point in her career Joan had already seen many of her female contemporaries quit the profession for various reasons. Several well-known budding actresses with whom Joan had shared early screen appearances famously chose to put family life before professional success, while many simply did not have the talent and versatility to maintain an acting career when their looks began to fade.

The Big Job was one of a couple of occasions when Joan was to work with Sylvia Syms, the leading screen actress four years Joan's junior who in later years would enjoy a successful career as a character actress.[109] Produced by Peter Rogers and directed by Gerald Thomas (and naturally filmed at Pinewood Studios) the film, which centred upon a group of 'inept bank robbers' who are released from prison after fifteen years to discover that the hollow tree in which they had hidden their loot now stands in the yard of a new police station, saw Joan playing a widowed landlady (Mildred Gamely). Various chums including Sid James, Dick Emery, Lance Percival and Jim Dale starred alongside Joan and Sylvia Syms and Edina Ronay, the future fashion designer, completed the main cast list playing Joan's daughter (Sally). Although Joan thought Mildred to be 'shrill' and 'overbearing' she ultimately turned out to be slightly more dynamic than some of Joan's other screen characters at the time.

Amazingly, despite acting in more than seventy feature films, Joan Sims never travelled further afield than Calais to shoot a picture. It was on the set of the 'silent' 1965 comedy *San Ferry Ann* that she first met Barbara Windsor, who had made her *Carry On* debut as Daphne Honeybutt in *Carry On Spying* in the previous year. The two ladies shared a room during their time in France and many laughs – never more so than when Barbara insisted upon buying postcards to send back home to her family who assumed that because she was abroad she had travelled to a 'posh' location. Despite the appalling setting and terrible weather Barbara duly wrote out the cards to her family while laid on her bed with Joan 'giggling' at her throughout. Over forty years later Barbara recalled her response to her colleague's bemusement and, in her typically honest way, remembers turning to Joan and saying, 'They're not to know it's a piss-hole, Joanie!'[110]

From this point in her career the *Carry On* series increasingly began to dominate Joan's film credits, and during the remainder of the 1960s and throughout most of the 1970s she remained loyal to the films which would ultimately make her an instantly recognisable face throughout the world.

4

Will Any Gent?

'I'm not doing anything wrong, am I?'

JOAN'S DISTINCTLY SHELTERED CHILDHOOD hardly prepared her for a life and career on the stage. Gladys and John's initial reluctance to allow Joan to pursue a career as an actress was threefold. Firstly, the profession was alien to the couple; and secondly, it was notoriously unstable. Furthermore, despite their ignorance of the stage, they must also have been aware that it would thrust Joan into a world of sex, drugs and alcohol which she had previously never dreamt of.

London in the 1950s and 1960s had its 'seedier' elements, and in the theatre drugs and alcohol were as much a part of day-to-day life as make-up and lighting. 'Uppers' and 'downers' were frequently used by actors and a number of Joan's contemporaries and even close friends were known to dabble with various drugs from marijuana to 'purple hearts' (a combination of amphetamine and barbiturate).

It must have been something of a relief to Joan's parents to know that she was living with Pat Clayfield (Hornsby) for several years in the 1950s. A vibrant, enthusiastic character with a natural zest for life, Pat was Joan's ideal flatmate. The pair, who labelled themselves the 'railway children', became extremely close; as Pat confirms, 'We really were like sisters. We never rowed, we always bailed each other out and I loved her.'[111] A great organiser, and above all great fun to be around, Pat was able to look after Joan and provide practical and moral support for her but never in a domineering or autocratic way. Small wonder, then, that Joan would recall their time living together as one of the happiest periods of her life.

The closeness of the two ladies certainly was immense. Until the mid 1960s they were able to share clothes (although not being exactly the same size precluded them from sharing shoes) and when living together at Jermyn Street shared the motto 'first up – best dressed'. Whenever either of them had an audition they invariably prayed that the other would not also have one on the same day since between them they only had one 'really good' dress suitable for such an occasion. When rushed for time the two ladies would even share a bath, jokingly fighting about who would sit at the 'tap end'. Their time spent living together was a blissful arrangement for both parties and a period remembered by Pat with deep affection: 'We were like genuine family.'[112] In later years, when Pat had left the acting profession and was working full-time in publishing, Joan would often spend holidays with Pat's parents, and when Molly Hornsby died in 1976 Joan would become good friends with Pat's stepmother.[113]

Despite moving out of the family home, Joan was not immune to the influence of her parents and in particular the almost suffocating grasp of her mother. Pat's closeness to Joan meant that she witnessed, first hand, the influence of Gladys both in person and over the telephone.

> Whenever Joanie had a boyfriend and 'Mummy Sims' thought it was getting too serious then the phone calls would start coming at half past eight at night when we were going to bed early because we were possibly filming early in the morning. I couldn't hear what was being said on the other end but tears started running down Joan's face and I would think, 'Oh no, no, no, she's only young, there's no need for her to be so difficult about it.' Nobody was good enough for Joan as far as her mother was concerned.[114]

Although Pat admits that 'Joan got on with everybody' there was a limit to her friendliness. While many actresses of the day gained reputations for having an endless string of lovers the same could never be said of Joan. Once she had left the family home in Laindon Joan experienced a new level of freedom, yet despite this she remained restrained in her lifestyle as Pat Clayfield remembers:

> Joan and I were very good – morally – we didn't hop in and out of bed with people and I think a lot of people were surprised by this.[115]

During the run of *Breath of Spring* in 1958 Joan met actor Antony Baird,[116] who was playing the policeman in the production. A divorcee, more than a decade older than Joan, according to his biography in the play's programme Antony Baird was living on his own yacht at Chiswick during the production of *Breath of Spring*. Joan would later recall that Antony's 'pride and joy' was little more than 'a peeling wreck'.[117] He had began his acting career in the early 1940s, appearing in minor roles in various 'B' films, and had also made a number of television appearances. Shortly before joining Joan on stage he played PC Wrothbury in six episodes of the serial *Big Guns* which was perhaps his most notable television work.

Nicholas Parsons remembers first meeting Antony Baird in Glasgow in 1945 and, although he considered him 'very good looking, charming and a delightful fellow', he was acutely aware even in those early days that Antony 'didn't have that extra *something* and as a result professional success eluded him'.[118]

Born Antony Broderick Baird on 1st January 1919 in Hillhead, Lanark, he married Evelyn Millicent Hardwick in August 1938 at the age of just nineteen. Six months later their first child, Patricia, was born followed quickly by three more children: Felicity, Antony Stephen and Peter.[119] Following the end of the Second World War Antony had left Scotland – and his young family – to pursue an acting career on stage and screen, and by 1945 he had already made the first of more than a dozen film appearances.

Anthony Baird's very sporadic acting career continued almost until the end of his life. He was still appearing on stage into the 1970s and during the 1960s featured in numerous television series, from *Crossroads* and *Z Cars* to *Danger Man* and *No Hiding Place*. Coincidentally he even managed to notch up an appearance in a *Carry On* film by playing an Amazon Guard in the James Bond spoof *Carry On Spying* in 1964. Notably, it was a *Carry On* romp that did not include Joan.

While admitting that initially she 'couldn't bear' Antony, Joan quickly became attracted to the man she would later recall as something of a 'black sheep' and a 'rogue'. In her late twenties Joan fell 'madly in love' with Antony and he moved in with her at the flat she was still renting at Wilton Place.[120]

Although described by Eleanor Fazan in a 2002 documentary as 'a bit of a ne'er-do-well' Antony was generally well liked by Joan's friends and indeed by Eleanor herself who would later admit that Baird was 'charming... a typical actor and very good at putting on a show of comfortable well-being'.[121]

For the first time in her life Joan was involved in a serious romantic relationship and she revelled in the normality of being part of a couple and enjoying nights at the cinema, dining out and meeting up with friends. It is interesting to note that in her film appearances during this time (particularly *Doctor in Love* and *Carry On Regardless*) Joan was slimmer than she had been for several years and appeared to positively glow. Sadly the carefree happiness of the relationship was not to last. Living with a man at the time was heavily frowned upon and 'living in sin' was relatively uncommon, even within Joan's liberally minded theatrical circle. Joan felt an underlying element of guilt throughout her relationship with Antony, perhaps because of her strict, conventional upbringing and also because of Baird's previous failed relationship and commitments.

Meanwhile there remained the problem of telling her parents about her liaison. Gladys Sims was no fool. She was aware very early on that her daughter was 'involved' with Antony Baird and took every opportunity to express her displeasure at her daughter's relationship with a divorcee. She was quick to remind Joan that she could 'do better' – despite the fact that she never actually met Baird. Although they were aware of Joan's relationship with Baird neither Gladys nor John realised that he was actually living with their daughter. Their visits to London would see Antony evacuate the flat he now shared with Joan. Each time Mr and Mrs Sims arrived Antony would be obliged to remove every trace of his existence in order not to upset Joan's parents who she felt were guaranteed to be horrified at her 'sinful' domestic arrangement.

Two years into their romance Joan decided to finally admit the truth of her relationship with Antony to her parents. Having travelled to Southchurch to spend Christmas with John and Gladys she plucked up the courage to reveal to her mother that she was living with Antony, informing Gladys that she was 'very happy' and asking her to 'accept' the situation.

Gladys's reaction to the news bordered on hysteria. From the family kitchen where she was sat with her daughter she screamed for her husband who was in his favourite position in the living room listening to the radio. Joan would later recall that while her father sat very quietly after Gladys had told him the news, her mother 'went absolutely bananas'.[122]

After a long period of silence John Sims turned to his wife and said, 'Well, Gladys, I suppose we can't expect our daughter to lead the life of a nun,' and with those words retired to bed.[123] Quite possibly John was aware that his own less than ideal marriage had not provided Joan with the best example of a truly happy relationship. Since Joan had always been 'morally' good it would appear Mr Sims had no reason to deny his daughter the chance of lasting happiness, regardless of the circumstances. Gladys, on the other hand, had completely different ideas. She felt that Joan should hold out for 'Mr Perfect' and held a very dim view of sexual relations, frequently saying 'there's nothing in sex – nothing at all'.

Once the announcement had been made Joan had to face a night of continual 'sobbing and wailing' from her mother – made all the worse by the fact that they were sharing a twin bedroom while John Sims slept alone in another room. The following morning Joan informed her mother that unless her hysteria stopped and she accepted the situation she would be forced to return to London – something she subsequently did. Joan was informed by her father that the situation would 'break her mother's heart', and with his words ringing in her ears Joan drove back to Wilton Place.

Just after Christmas a letter arrived from Joan's parents, as she later recalled in her autobiography:

> It was in my father's handwriting, but the words were certainly my mother's: 'Fingers of shame will be pointing at you... Remove this seducer from your home... God knows how you have persecuted us.'[124]

The lengthy (four-page) diatribe left Joan bewildered and deeply upset.

This difficult time left a great impression on the few people who were privy to it. Joan's younger cousin, Yvonne, remembers that Joan had previously thought of taking Antony to Southchurch to meet Mr and Mrs Sims and following her revelation a series of letters were exchanged between Joan and her parents. Yvonne recalls '*the*' letter from John Sims to his daughter as 'terrible' and she was well aware that her Aunt Gladys was adept at working her husband into a 'right rage'. Equally, whenever Gladys wanted something 'horrible' done, she would invariably persuade her husband to do it.[125]

On the advice of Peter Eade Joan wrote back to her parents informing them that she would not give up her relationship with Antony. Gladys and John did not reply to their daughter's letter. The situation had reached a stalemate. Joan would not give up Antony. Her parents would not see their daughter until she did. For six months there was no contact at all between Joan and her parents.

Sadly the highly emotional situation only served to emphasise Joan's guilt at living with Antony and the deception she had created. The relationship slowly began to unravel and Joan's infatuation began to fade as she increasingly had to support Antony who was frequently out of work. Things finally came to a head when Joan returned home to their rented flat following her tour of *The Lord Chamberlain Regrets...!* in the summer of 1961. She found the flat unkempt with piles of dirty laundry sat waiting for her. It seemed that Antony had spent most of his time in the local pub or sitting around 'with his feet up' whilst she was working to keep him. By the time she ended her run in the play Joan had informed Antony that she wanted the relationship to end – something which left both of them heartbroken.

Pat Clayfield looks back on Joan and Antony's relationship with mixed emotions. She remembers the couple's time living together at Wilton Place while she herself was residing in Wembley. Pat maintains that without the interference of Gladys in particular the relationship had the potential to succeed: 'Joan absolutely adored Tony and everything would have been alright... I don't think they [her parents] ever wanted Joan to marry. If they had allowed it I think she would have been a different person.'[126]

Eleanor Fazan rather thought that Joan's relationship with Antony ended not purely because of her parents but because of Joan herself. Fazan felt that Joan, who had been 'adored' and slightly 'spoilt' by her parents, found it difficult to sustain a relationship with a man. In addition Joan always remained conscious of her status as a 'star'. By the time Joan met Antony she was a leading lady and since Baird never rose above being a supporting actor he was perhaps 'just not successful enough' for someone of Joan's professional stature. Likewise Joan would have 'found it impossible' to give up her career to become a full-time wife and mother and the love of her life would remain her work.[127] Anything which interfered with Joan's passion for acting, even an intimate relationship, was viewed by her with some degree of scepticism. Another major factor during her relationship with Antony was a financial one. Throughout their time together Joan had been the main 'breadwinner' in the household, something her upbringing simply did not allow her to feel comfortable about. 'If we'd had househusbands in those days it wouldn't have mattered,' she would later comment.[128] At the time, however, it was largely unheard of that a woman should support a man.

While Joan maintained that the break-up was necessary for her own 'survival' the relationship was perhaps doomed from the start, not just because of Joan's parents and her own demons but also because of Antony's tainted past. He had after all left behind a young wife and three young children in Scotland to pursue a career on stage in London and was perhaps 'embarrassed that he had abandoned them for Joan'.[129] Antony's family and past life would largely remain something of a mystery to Joan and her inner circle. She was certainly never called upon to play the role of stepmother to his three children.

After the couple split Antony carried on acting on stage and television and doing occasional work as a compere. He never became a 'star' and indeed never managed to rise above playing minor supporting roles in further television series such as *Special Branch* and Diana Dors' series *Queenie's Castle* (in which he played a policeman in four episodes in 1970). His acting work became more and more infrequent although he is credited with television appearances as late as 1981. In the same year, however, he was no longer a member of Equity (the actor's union) who were attempting to contact him regarding royalties' payments via the actor's newspaper, *The Stage*. His final film role came in the Disney production, *Cheetah*, in 1989, an appearance I have been unable to verify.

Joan did not keep in touch with Antony Baird after their relationship ended. It was tragically ironic that both parties would end their days alone. Antony's final years were spent living in sheltered accommodation at Ada Court in Maida Vale, London. He died from lung cancer at the hospital of St John and St Elizabeth, Westminster, on 27th August 1995, aged seventy-six. Seemingly without any family or even close friends with him at the end of his life, Baird's death was registered by Westminster City Council's funeral director who also organised his burial.[130]

*

It is fair to say that Antony Baird was the only serious romance Joan ever experienced. Arguably the break-up of their relationship was the most catastrophic event of Joan's personal life. After they parted ways she began a slow decline into regular bouts of depression, a reliance on alcohol and an increasing battle with her weight which would blight the next four decades.

Joan's involvement with Antony – kept secret from her parents for so long – had a major impact on her life and particularly her relationship with her mother. By the time the couple split Joan was over thirty and possibly realised that the chances of another long-term (or lifelong) relationship were slim. Almost inevitably this rather sad realisation led Joan to look for comfort and she found this in alcohol.

Pat Clayfield, who was privy to Joan's deepest feelings at this point in her life, explains the change which occurred in her friend after Antony had left her life:

> It was round about that time the depression really began. She started one or two bouts prior to that – but when that happened the whole change came. It was almost as if she was saying, 'Well if you're doing that to me, I'm going to do what I want,' and wouldn't actually say this or couldn't – but just drank.[131]

Like her mother before her, Joan had experienced periods of depression in her twenties; but the real beginnings of her battle with mental illness can be pinpointed to this time in her life.

At times Joan had an almost child-like nature and in some ways it is not surprising that she retaliated against her parents by drinking heavily following her break-up with Baird. Her reaction to their key role in sabotaging her romance was very much the reaction a teenage girl would have in a similar situation. Sadly this retaliation would become a habit and eventually an addiction – although to the end of her days Joan refused to label herself an alcoholic. In times of unhappiness and loneliness Joan would increasingly take solace in alcohol, allowing herself to 'blot out' whatever was troubling her at the time.

It is also slightly ironic that Antony was the person credited with 'introducing' Joan to alcohol. In her autobiography Joan remembered his 'love' of Scotch whisky and how she tried to 'emulate both his taste and his intake'.[132] Pat Clayfield confirms he enjoyed a drink in social situations and remembers his ability to cope with its effects: 'He could hold his drink.'[133]

Throughout her twenties alcohol had not featured heavily in Joan's life. Although it appears that Gladys may have sought comfort in the occasional drink in her latter years, neither of Joan's parents drank heavily and they rarely socialised. Even after she had moved out of the Stationmaster's House at Laindon and set up home permanently in London Joan rarely drank. Aside from the sheer cost of alcohol, Pat Clayfield remembers how much things have changed since she first met Joan: 'In those days we didn't have wine. You couldn't go to the pub and ask for a glass of wine... everything was so different.'[134] In their early days if the friends did drink together it would be in a light-hearted way. Once such example of this is worth recording; during their time together at Jermyn Street Pat remembers she and Joan decided to try and make the 'new' cocktail at the time – 'Between the Sheets'. Having gone out at lunchtime to buy the ingredients the two friends completed their mission and decided there was only once place to drink the concoction – in bed![135] It was only after her split with Tony that Joan's relationship with alcohol suddenly changed.

Not long after Baird had left Joan's world at Wilton Place she went on to have a relationship, as 'boyfriend and girlfriend', with John Walters, a stage manager who was also well-liked by Joan's inner circle. The couple had known each other for years – John was assistant stage manager for *High Spirits* – and Joan admitted to 'an innocent romance' with him in the 1950s. She seemed to almost rebound into her secret relationship with John, who lived with her for nearly two years, but her heart was never truly captured and she later wrote:

> John, who had been brought up in a children's home, was much more moody than Tony had been, and somehow I never felt that ours would be a long-term relationship: I simply couldn't have lived with those wildly varying changes in his temperament.

It was while living with John that the idea of motherhood raised its head, as Joan went through the one and only 'broody' phase of her life:

> At one point we did talk of getting married and having children – the only time I have ever thought seriously about it – but we agreed that we both had too many reservations.[136]

It seems this was never more than a casual relationship and again would end in tears after a relatively short period. Above all else Joan desperately wanted to remain a 'star' and was unable to combine a successful career with a successful relationship. In this, of course, she was not alone. So many of her contemporaries sacrificed personal happiness for professional success.

Painfully aware of her unmarried state after her break-up with Antony and John Walters, Joan would remain optimistic that she would meet someone: 'I'm hoping the spinster state won't go on for too long. When a girl gets to 34 she starts worrying about things like that... But the right chap hasn't come along yet. So we'll just have to wait and see,' she said in 1964.[137]

During the remainder of the 1960s Joan had a number of 'boyfriends' without ever getting involved in another serious relationship. She had never been very confident around potential suitors and what little confidence she had was seemingly shattered at every opportunity by Gladys. By the time she reached her mid thirties Joan had become increasingly unsure of herself when it came to men. Although during their RADA days Pat Clayfield remembers Joan being much more confident than many of their contemporaries, she feels that by the late 1950s a certain shyness (perhaps lingering from her childhood) had began to engulf Joan. It says much for her growing insecurity that Joan would often question, 'I'm not doing anything wrong, am I Pat?' especially after the 'bust up with Tony [Antony]'. Summing up Joan's decline from this point onwards Pat Clayfield states: 'She was the kind of person who just couldn't live on her own... that was when the rot set in.'[138]

*

At the age of thirty-three and following the collapse of her relationships with Antony Baird and John Walters, Joan bought her first home: an elegant, spacious Victorian terraced house in Hurlingham Road, Fulham. After living in a succession of flats for more than a decade Joan revelled in the space of her new residence which was set out over five levels and cost £8,000.[139] It was a shrewd investment, although sadly Joan did not reap the financial benefits of her venture into property. In June 1996 the property sold for £325,000 and by 2013 the estimated value of the property was £1,636,988.[140] Joan moved into the house shortly before Christmas 1963 and immediately started work to improve her first real home. Ten workmen were duly employed to carry out the work and the house became a hive of activity, although as Joan later remembered her hospitality may have slowed down proceedings:

> The place rapidly became an all-day canteen with me serving tea and cakes and keeping the men chuckling at my chatter. No wonder they took so long to finish the job![141]

Not long after moving in Joan granted a rare interview and revealed that 'a very famous actor' was about to become one of her neighbours, but discreetly declined to name him since contracts had not been signed.[142] The actor was Sir Tom Courtenay[143] who remembers that estate agent Bernard Walsh found homes in Hurlingham Road for both him and Joan and that she was already living there when he moved in.[144] Joan was photographed at home in various poses: relaxing with a cigarette, making a cup of tea dressed in a pinafore and in the driver's seat of her car on her way to the BBC television studios to film *The Dick Emery Show*. It was one of only a handful of occasions during her life that Joan allowed herself to be photographed at home.

Over the course of the next sixteen years the house, which overlooked a large, tree-filled playground, would see Joan play hostess at numerous parties. Although she never gained the same reputation as Hattie Jacques, who was well known in the acting fraternity for her culinary skills and generosity as a hostess, Joan's gatherings were invariably star-studded affairs and certainly impressed her young cousin, Yvonne, who was often added to the guest list. In addition to Tom Courtenay, Joan's neighbours included Noel Harrison[145] and actress Joan Heal (who had co-starred with Joan in revue a decade earlier). Along with many other famous faces, including writers Ian La Frenais and Dick Clement, they would be Joan's guests at house parties from time to time. In later years chums from the *Carry On* series, in particular Kenneth Williams, would often gather at Joan's home for dinner, drinks and much hilarity. The chance to see Kenneth and Joan perform their 'star turns' never failed to entice would-be guests, and in the company of close friends Joan was at her best – happy, relaxed and hugely entertaining.

During the early years of her time in Hurlingham Road Joan was intensely busy with film and television work which suited both her nature and her bank balance. Despite investing in property her financial situation was comfortable and she could even afford the occasional extravagance. Her spare time was spent 'cooking and watching television… plays, old films and documentaries' and when the weather was fine she would drive into the country in her Mini car 'to get away from it all'.[146]

Joan's increasingly well-known profile brought with it the occasional 'public' appearance. In November 1963 she was a special guest at the Bowater-Scott Mill where she presented a transistor radio to eighteen-year-old Patricia Wenman for being 'the Smartest Girl in the Mill'. Joan's visit to the Mill saw her 'setting an excellent example of smartness in a black coat, trimmed with fur'.[147] She was accompanied by Ted Dicks and Myles Rudge who along with Joan were treated to a tour of the paper mill. Relatively speaking this was a rare chance for members of the general public to encounter Joan Sims since she always remained reluctant to attend public events.

*

An interesting afterword to Joan's romances is provided in the unlikely form of Kenneth Williams. Joan and Kenneth were both clients of Peter Eade and had met briefly in his office in the 1950s but did not become great friends until the filming of *Carry On Nurse* at the end of 1958. They remained close until his death twenty years later. Kenneth openly adored Hattie Jacques, who was a huge calming influence in his life, but enjoyed a slightly more volatile relationship with Joan. He loved 'strong' leading ladies who were able to match his forthright personality and thus revelled in the company of Dame Maggie Smith, Sheila Hancock and Barbara Windsor. Joan too was more than a match for Kenneth. Director Nicholas Ferguson, who became good friends with Joan in the early 1980s, clearly remembers her more forthright side:

> She could be quite strong. I remember once when we were out with a friend of mine and he and I were quarrelling about something and she got very strict and told us both to shut up. One always thinks of her as sweet and gentle but if it was needed and necessary she could make her voice heard.[148]

Joan was well aware of Kenneth's 'twin obsessions' – his privacy and hygiene. Joan (along with Hattie) was one of the few friends to see inside Kenneth's home – a sparsely furnished flat on Osnaburgh Street in London where he lived from 1972 until his death. Joan considered her visit to the flat something of a triumph, she and Hattie having used their 'combined weight' to more or less force their way into Williams' abode. Having succeeded in their mission to get inside the flat the pair did not force the issue of using Kenneth's lavatory, knowing that he invariably directed visitors to a public convenience down the road if they asked to use his loo! Joan was equally aware that Kenneth was gay – 'spiritually' if not physically. His homosexual leanings, however, did not prevent him from asking Joan to be his wife.

By the time Kenneth Williams proposed to Joan, possibly during the filming of *Carry On Loving,* she was over forty. It was, as he candidly told her, a last chance for both of them to start a family of their own (or in Kenneth's words: 'I'd give you a child if you wanted one'). Although Joan claimed never to be particularly maternal, the issue of children had cropped up in her life from time to time. Now her biological clock was 'ticking' – a fact played upon by Williams.

Kenneth's official biographer suggests that, contrary to Joan's recollections, the proposal probably took place in August 1973 when Kenneth recorded in his diary that he had spent an evening with Joan in a 'lousy' restaurant:

> In the middle of the meal (half of which was uneaten) Joan burst into tears and said, 'I need somebody in my life, Kenny!' […] I gave her my handkerchief and she kept squashing it into a sodden ball and crying convulsively.[149]

Kenneth felt that they would make a 'wonderful couple' and be able to host 'fabulous parties'. His offer of fathering a child with Joan was followed by what Joan later described as 'small print' – since he insisted he would need to carry on leading his own life afterwards. In this respect his proposal was not dissimilar to a proposition he had put to Barbara Windsor some years earlier. When Kenneth asked if Barbara would marry him if she were to ever leave Ronnie Knight (her first husband) she was initially flattered. His proposal was quickly followed by a clause: 'Mind you, there'd be no sex!' [150]

Joan would admit she thought the proposal was 'bizarre' and it left her confused and somewhat uncomfortable. Without wanting to hurt Kenneth's feelings Joan asked what was in the offer for her, to which Williams replied: 'Oh, nothing but sand!'[151] It was a reply Joan never quite understood – but it was enough to break the tension of the moment as the two friends burst into laughter.[152]

Kenneth's marriage proposal to Joan became a well-known and oft repeated story among their friends and colleagues within the profession. It was well known that the pair were great friends and 'liked each other enormously'.[153] Nicholas Parsons, who worked with Williams for years on radio in *Just a Minute*, remembers Joan telling him about the event:

> She got on very well with Kenneth Williams – I think because they both came from working-class backgrounds. They certainly laughed a lot together. She told me that he did propose to her once but warned her 'there will be no nonsense in the bed'. Joan admitted to having normal desires in that department and concluded that the arrangement just wouldn't suit her.[154]

Joe Grossi, who worked with Joan in the late 1980s, was also privy to the story: 'She spoke fondly of Kenny and told a small group of us at lunch one day that he had proposed to her once.'[155]

Bruce Copp, Hattie Jacques' one-time lodger and dear friend, was well placed to confirm that Joan and Kenneth were 'very fond of each other'. A war hero and culinary expert, Bruce ran his own restaurants for many years and later became manager of the Establishment Club. He was devoted to Hattie Jacques and as a result frequently saw Joan at Hattie's home in Eardley Crescent for 'lunch or dinner or some kind of meal' and found her to be 'adorable and intelligent and always prepared to talk about anything connected to the arts'. Kenneth Williams was another frequent visitor. Remembered by Bruce as 'intellectual, agreeable over lunch and jolly and funny – although he wasn't normally funny', Kenneth along with Hattie and Joan made a 'good trio'. On the subject of Joan and Kenneth marrying Bruce felt that Joan 'wouldn't have minded a sexless marriage' although he admits 'it would have been complicated'.[156]

Interestingly, children adored Kenneth Williams and they brought out the best in his multi-faceted character. A significant amount of his later work on television was providing 'voices' for classic children's programmes including *Willo the Wisp* and *Galloping Galaxies*, both of which brought him a new generation of fans. His affection for his thirteen-year-old godson, Robert Chiddell, was demonstrated when it was revealed that Kenneth had left a quarter of his £538,000 estate to the boy in his last will and testament in 1988.

Privately Joan was deemed equally 'marvellous' with children and loved by youngsters who were lucky enough to encounter her. One of Pat Clayfield's grandsons 'absolutely adored' Joan and has never forgotten her – despite the fact that she died when he was just six years old. Despite Joan professing to being un-maternal the under-lying question of whether she would have wanted children *if* she had ever married is one we can only speculate on, although Pat Clayfield believes the answer would have been 'yes' and that Joan 'would have been a good mother'.[157]

Inevitably, because she remained single and after the 1960s boyfriends began to dwindle, there was some speculation regarding Joan's sexuality. Ronnie Barker was more open than most and during their time together on stage in 1971 'looked at Joan very seriously' and asked if she was a lesbian. He admitted that his questioning was based purely on the fact that Joan had never married and that he had never seen her date any men.[158] Joan's apparent lack of boyfriends was also noted by other contemporaries, and Sir Tom Courtenay recalls: 'My impression was she was lonely. I didn't know any boyfriends… I never saw her with anyone.'[159]

Those closest to Joan confirm there was never any question that she was undoubtedly strictly heterosexual and it was a misconception that she did not have boyfriends following Antony Baird and John Walters. Despite the weight gain she was so blatantly conscious of, Joan remained attractive to the opposite sex into her fifties. Stylish, well dressed and immaculately groomed, her shapely legs and porcelain complexion remained her best physical attributes even at the end of her life. Her doll-like prettiness likewise never left her. Boyfriends – and occasional physical interludes – would certainly continue to some degree until at least 1980.[160] Thereafter she would only joke of romance and passion – admitting for example (at the age of seventy) her fondness for the American actor George Clooney: 'Isn't he divine? I could eat him on toast.'[161]

The great influence inflicted upon Joan by her mother would have a massive impact on her self-esteem and mindset. Pat Clayfield held out hopes that Joan would meet another long-term partner following her split with Antony Baird but with the passage of time watched her friend increasingly lose her confidence.

> When asked if she'd like to marry and have children she would reply, 'Yes, but who could I marry?' – it got like that. There were some other boyfriends after Tony and I remember Bill saying, 'Don't tell your mother, Joan.' He'd say: 'We'll sneak you off and get you married,' to which Joan replied, 'Whatever would mother say?' If she'd met the Earl of something Gladys would probably have approved.[162]

Painfully aware of Gladys's underlying snobbery, the two friends would frequently remember their encounter with Tyrone Power and would jokingly question what Gladys would have said if Joan had married him. Suffice to say Pat admits, 'We never came to a conclusion!'[163]

Joan's profession inevitably brought her into close contact with many gay men. Aside from Kenneth Williams, Charles Hawtrey and Frankie Howerd, she had many other gay friends. It was a two-way attraction; they revelled in her company and she was completely happy being revered in their presence, so much so that in later years she would proudly label herself 'a Queens' Pudding'. In 1998 while discussing her love life she also revealed that she had fallen in love with a gay man, 'thinking that I could change him; but of course I couldn't'.[164] Nicholas Ferguson confirms Joan's affinity with gay men:

> I think she had crushes on homosexuals because possibly they were safer and I think there was a pattern there – possibly. I don't know that for a fact but I'm pretty sure. Perhaps she feared men, I don't know. She liked men and she liked the company of men enormously but I think she felt safer with gay people.[165]

Although she never took on the mantle of a gay 'icon', *à la* Judy Garland or Dame Shirley Bassey, Joan nevertheless had a large gay following, especially at the end of her life (a two-page tribute to Joan would appear in edition 95 of the gay men's magazine, *Attitude*, following her death).

On the subject of boyfriends Joan Le Mesurier recalls, 'Some of them didn't make her very happy but she didn't talk about that... Bless her heart I don't think she had much luck in the male department. She ended up with no one but she needed a family and a home.'[166]

After working with Joan in the theatre in the 1950s and on screen and radio in the 1960s, Fenella Fielding was also aware of Joan's private unhappiness:

> She didn't have a very nice love life. She had this guy who I think was her boyfriend but when he moved in he suddenly went cold on her.[167]

Many, including Pat Clayfield, felt it was a great shame that Joan never did marry: 'She had the cat to say hello to but that was it... It was sad because that girl had such a lot to offer. She deserved somebody.'[168] Nicholas Parsons echoed Pat's sentiments: 'It was very sad she didn't find "Mr Right" because she would have made a loyal, loving wife. She just never met the right fellow.'[169]

Joan herself remained philosophical and matter-of-fact about the issue, writing in her autobiography:

> I never married because the right person never came along... I leave others to see for darker explanations. For me it's extremely simple!

Throughout her life Joan was frequently questioned about why she had never married. By 1988 when she discussed the matter in a newspaper interview boyfriends had become a thing of the past and her male friendships were purely platonic. It is fair to say that by this point her career had firmly become her life:

> This is a very testing career to be in, and yes, maybe I have seen too many of my colleagues and friends in marriages that haven't worked. Really I'm a workaholic. Of course I get lonely but everyone does – I guess. I'm at my best when I'm working.[170]

The failure of so many of her colleagues' marriages was clear to see and the list was extensive: Hattie Jacques was John Le Mesurier's second wife and they divorced in 1965 (with Hattie's subsequent relationship with John Schofield also ending disastrously), Dilys Laye was twice divorced before finding happiness with her third husband Alan Downer, Barbara Windsor was twice divorced; and it seemed a rarity, particularly within Joan's circle of female friends and colleagues, if a marriage could stand the test of time (a notable exception being June Whitfield who was happily married to her husband, Tim Aitchison, from 1955 until his death in 2001).[171]

Aside from her career, which was the abiding love of her life, Joan had few real interests away from the stage. She listed her hobbies as 'cooking' in the 1980 Theatre Guide and friends confirmed that in her early days she was indeed a natural 'homemaker'.[172] Her homes had a warm, cosy feeling about them and her flat in Thackeray Street was described as 'inviting' with a fine selection of bone china and paintings. She found some domestic chores 'therapeutic', admitting she could get lost in thought while washing up, and until her final years did all of her own housework. Joan was also a fine cook, a trait inherited from her mother, and was particularly adept at preparing 'plain' English food of the 1950s such as steamed puddings and blancmange.[173]

In her thirties Joan freely admitted to being a 'simple' girl – happiest 'pottering' around her home and listening to records 'from the popular shows'.[174] After moving into Hurlingham Road the novelty of having a garden was something she enjoyed for a while, although her interest in horticulture was by no means an avid one. Likewise, unlike many of her friends, Joan was not a great letter-writer. Indeed the most she tended to write were cards at Christmastime: her Christmas card list in the 1980s numbered around 100 names, including Dilys Laye, Angela More (Angela Douglas), John and Joan Le Mesurier, Hattie Jacques' two sons, Gerald Thomas, Peter Rogers, Ronnie Barker and even Martin Christopherson (Hattie Jacques' friend and one-time employee).

Cards among Joan's personal possessions at least give some clue as to the relationship she shared with her mother in the latter half of the 1960s. Visits to and from Gladys would frequently be followed by 'thank you' messages and affectionate greetings would be sent on birthdays and Mother's Day from Joan and also from her cat, Amanda (Mandy). These slight pieces of correspondence from Mandy, addressing Gladys as 'Gran', say much about Joan's child-like personality:

> Dear Gran,
>
> Thank you for all your kindness to me when my Mother has to go away. I do enjoy my titbits with you – I don't always get them here in London. Hope to see you very soon. Have a lovely birthday and many happy returns.
>
> From Mandy x[175]

Each card sent from Mandy, in Joan's handwriting, would be accompanied by a hand-drawn sketch of a cat beneath her 'signature'. Although she always regarded herself as un-maternal it is clear that Joan still needed an outlet for her affections, even if this was merely being 'mother' to her feline friend. Generally, however, Joan was regarded as someone who needed to be looked after and this was a trait which never really left her. In her late fifties she would admit:

> This may sound daft but I've been someone who's very late in maturing; possibly because I've been cosseted in many ways in my life, with people doing things for me that I should have been doing myself.[176]

Although aware of her own shortcomings when it came to her 'neediness' it wasn't until the very end of her life that Joan was able to cast off her insecurities and develop a true sense of personal independence and self-confidence.

5

What a Carry On

'We were like kids at school'

To FULLY CRITIQUE EVERY ONE of Joan's thirty-seven appearances in the *Carry On* series, including starring roles in twenty-four of the feature films, would be to create a book in itself. Each one of her roles in the classic film series was different and truly illustrated her versatility as a star character actress. Although often labelled 'the nagging wife' of the series (and she did indeed play this role, more or less, in at least a dozen of the films) Joan nevertheless managed to add fresh nuances to every one of her portrayals. Despite the regularity of playing harridan-type characters in the films she was never typecast in the series, unlike many of her co-stars. It is hard to imagine any other actress portraying the cheeky, glamorous, buxom Désirée Dubarry in *Carry On Don't Lose Your Head* and the dowdy, downtrodden, chronically deaf Chloe Gibson in *Carry On Doctor* less than a year later. The two characters are poles apart in every way possible – so much so that it seems incredible that they were played by the same person.

As a result of her versatility and ever-changing image in the *Carry On* films, Joan is perhaps less well-recognised for her work in the series than some of her contemporaries. Kenneth Williams is forever remembered as the acidulous 'doctor', Sid James as the lecherous but lovable rogue, Hattie Jacques as matron, Charles Hawtrey as the bespectacled eccentric and Barbara Windsor as the buxom blonde love-interest. Joan's contribution to the beloved comedy institution is less easy to define.

The *Carry On* series began with *Carry On Sergeant* in 1958. Produced by Peter Rogers and directed by Gerald Thomas the film was made on a modest budget of just over £70,000 at Pinewood Studios in Buckinghamshire and would set the precedent for another thirty films – all filmed at Pinewood on a shoestring budget, usually within the space of six weeks.

The commercial success of *Carry On Sergeant* immediately saw Rogers and Thomas casting for a second film, which began production within months of *Sergeant* being released. Joan had previously worked on several Betty Box films so was already familiar to Peter Rogers (Betty's husband) as a reliable and versatile actress.

Joan's *Carry On* debut saw her make an immediate impact in a scene-stealing role as trainee Nurse Stella Dawson in *Carry On Nurse*. Her wonderfully naïve performance, combined with her rounded face, almost made Joan into the 'juvenile lead' of the film, despite being years older than the other nurses: Shirley Eaton, Ann Firbank and Susan Beaumont.

Carry On Nurse brought Joan back into contact with Hattie Jacques (playing Matron) and secured a friendship which would last until Hattie's death. Although Joan had encountered Kenneth Williams from time to time as a fellow client of Peter Eade, their time on the set of *Carry On Nurse* was the first time they had worked together. They became instant friends. Other important friendships were also formed during the hectic six-week shoot – notably with Charles Hawtrey (the eccentric bespectacled character actor who made his film debut in 1922) and Kenneth Connor (then a well-known radio star who ultimately starred in seventeen *Carry On* films) with whom she had already worked on a couple of occasions. Joan would also be reacquainted with character actress Joan Hickson (who had played her mother in *Doctor at Sea*) whom she would act alongside on both screen and television over the next twenty-five years.

Diminutive character actress Christine Ozanne made her screen debut as the 'Fat Maid' in *Carry On Nurse,* a role she remembers fondly as 'a first in so many ways'. Six years younger than Joan, she recalled her co-star forty years after they had first worked together:

> At the end of the day Joan Sims offered me a lift in her chauffeur-driven limousine. She was appearing in *Breath of Spring* at the Duke of York's every evening, and as we arrived at the theatre she instructed the driver to 'take this young lady wherever she wants to

go'. (I met up with Joan again about 30 years later on a TV show, and I reminded her of her kindness. She didn't remember it at all.)[177]

For Joan at the time her appearance as the accident-prone trainee nurse was relatively insignificant, at least professionally speaking. Having already appeared in over twenty films and with other screen appearances already lined up there was no reason to suspect that *Carry On Nurse* would mark a turning point in her career as a film actress.

Carry On Nurse was released in 1959 and went on to become the most popular film at the box office in that year. It also proved to be a surprise hit in America where it was reportedly screened at some cinemas for a staggering three years. On a more personal note Joan would recall that her first *Carry On* appearance was also the first (if not the last) time that she shed blood on a film set. In one scene she was required to collide with a hospital surgical trolley and fall to the ground. The gag would result in Joan hitting a sharp edge of the trolley and as a result she was left with a deep gash in her shin which saw her rushed to the medical room at Pinewood for stitches. As the films were shot very quickly, with no room for errors, in typical *Carry On* fashion Joan was back to work before the end of the day filming additional scenes.

Before beginning work on a second *Carry On* film Joan suffered another accident on the set of *Upstairs and Downstairs* (directed by Ralph Thomas and produced by Betty Box) when she was required to fall over a suitcase and ended up with a bruised leg, of which she made little. By the time shooting began on *Carry On Teacher* Joan was in considerable pain and a visit to the medical room at Pinewood resulted in her being diagnosed with thrombophlebitis (a circulatory problem that develops when a blood clot slows the circulation in a vein) in her right leg. For the first few days on set Joan was required to sit with her leg propped up on a chair, out of shot of the camera, before being taken to hospital where she remained for almost two weeks.

Carry On Teacher saw Joan cast as the shapely gym mistress Miss Allcock, the love interest of school inspector Leslie Phillips (as Alistair Grigg), with whom Joan had worked four years previously on *As Long As They're Happy* and more recently in *Please Turn Over* (directed by Gerald Thomas). The pair would subsequently work together on a number of occasions over the next three decades and became good friends. Phillips would remember Joan in his 2006 autobiography as 'hysterically funny' and 'admired' her 'madness and joy in her work'.[178] Having already met some time earlier via their mutual agent, Peter Eade, Joan was pleased to work again with actress Rosalind Knight (who had also appeared in *Carry On Nurse*) on the set of *Carry On Teacher* – when they were required to have a drunken 'cat-fight' in the staff room.[179] The film also featured the esteemed radio star Ted Ray,[180] in his only appearance on the series; and not for the last time the script caused eyebrows to be raised by the censor (resulting in Leslie Phillips not being allowed to place emphasis on either the beginning or the end of 'Allcock'). Shirley Eaton was absent from the film (having featured in leading roles in both *Sergeant* and *Nurse*) and it was left to Joan to admirably play the leading lady.

On the set of the film the cast was visited by Charles Hawtrey's mother, and there is an oft-repeated story involving Joan as she sat with his mum listening to one of Charlie's stories:

> … while he was recounting his story, his mother… was enjoying a cigarette and listening so intently that she inadvertently dropped the end of her lit cigarette into her open handbag. Joan Sims, who was the first to spot what had happened, cried out, 'Charlie, Charlie, your mother's bag is on fire!' Without pausing for breath, Charlie tipped what was left of his tea into the bag, snapped it shut and carried on the conversation as though nothing had happened.[181]

Carry On Teacher, made on a budget of less than £80,000, proved to be another smash hit for Rogers and Thomas and thus ensured that the series would continue to run.

Amid the early success of the *Carry Ons* came *Our House*, a hugely successful television series produced for Thames Television (ITV), which reunited Joan with Hattie Jacques, Charles Hawtrey and Norman Rossington. Essentially a vehicle for Hattie Jacques, the sitcom was principally written by Norman Hudis who by this point had scripted the first six *Carry On* films (*Sergeant, Nurse, Teacher, Constable, Regardless* and *Cruising*). The series saw nine people, from various walks of life, brought together by 'an urgent need to find a place to live'. In the first episode all nine characters decide to pool their resources to buy a large house where they can all live together.[182]

Ernest Maxin, who produced and directed the series, recalled the cast with fond memories in his ninetieth year. He found Joan 'delightful to work with and quite funny when being herself' and admitted she 'took direction very well, never questioned my ideas and was a real pro'. Like the *Carry Ons,* the series was produced at breakneck pace; a total of thirty-nine episodes filmed like a live stage show with the cast and crew sometimes working up to seven days a week. Ernest remembers the actors as already being 'very good friends'; and, while Joan was a director's dream, the same could not be said of Charles Hawtrey, who played Simon Willow in every episode of the sitcom. 'He was a strange character and basically exactly the same on screen as off. He'd always stick to the dialogue but despite direction he'd still do things his own way. What you saw on screen was him,' remembers Maxin.[183]

While Norman Hudis wrote the dialogue for each episode it was Ernest Maxin who helped provide ideas for the stories. His own career started at the tender age of six and peaked while working with Morecambe and Wise when ratings for their series rose from 11 million viewers to a record-breaking 30 million viewers. The cosy atmosphere on the set, despite the hectic pace, was helped not only by the cast already being good friends but also by the fact that Leigh Madison, who became Ernest's beloved wife during the course of the series, was also in the cast as Marcia Hatton (alongside Australian-born actor Trader Faulkner as her newly-wed husband Stephen). The couple had met three years previously and reacquainted when Leigh was among thirty actresses to audition for the role of Marcia. They sensibly kept the date and location of their wedding a secret thus ensuring the event remained 'a quiet family affair with no fuss'.[184]

The series was extremely well received by the public with reviews rating it 'hilarious' and 'a howl'. The stellar cast ensured that *Our House* 'crushed all records for television viewing' and became 'a shattering success'.[185] While Hattie and Charles Hawtrey would go on to make a second series of *Our House* – joined by comedy legend Hylda Baker and future *Carry On* star Bernard Bresslaw – Joan's character of Daisy Burke lasted only for the first thirteen episodes due to her commitments in the theatre.

Sid James arrived in Britain from South Africa on Christmas Day 1946. Within nine days he had secured a role in the feature film *Black Memory*, and by the time he made his *Carry On* debut in *Carry On*

Constable he was one of the country's best-known actors thanks to over eighty film appearances and a string of hits both on television (notably in six series of *Hancock's Half Hour*, with Tony Hancock) and radio. With Sid taking the lead role of Sergeant Frank Wilkins the film was another commercial success for Rogers and Thomas. Joan, cast as the efficient WPC Gloria Passworthy, played the love interest of Constable Charlie Constable (Kenneth Connor) and happily this time managed to complete the six-week shoot without accident or incident!

As Lily Duveen, a member of the Helping Hands agency, Joan's appearance in *Carry On Regardless* (filmed in the winter of 1960-61) saw her working alongside Liz Fraser just months after they had completed their youthful double-act in *Doctor in Love*. Joan's overriding memory of *Regardless* involved the wine-tasting session where she was required to collect tickets at the door but ultimately ends up joining the tasting session and sampling the goods. Having rehearsed the scene the night before Joan was on set the following morning and by 8.30am had completed a run-through and was ready for her take. Unbeknown to Joan, one of the 'samples' of wine was replaced by Gerald Thomas with neat gin. She would later recall her (genuine) reaction to the alcohol was the one used in the final film release and jokingly admitted that she was 'out for the count' for the rest of the day.[186]

Nicholas Parsons was among a large number of guest actors called upon to star in cameo roles in *Carry On Regardless,* in which he played the 'wolf' encountered by Joan during the infamous wine-tasting session. Over fifty years later he would recall his co-star:

> I was very fond of darling Joanie. I first met her in the fifties in intimate revue and worked with her in *Carry On Regardless*, in that very funny scene where she hit me with the wine bottle, and again in *Uproar in the House*, and she never changed. She was a genuine, warm, giving person and very professional – what we call in the business a real pro.

He considered Joan to be a 'superb character actress with genuine talent and certainly one of the strongest members of the [*Carry On*] team'.[187]

Regardless saw Joan's hourglass figure shown off to its full potential. Personally and professionally she was possibly at the happiest of her entire life and it showed in her physical appearance as she positively glowed on screen.

Having starred in four consecutive *Carry On* films made between 1958 and 1961 Joan then missed out on a further four films (*Cruising*, *Cabby*, *Jack* and *Spying*) as she was busy with other productions. It is often stated that Joan was cast to appear in *Carry On Cruising* but had to be replaced just days before filming began due to illness (Joan's old chum Dilys Laye dyed her hair blonde and stepped into the fold opposite Liz Fraser). Since Joan had only just finished her hectic run in *The Lord Chamberlain Regrets...!* this has always seemed like a valid reason for absence from the film. It has also been stated that during production of *Carry On Regardless* the previous year, Joan had become romantically involved with a carpenter on the set to the displeasure of Peter Rogers.[188] Whether Joan was 'dropped' from *Cruising* because of an apparently innocent fling is questionable, since she herself never made any reference to it. If she had indeed incurred Rogers' displeasure it would not be especially long-lasting.

When Joan returned to the *Carry On* series, which was by now well established, it was to star as Calpurnia, the wife of Julius Caesar (played by Kenneth Williams) in *Carry On Cleo*, one of the most lavish entries in the series thanks mainly to Peter Rogers using sets, props and costumes left behind from the Elizabeth Taylor/Richard Burton production *Cleopatra* which had cost $44 million in 1963. *Carry On Cleo* marked a turning point in Joan's role in the series. From here on in she would frequently be called upon to play the 'nagging wife' in the *Carry On* films. Joan's youthful, slapstick antics of the earlier films slowly began to be replaced by more domineering portrayals, possibly due to Joan's increasing maturity but also because of a change in the series' scriptwriter: Norman Hudis was the scriptwriter for the first six films in the series, while Talbot Rothwell took over from 1963 until 1974.

Joan considered *Carry On Cleo* one of the very best of the *Carry On* films. She was duly impressed with the luxurious sets and thrilled to have costumes especially made for her (a rarity in the *Carry On* world). The costume designer on the film was the beautiful and elegant Julie Harris (who won an Oscar in 1965 for her work in the black-and-white film *Darling*) who found both Joan and Amanda Barrie 'delightful to work with and good at wearing their Roman/Egyptian costumes'.[189] Ironically, in later years Joan and Julie Harris would share the same cleaning lady and as a result would occasionally chat on the telephone.

Interestingly *Carry On Cleo* was the only time in the series when Joan was required to swear – although the deed was very brief (she can be seen mouthing 'piss off' to Kenneth Connor when she realises he is on top of her bed). It was one of the few occasions in the entire series when an expletive was used.

Once Antony Baird had left her life for good, Joan's relationship with her parents eventually returned to normal although it took some time for the emotional wounds to be healed. Following his retirement from his position as stationmaster in the early 1950s, John Sims had spent his days indulging his passion for gardening and the radio and there were frequent visits to and from Joan. To the end of his life he continued to take delight in showing visitors his collection of press cuttings charting his daughter's success, often to his wife's annoyance. In the spring of 1964 Joan received word that her father had been admitted to hospital in Essex suffering from bronchitis. Peter Eade subsequently drove Joan to her father's bedside where she found him to be gravely ill. John's final words to his daughter were a request to 'look after' Gladys. He died later that night on 21st March 1964, aged seventy-five. It was only after John's death that Joan and Gladys discovered he was suffering from terminal cancer of the stomach and lungs.

John's funeral took place five days after his death, on 26th March. Gladys was a notable absentee from the proceedings. She could not bring herself to attend the ceremony and stayed behind at the couple's home to prepare refreshments for mourners who had attended the funeral. Her father's funeral bill remained among Joan's possessions at the time of her own death in a box labelled 'Mother and Father – Personal'. It showed the cost of the funeral (a cremation at Southend-on-Sea Crematorium) to total £54, 13 shillings and 6 pence. John had left strict instructions written on the envelope of his Last Will and Testament (signed and dated 14th April 1963), 'My body to be cremated. No flowers and wear no mourning please.' The executor of his estate was Malcolm Mumford, Gladys's brother-in-law. John's Post Office savings amounted to £104, 8 shillings and 10 pence.[190]

The death of John Sims left a huge void in the lives of his wife and daughter. Although John and Gladys were not an ideal match their marriage had survived for over forty years. John had worked hard to provide for his wife and daughter. Now, for the first time in her life, Gladys had to face ordinary, everyday tasks (such as paying household bills) that had previously been taken care of so diligently by her husband. To her credit Gladys, by then in her late sixties, did manage to adjust to life on her own, and even took on new hobbies such as pottery classes to help fill her days.

During John's life, laughter, to some degree or another, had been almost guaranteed. As Pat Clayfield recalled, Mr Sims was 'full of fun and it was normally the three of us laughing and not Mummy Sims'. It brought Joan great pleasure to know that she was far more like her father in personality than her mother and many felt Joan's 'lovely sense of humour' was a quality inherited from the former station-master.[191] Joan's career brought her father a great deal of pride and opened up a world previously unknown to him. Whenever he was with his daughter's friends he tried to mimic 'what he rather quaintly thought was the "in" language of the London theatre', and during Joan's days in rep would ask, 'Any dead wood in this show of yours Joan?' – a catchphrase remembered both by Joan in her autobiography and Eleanor Fazan to the author.[192]

John's demise inevitably brought a change in Joan's relationship with her mother and sensibly, following her father's death, Joan made a firm stance and did not allow Gladys to move in with her. Just months after John's death Joan revealed:

> When my dad died last Easter I thought my mother might want to sell her place at Thorpe Bay and live with me. But she told me she wouldn't want to leave her friends. And besides with her here I wouldn't be able to find room for a husband![193]

Those closest to Joan seem to recall this situation differently and remember Joan being very adamant that Gladys would not move to London, realising the catastrophic impact this would have on her life. Gladys would remain in Southend during her widowhood (where her sister 'Floss' also lived until her death in the mid 1970s), although her visits to Joan became increasingly frequent and often prolonged.

By the mid 1960s Joan was well established as one of Britain's best-known character comediennes. Having already made over forty film appearances – in addition to her work on stage, television and radio – as she reached her mid thirties Joan was certainly in a good position to offer words of professional advice to other aspiring actresses:

You must make absolutely certain that it is the one thing in life you really want. You must love the work and have no illusions about it being a glamorous life. There is glamour attached to it, but there is a great deal of hard work as well. Hard knocks are sure to come along on the road to success, but you must take them and come up for more.[194]

*

As early as 1959 Joan's weight had been a talking point for the press when she freely admitted, 'I like all the wrong things, like fatty roast potatoes, Yorkshire pud and my pressure-cooker stews.'[195] Joan's fondness for 'the wrong things' combined with a work schedule that at times saw her filming throughout the day and working on stage at night did nothing to help her figure. Between filming *Carry On Nurse* and *Carry On Teacher* she attempted to lose a stone and booked herself into a 'Nature Cure resort' at Tring.[196] Plenty of rest, living on fruit juices and enjoying regular massage sessions proved to be something Joan enjoyed and visits to health farms would become a feature of her life for the next thirty years. Grayshott Hall in Surrey was her favourite health retreat and she became well known within the profession for her frequent visits to the health and fitness centre, as recalled by Fenella Fielding:

> My memory of her is that every now and again she would go off to a health farm and lose all the weight and look absolutely smashing and then she'd suddenly put it all back on again and had to go away again. She was always doing that. It was a constant battle with the weight and especially in films it matters terribly. It's maddening to think she could only play character parts – not that anyone minds because she was brilliant but it is lovely to play the love interest now and again! I know that did upset her.[197]

Following her heartbreak at being recast in *Nurse On Wheels*, Joan's weight increasingly began to cause her concern and was again noted in a rare newspaper interview she granted in 1964: 'She now carries a few extra pounds.'[198] In the same year she went on to say, 'I've always had a weight problem. But life gets so miserable when you're on an endless round of either starting a diet, suffering because of a diet, or breaking off a diet because your will power is sagging!' At this stage in her life Joan weighed 10 stone and hoped to slim down to 9 stone and 3 pounds; 'I doubt if I'll ever make it. I get so hungry between takes!' [199]

Joan embraced her curvaceous figure for one of her all-time favourite roles in the series when she played Belle – the sharp-shooting, gutsy saloon owner – in *Carry On Cowboy*. Once again she was thrilled with her costume and hairstyle for the shoot and revelled in one of her finest film appearances. Her fondness for her role in *Cowboy* was clearly mirrored in the number of publicity photographs she had printed of herself in costume which were subsequently sent out for friends and fans. Many (unsigned) prints still remained in Joan's collection at the time of her death.

In the final scenes of *Carry On Cowboy* she was required to ride a horse as she rescues the Rumpo Kid, and stills of the scene clearly show that it was indeed Joan on horseback rather than a stunt double (at least for the initial part of the shot). In 1975 Joan would recall the film as one of her favourites: 'I hadn't seen the completed film until I saw it on television. I loved it. I must admit it really was quite impressive.' [200] Her sentiments would be echoed twenty-three years later in the 1998 television documentary, *What's a Carry On?*, when she recalled walking down the staircase of the saloon towards a captivated Sid James, a subservient Peter Butterworth and gobsmacked Kenneth Williams.

Another of Joan's memorable scenes was her cat-fight with Angela Douglas (and Edina Ronay) with whom she became friends. Angela would later recall her co-star as 'wonderfully gifted' while remembering her difficulty in keeping a straight face throughout the fight scene (Angela would spent quite some time with her face buried in Joan's shoulder to avoid ruining the shot). [201]

In the midst of her return to the *Carry On* series, Joan was still also appearing in other screen comedies, notably as the prickly hospital matron overcome by laughing gas in *Doctor in Clover* alongside the redoubtable James Robertson Justice. The film saw Joan on screen with Fenella Fielding, who would make an iconic appearance in *Carry On Screaming* shortly afterwards, and who recalled the appearance over forty years later:

> She was still terribly nice when we did *Doctor in Clover* – we only had one brief scene and she had to be very stern with me! [202]

Joan's fourth and penultimate role in a *Doctor* film was another happy project (despite having to be submerged fully clothed in a swimming pool) since she was also reunited with Leslie Phillips and given the chance to work alongside Arthur Haynes, whom she greatly admired, prior to his premature death from a heart attack at the age of just fifty-two.[203]

Carry On Screaming has stood the test of time as one of the one of the best – and best-loved – of all the *Carry On* films. A parody of the popular Hammer House of Horror films (in much the same way as *Carry On Spying* was a send-up of the James Bond '007' films) it featured a handful of the main team, including Kenneth Williams, Bernard Bresslaw and Jim Dale, as well as Harry H. Corbett in a one-off guest-starring role.

Joan's role in the film saw her cast as Mrs Emily Bung (Corbett's wife). It was probably the most vitriolic role of Joan's entire career. Her shrill, nagging tirades directed towards Corbett culminate in her following him to Oakham Woods where she is subsequently kidnapped by Oddbod Junior (played by Billy Cornelius) and turned into a shop mannequin. This particular part of the storyline involved a life-size plaster cast of Joan's body and face being made (with Joan suffering for her art under layers of plaster of Paris for approximately one hour) to feature in several shots. Following Emily's 'demise' Corbett is looked after by Valeria, the stunning *femme fatale* of the film, played by Fenella Fielding in her finest screen appearance. The final shot of *Carry On Screaming* is notably left to Joan (in mannequin form) as she winks knowingly to the camera at her on-screen husband's antics.

The new year of 1966 saw Joan depart Britain for sunnier climes when she agreed to travel to Cartagena in South America to attend a Columbian film festival. It was originally intended that Julie Christie and Joan's neighbour (Sir) Tom Courtenay would be star guests at the event which would screen their latest film, *Billy Liar*. When Julie was forced to withdraw from the event Joan was deemed to be a suitable replacement since the *Carry On*s already had an international audience which included cinema-goers in South America. Subsequently Tom Courtenay was also forced to withdraw from the festival and it was left to Joan to fly the British flag at the event.

As ever Joan needed help in preparing for her journey and after enlisting the assistance of Pinewood's wardrobe department to advise her in buying a selection of new clothes for the trip she embarked on a long, champagne-filled flight across the Atlantic. Her main official task was to address guests attending the festival. Suitably dressed in a simple white sleeveless dress which showed off her shapely legs, Joan brought the house down by simply going on stage and uttering the words '*Viva Cartagena!*'

Joan's time in South America was incredibly relaxed and happy. She was labelled 'the little English girl' and the local press adored her. The trip did wonders for Joan's self-esteem and for the first and last time she revelled in her celebrity status. Casting aside her demons regarding her weight and figure she was photographed posing in a one-piece bathing costume on the beach at Bocagrande sitting on a rock by the sea. It was reported that 'without speaking Spanish, Joan makes herself understood by admirers by mime, when she has no interpreter at her side'. The locals embraced Joan and she was 'followed by a group of schoolgirls who were asking her questions, admiring her and wanted to go with her everywhere'.[204]

Publicity director John Troke meanwhile commented about Joan, 'She is a special actress. She is not the only comic in England, but she is the best. Moreover, she is a magnificent theatre actress.'[205]

The film festival itself lasted a mere week but Joan loved Cartagena so much that she decided to stay on. Having always enjoyed being looked after, the holiday suited Joan perfectly. She admitted to being treated like royalty and in addition to receiving the freedom of the city of Cartagena was also a frequent guest at local hotel and beach parties. One of her fondest memories was being awakened by the music of a band outside her bedroom door, which had been sent by an admirer to serenade her.

Joan's blissful time in South America – which ended up escalating to five weeks – was ended only when she received a telegram from Peter Eade insisting that she return home in order to 'earn some money'. So loved was she by the staff at the Hotel Americano that when she checked out Joan would receive a special certificate for being such an 'exemplary guest'.

A return to the kind of dizzy blonde characters she had played during her early screen appearances was required for Joan's role as the buxom Désirée Dubarry in *Carry On Don't Lose Your Head*. Taking on an endearingly girlish Essex accent, full of giggles and mischief, Joan not only looked stunning throughout the film but also provided some of its finest moments. Inadvertently the production also illustrated her great versatility as an actress. In 1966 alone she had appeared in lead roles in three of the country's biggest screen comedies. Each characterisation was poles apart and it is difficult to believe not only the physical transformations which took place but also the range needed to convincingly portray such very different characters. At her best in eighteenth-century period finery Joan delivered a series of superb one-liners, while her carefully spoken quip to Charles Hawtrey (as the Duc de Pommfrit) in the arbour scene was famously lucky to escape the eagle eye of the censor. *Don't Lose Your Head* was Joan's eighth *Carry On* appearance. It would remain a personal favourite for her.

By now the main team had become an on-screen family, familiar and comfortable with each other and lucky enough to have many of the same crew members for each film. This ensemble cast and crew ensured that each *Carry On* shoot became like a well-oiled machine – efficient, organised and above all economical in its production. Leon Greene who appeared in supporting roles in three of the films, including playing Malabonce the executioner in *Don't Lose Your Head*, confirmed the happy atmosphere on the set of the films:

> … no matter how big or small your role in the film you were made to feel very welcome by the main cast. From being invited to join their table at lunch, to being included in their conversations and joke sessions (and there were many) on set, you felt you were part of a large and very happy family.[206]

It was during the early years of the *Carry On* series that Joan met Norah Holland, a stunt driver and double, who would become Joan's stand-in on many of the films and ultimately one of her best friends. Norah evidently fitted in well with the cast and crew of the *Carry Ons* – often playing poker with Sid James and his 'long-running poker school'[207] – and supplying Joan with bacon and mushroom sandwiches 'dripping with butter' (a speciality of the canteen at Pinewood Studios).[208]

Although her friendship with Norah was different to her relationship with Hattie Jacques, Joan often relied on Holland in many different ways. On the set of *Carry On Don't Lose Your Head*, for example, Joan's large costume and hooped skirts made it impossible for her to remove her underwear to go to the toilet. It was subsequently left to Norah to assist Joan in the process, causing the former to joke: 'I've never been called upon to pull down an artist's knickers so that she can have a wee.'[209] Joan also became good friends with Norah's husband, Leslie (known as 'Dutch'), a former pilot, and would often spend weekends with the couple, particularly in her latter years.

As well as appearances on the big screen Joan also continued her work on television and radio throughout the 1960s, for which she could earn comparatively more than she did for her work in the *Carry On* series. For her first appearances on the small screen in the early 1950s Joan was earning amounts of anything between £21 and £66 while her appearance in *Space*, the 1957 experimental colour transmission, earned her the sum of £126.[210] By the mid 1960s she could command £120 for one appearance in a sitcom,[211] and a decade later this amount had trebled.[212] In comparison to £2,500, the average amount she received for six weeks starring in a *Carry On* film (filmed at breakneck pace, often in less than comfortable conditions), it is not surprising that Joan was happy to accept as much work on the small screen as possible.

One of her happiest assignments on television was co-starring with Dick Emery over a period of nine months in twelve episodes of his popular television series, *The Dick Emery Show*. The pair's friendship was cemented by their schoolboy sense of humour: Joan would recall that Dick would record his 'bouts of flatulence' at home and bring them to the studio to play to her via a large reel-to-reel tape recorder, saying 'I've got some beauties for you today, Joan' – much to her amusement! With some episodes produced by David Croft (of *Dad's Army* fame) and featuring the likes of Una Stubbs, Deryck Guyler and singer and actress Mary Millar[213] the series was extremely popular and provided the perfect opportunity for Emery to show off his 'flair for costume and make-up'.[214]

Stanley Baxter was another leading comedian with whom Joan was delighted to work in the sixties – a decade after they had first met at the Glasgow Citizen's Theatre. It was while buying cod and chips for lunch on the Edgware Road with Stanley that Joan was inadvertently mistaken by a member of the general public for Hollywood leading lady Shirley MacLaine. This was certainly somewhat different to being taken for Dora Bryan or Beryl Reid with whom she was most frequently confused by film and television viewers.

Alongside David Kossoff, Joan also starred in the radio series *Sam and Janet*, written by David Cumming and produced by Bill

Worsley, in the mid 1960s. Playing a suburban couple who had been married for nineteen years and had two children, both David and Joan received glowing reviews for their roles in the series, which also featured Alan Curtis and Kim Grant. While David Kossoff admitted the performance was nothing like his own private life, Joan was credited with playing Janet 'with great sympathy and under-standing'[215] – a far cry from the harridans she had recently played on the big screen. Another notable performance at around the same time was her role as Beryl in *That Old Black Magic* (filmed for Rediffusion and screened in January 1967). This topical television play saw Joan playing the mother of a teenage daughter, Cherry (Julia Foster), alongside George Cole (as Joan's husband, Frank). The plot centred on the couple's 'nice, safe suburban' world being shaken up when they take in a 'coloured' lodger (Ambrose) played by Johnny Sekka, the RADA-trained actor who arrived in Britain in 1952. The production was considered by *The Stage* to be an 'intelligent and humorous play'[216] and was certainly poles apart from Joan's more recent light-hearted work on the big screen. There were also well-paid appearances in productions such as *Iolanthe* – produced by David Croft and starring Patrick Cargill, Jimmy Logan, David Kernan and Trisha Noble – which screened on BBC2 on Christmas Day and *Love At Law*, produced by Wallace Douglas.[217]

Carry On Doctor saw Joan as Chloe Gibson, the put-upon assistant of charlatan faith-healer Francis Bigger (played with gusto by Frankie Howerd). The pair had first met in the fifties and Joan had made a guest appearance in Frankie's television series in November 1956, for which she was paid the princely sum of £49.[218] Joan adored working with Frankie Howerd who was more than capable of reducing her to hysterics. In the end the only way Joan could avoid 'corpsing' while working with Howerd was to look at his eyebrows, rather than directly into his eyes. Although disliked by Kenneth Williams, Joan enjoyed Frankie's company both on screen and off. Their antics together invariably resulted in uncontrollable laughter from the crew and caused Frankie to jokingly tell Gerald Thomas he needed Valium before working with Joan! The pair frequently dined out together[219] and although they became good friends Joan was aware of Frankie's hidden demons and conceded that there was a part of his personality that remained 'impenetrable'.

Anita Harris, who also starred in *Carry On Doctor*, happily admits that she adored Joan and although her older contemporary was already well-established as a 'star' of the series, she was 'incredibly easy to get along with and a master at her craft'. Joan's immense versatility as an actress also struck Anita – particularly as she saw first hand how her colleague transformed from the fiery, curvaceous, liberated Zig-Zig in *Carry On Follow That Camel* to the frumpy would-be harridan Chloe Gibson in *Carry On Doctor*.[220]

Although they rarely shared time together on screen in the *Carry Ons* Barbara Windsor was well placed to observe Joan on the set of the eight *Carry On* films in which they co-starred.[221] She recalls how happy Joan seemed on the set of *Carry On Doctor* (perhaps as a result of her non-stop laughter with Frankie Howerd) but by the time they came to film *Carry On Camping* things had clearly changed. Although, as Barbara admits, Joan was still 'very attractive' she was 'unhappy with her appearance' and vehemently refused to be seen in a bathing costume for her role as Joan Fussey, the straight-laced girlfriend of Sid Boggle (played by Sid James). As Barbara points out, it was now the age of Twiggy and pencil-slim models, and Joan's curvaceous figure – which had noticeably gained weight in recent years – was now most definitely out of fashion.[222]

Carry On Camping saw Dilys Laye (playing Joan's best friend, the car-sick Anthea Meeks) return to the fold for her fourth and final *Carry On* appearance, and welcomed several new additions including Sandra Caron, the sister of singer Alma Cogan and a former classmate of Barbara Windsor, who remembered Joan as 'a consummate comedienne'.[223] The film proved to be one of the best and most popular of the entire series and featured almost the entire team of *Carry On* 'regulars' along with veteran actress and comedienne Betty Marsden in a memorable supporting role as Harriet Potter.

Stories about the conditions on the set of *Carry On Camping* – which was supposed to be set on a Devon campsite in the middle of summer – have now become the stuff of legend. Filmed in October and November 1968 it is well known that members of the props team were required to spray the grass (which had turned to mud) green and that leaves were stuck back onto trees from which they had fallen. Dilys Laye would recall filming a scene where she and Joan had to sit in a car while Sid James and Bernard Bresslaw (as Bernie

Lugg) tried their best to put up a tent. Although it was meant to be raining it was ultimately left to the fire brigade to lend their support. As Dilys admitted 'the car was inches deep with water!'[224] Despite such conditions the film is a gem of British comedy and fondly remembered by schoolboys around the world because of Barbara Windsor's infamous bra-popping exercise routine.

Amid filming her latest *Carry On* role Joan received word that her uncle and godfather, Cecil Edgar Smith, had died peacefully on 26th October 1968. It was another break with the past and involved a family gathering at Southend crematorium.

Joan's performance as Lady Ruff-Diamond in *Carry On Up the Khyber* perhaps epitomised her entire *Carry On* career and certainly showed to full advantage her ability to play mock-refined characters. Grand, almost majestic, Lady Ruff-Diamond is a fully formed character – sensual, fiery, dignified and down to earth, she is more than a match for her male counterparts, as indeed Joan's characters invariably were throughout the *Carry On*s.

Scenes with Kenneth Williams in *Up the Khyber* invariably led to a series of antics which, like many *Carry On* anecdotes, have now become legendary and told in various different versions. While Joan and Kenneth remained great friends over three decades, their relationship was not always harmonious. When Kenneth broke wind during one of their scenes he was jokingly reprimanded by Joan, who called him a 'dirty sod',[225] only to be told by Kenneth that Rudolph Valentino always broke wind in front of his leading ladies. 'Yes,' replied Joan, 'but they were silent films, Kenny!'[226]

She often 'scolded' Williams for his behaviour – labelling her friend a 'demonic little sod' after witnessing his rudeness towards an elderly wardrobe assistant on the set of *Up the Khyber*. Joan was especially hurt when Kenneth refused to leave his dressing room to meet Norah Holland's mother-in-law on the set of *Don't Lose Your Head*. After she called him 'an evil little bastard' Williams then refused to speak to Joan for three days until Gerald Thomas intervened.[227] Never one to actually apologise for his childish behaviour, Kenneth patched things over with Joan by giving her his cloak to keep her warm during one of their outdoor scenes together and so harmony was restored.

Away from Pinewood their relationship continued and without the pressures of filming was often more joyous. Joan loved to lunch with Kenneth and he would recall one such occasion in his diary, when they were joined by Angela Douglas, and ended up a 'trio of gigglers' around the table.[228]

Carry On Again Doctor was another significant entry in the series since it allowed Joan to once again film a number of scenes with Kenneth Williams. Inevitably, since Joan always refused to tolerate his rudeness and changeability, they 'clashed' as he recorded in his diary on 15th April 1969:

> At lunch I had the great shouting match with Joan Sims. Her patronage and assumption at times that she should tell me what to do is intolerable. Hattie intervened & told me to stop it.[229]

The quarrels between the pair could be 'violent' but always blew over (with Kenneth invariably apologising in his own unique way) and grudges were never held between the two co-stars for very long. While Joan absolutely adored Kenneth she was certainly not blind to his foibles:

> Kenny was certainly the most complex character – and at the same time the most talented, most imaginative, most intellectual actor – with whom I worked regularly. He was not difficult to get on with when performing a show or filming a scene, but he could be maddening off the set, and the trouble was that it was impossible to predict his mood.[230]

Having seen Joan's unhappiness at the prospect of wearing a bathing costume on the set of *Carry On Camping*, Barbara Windsor recalls her co-star 'bursting into tears' on the set of *Carry On Again Doctor* when she was required to wear a black corset. The scene – where Joan is seen sharing a bedroom with Lady Puddleton (Charles Hawtrey) – was discreetly shot with Joan covered for the most part by a black negligee. A 'still' photograph from the scene shows Joan's justly famous legs to their full advantage and in retrospect Joan must have realised just how attractive she was at the time since the photograph was later included in her autobiography.

As a point of interest for *Carry On* fans, the black corset worn by Joan in *Carry On Again Doctor* was listed on an online auction site in 2013 with a starting price of £600. Other items to have been worn by Joan to have sold in recent years include the wig she wore in *Carry On Emmannuelle* and the dress she wore during the polo match in *Carry On Up the Khyber*.

As Joan became more and more conscious of her weight gain she was particularly grateful to cinematographer Alan Hume for his superb lighting skills and clever camera angles, never more so than in the scene where she was disguised as a belly dancer in *Carry On Up the Khyber* opposite Angela Douglas (ten years Joan's junior and a good deal slimmer). A quiet, modest man with the bluest of blue eyes and a keen sense of humour, Alan was adored by the *Carry On* team and especially by Joan for his professionalism and ability to present the stars of the films in the best possible way. While panels now often had to be sewn into the sides of Joan's dresses to accommodate her increasing waistline, feather boas and scarves also became a key feature of her wardrobe (and would remain so), especially for formal photo shoots, in an attempt to disguise added weight around her neck.

Although their living arrangements had long since changed, Joan's close friendship with Pat Clayfield remained as strong as ever throughout the 1960s. Pat would often meet up with Joan and would also regularly lunch with Peter Eade, whom she considered to be 'a very, very special person' at a little Italian restaurant they were fond of. On occasion they would be joined by Kenneth Williams. At the very end of the 1960s after Pat had broken up with her boyfriend she would visit Joan at Hurlingham Road nearly every weekend. It was around this time that Peter Eade pleaded with Pat to move in with Joan again. Having seen how happy Joan had been living with 'Jerry' in the 1950s at Jermyn Street, Peter felt a live-in friend would be the ideal solution to Joan's increasing loneliness. 'Peter Eade liked it very much indeed when we were sharing a flat,' remembers Pat who was then living in St James' Place and working in Wembley. Despite their closeness Pat felt unable to regress in time to once again share living accommodation with Joan.[231] Life had inevitably moved on and Joan was left to a largely solitary private existence.

The regularity of the *Carry On* films at least alleviated some of Joan's solitude. Barbara Windsor, now one of the last surviving stars of the *Carry On* series, recalled in 2012 how the actors would spend their time on set between takes:

> Charlie Hawtrey would often be sat alone smoking his Woodbines while Hattie Jacques and Bernie Bresslaw would usually sit together doing some highbrow crossword. Sid James would be playing poker with the crew and Kenny Connor and Peter Butterworth would be

larking about somewhere. I was normally with Kenny [Williams] listening to his jokes and Joan was usually with Norah Holland. She was very down to earth and would probably be discussing the price of meat at Sainsbury's! Kenny always used to call Joan very 'suburban'.

The term 'suburban' was frequently used by Kenneth Williams to describe Joan. It must be said that it is a description which baffles those nearest to her. However, in comparison to some of his other closest friends, Joan was certainly more grounded and less arty than many of the theatrical types Williams chose to spent time with so one can only assume the word 'suburban' was his way of summing up her lack of pretentiousness. Although Joan was always a star she could never have been accused of being 'starry'. Throughout her career she avoided celebrity gatherings and practically any kind of media attention. This was in contrast to Kenneth who was always willing to grant interviews and heavily relied upon chat shows in his latter career as a source of work and income.

Kenneth's authorised biographer Christopher Stevens wrote that Williams thought Joan to be 'hopelessly suburban – so morally conventional that she was neutered'.[232] Despite this, Joan was a great friend to Kenneth for thirty years. Many of his female co-stars became the victim of his acid tongue and he could be extremely hurtful towards anyone he considered a 'threat' or, equally, to anyone who was 'indifferent' towards him. Joan was strong enough to stand up to Kenneth and he admired her for this. A typical example of how Joan was able to curb Kenneth's bad behaviour was recalled in her autobiography and again by Christopher Stevens:

> When, during *Carry On Camping*, he had refused to let a young actress named Liz [Elizabeth] Knight join the 'regulars' in the canteen, Sims called him 'a demonic little sod' and pointedly led the newcomer away to sit with her at another table. That sort of reproach – direct, rude, practical – was the sort Williams appreciated best, and he never resented it.[233]

If Joan, in Kenneth's eyes, was 'neutered' then he was certainly in no position to pass judgement – although this never stopped him. His own demons regarding his sexuality prevented him from ever having a long-term sexual relationship. Indeed his brief sexual dalliances over the years inevitably ended catastrophically. Like Joan, he was very close to his mother, Louisa (Louie) – even to the point of living in adjoining flats. Unlike Gladys, however, Louie was vivacious, fun-loving and devoted to Kenneth. It was only in the last few years of Kenneth's life that his mother's increasing infirmities began to test their relationship. Arguably Kenneth's devotion to his mother had a massive impact on his inability to form close relationships with anyone else and he would admit to being 'asexual', although he did have occasional homosexual encounters. In his later years he lived a life of celibacy (if not chastity) and wasn't interested in 'the other' which he considered to be a 'very messy business'. In fairness Kenneth was also a man of massive contradictions and his opinions on people and subjects were rarely static.

Joan's strict middle-class upbringing and fiercely protective parents ensured that she was, morally speaking, a 'good girl'. Even in her thirties and beyond when she was living in her own home and a 'free agent', she did not take advantage of her circumstances as far as the opposite sex was concerned. Williams was wrong to criticise her on this point, since it was not through lack of opportunity or indeed desire. Quite simply it was not in Joan's nature.

Whatever his private opinions of Joan were, they did not prevent their close friendship from enduring over the decades. Joan revelled in his rude stories which invariably reduced her to hysterics and tears of laughter. Joan's inner circle also frequently encountered Williams, with varying degrees of success. To Eleanor Fazan he was 'very brilliant but not an easy person – he could be difficult'[234] while Nicholas Ferguson would recall: 'He could be sharp and rude and everything else but actually privately he was very sweet but very rarely publicly – he would always just be the same "act" all the time.'[235]

*

During the 1960s and 1970s Pinewood Studios played host to some of the world's biggest stars and Barbara Windsor and Joan were both completely star-struck when they met Hollywood actor Gregory Peck. Barbara recalls looking at Joan and asking 'What do we do?' at the sight of the legend of the silver screen and the two ladies ending up in a fit of girlish giggles.[236] Joan was slightly more restrained on the set of *Up the Khyber*, when she and Sid James were photographed between takes with the American actor Dick Van Dyke (then at Pinewood Studios filming *Chitty Chitty Bang Bang*). Her encounter with another Hollywood legend several years later, in the formidable form of leading lady Bette Davis, would be much less agreeable (see page 86). By this time, although Joan was a star at Pinewood in her own right, she still remained rather overwhelmed whenever encountering Hollywood stars, particularly those who were famous during her youth and the Golden Age of Hollywood.

The continued success of the *Carry On* series brought Joan some degree of financial security. As well as being able to buy her own home in Hurlingham Road she was occasionally able to treat herself and those around her. Joan's generosity towards her parents was well known and even after Harry's death she continued to provide for Gladys in her old age. A rare surviving letter from Joan to her mother from Christmas 1969 demonstrates:

> Here is a little something to have a lot of fun with – now enjoy it!
> Throw caution to the wind!!! For once!
> Much Love, Joan x

As was often the case Gladys used the letter to reply to her daughter, writing at the bottom of the page: 'I did. My sincere thanks. Bless you always. Mum.' [237]

Unlike her *Carry On* co-stars Kenneth Williams and Charles Hawtrey (who was well known for his penny-pinching ways) Joan was not frugal. Like Hattie, Joan was giving and almost carefree when it came to money. Safe in the knowledge that Peter Eade and her accountant were managing her finances, Joan's money was hers to do with as she chose. She was more than happy to splash out on extravagances and in later years admitted to spending £600 on two dresses and then treating herself to tea at the Hyde Park Hotel while filming *The Kenneth Williams Show* in 1970.[238]

By 1970 the *Carry On* series had been running for more than a decade. Almost inevitably it was decided that a new generation of actors should be recruited to join the team. Among them, making her *Carry On* debut in *Carry On Up the Jungle*, was Birmingham-born light leading lady Jacki Piper.[239] Cast as June, Lady Baggley's maid, in the twenty-seventh *Carry On* film, Jacki made an immediate impact with Peter Rogers who quickly placed her under contract for the next two years (she remains the only actress ever to be placed under contract in the *Carry On* series). Her transformation from 'a sort of female version of Charles Hawtrey to a very glamorous character' thrilled Jacki who was delighted to have a 'huge lead role' in a *Carry On* film. The main team welcomed her with open arms including Joan, whom Jacki remembers as 'a brilliant, understated actress'.[240] *Up the Jungle* allowed Joan to work closely again with Frankie Howerd. Stills from the production show the continued hilarity between the pair while Joan's infamous scene with the 'vinscreen viper' has gone down in cinema history.

Despite the intake of younger actors now joining the series it was more or less left to Joan to play the female lead in both *Carry On Loving* (as Esme Crowfoot) and *Carry On At Your Convenience*. In both films she was the recipient of the lead man's (Sid James) wandering eye. Neither film had much of an impact upon Joan and she was much happier playing Queen Marie in *Carry On Henry*. The film, which was a lavish affair by *Carry On* standards, not only allowed her the chance to dress in Tudor finery but also gave Joan opportunity to show off her fine French accent. Standing out as one of the better films in the second half of the series, Joan gave a magnificent performance as the haughty, imperious consort to Sid James' King Henry.

In between the *Carry On* films, which by now had become at least an annual event for Joan, there was plenty of other work to be had. *Doctor in Trouble* was Joan's fifth and final appearance in that series and saw her playing a man-hungry Russian sea captain (a far cry from Dawn in *Doctor in Love* a decade earlier) and shortly afterwards she featured as a policewoman in the rather bizarre *Magnificent Seven Deadly Sins*, directed by Graham Stark. One of Joan's happiest television assignments of the 1970s was working with Kenneth Williams in *The Kenneth Williams Show*. A joint interview with Denis Curtis, published in the *Radio Times*, confirmed the affection between the pair. Despite a great deal of tongue-in-cheek innuendo throughout their conversation with Curtis they were 'completely sincere' in their praise of each other:

> Joan says Kenneth is the nicest actor she's ever played to; and Kenneth says Joan is the warmest brightest actress he's ever worked with.

Joan went on to reiterate, 'We always have fun working together… right from the beginning with the *Carry On* series,' with Kenneth intervening: 'You've got to keep the ball in the air. Drop it and it becomes dirty. But we're never dirty, are we dear?'[241]

Despite the merriment between Joan and Kenneth during production the series, which also featured Lance Percival, was not well received. Anna Karen, who also made guest appearances in the show, recalled that the line-up of other actors depended almost entirely on Kenneth Williams' mood from week to week and that co-stars would be 'dropped' at a moment's notice if they were unlucky enough to fall out of favour with the notoriously changeable Williams.[242]

Joan was wise enough to realise that a *Carry On* budget would never stretch to an exotic location abroad and as a result *Carry On Abroad*, supposedly set somewhere in the Mediterranean, was filmed at Pinewood under typical testing conditions in April 1972. Joan later recalled being so cold during one outdoor scene (filmed in the car park at the studios) that her nose turned blue!

Once again several new actors were brought in for the film including Sally Geeson and Carol Hawkins (as Sally and Marge). Ray Brooks was another new addition to the cast. He would later remember Joan as 'a quiet person compared to the rest of the team'.[243] Jimmy Logan, the well-known Scottish comedian with whom Joan had previously worked on television, was also drafted in to play the raucous Bert Conway and recalled Joan quite simply as 'lovely'.[244] David Kernan, in his only *Carry On* appearance as Nicholas, recounted working with Joan for the first time four years after they had first met:

> We were reunited on the set of *Carry On Abroad*. A pathetic fee but I wouldn't have missed it for the world. One afternoon during a break Joan and I found ourselves in the makeup department. I reminded her of her performance of 'The Man That Got Away'. We then both launched ourselves into the song. We got to the line 'good riddance, goodbye' when, of all people, Bette Davis marched into the room… She boomed out to us, 'I certainly wish *you* good riddance, goodbye. You have woken me from my nap. I have a very heavy schedule.' As she stormed out we timidly offered apologies.

When filming wrapped on *Carry On Abroad* Joan and David Kernan had their own foreign holiday, which thankfully involved travelling further than the car park at Pinewood Studios. Under David's suggestion they travelled to the South of France.

Two memories of that holiday. We were sunning ourselves on the beach at Cannes. Joan was closer to the waves than I when a tsunami-like wave hit the shore soaking poor Joan. I immediately went to her aid. Dripping with sea water she said, 'I must look like a bloody beached whale!'

The other occasion was at a restaurant near Cannes. It was the last night so we pushed the boat out and had a delicious but expensive supper. When it came to splitting the bill we found to our embarrassment that we did not have sufficient funds. I immediately told Joan to do her renowned mother and baby act. So without wasting time up came the knee covered with a napkin and there was the baby nestling lifelike in her arms. Like the pro she was she went into her routine: an exhausted Mum with her noisy baby… Within minutes the mostly French customers were totally enchanted by the act. The *patron* equally enchanted dramatically tore up our bill… and a great evening was had by all.[245]

Carry On Matron would be the final time the gang would gather in a hospital setting. It was by far Joan's easiest role in a *Carry On* film since she spent all of her scenes in bed. As Mrs Tidey, a heavily expectant (and long overdue) mother, Joan had the pleasure of devouring her way through the hospital menu as her impatient husband (Kenneth Connor) sat anxiously awaiting the birth of their first child. It was one of the few times she was required to share scenes on screen with Hattie Jacques who inevitably was cast in the title role of the film. Ironically Joan would reveal years later that 'if I had been more academic I would have liked to have gone into the medical profession'.[246]

It says a great deal for Joan's talent (and continued lack of vanity) that at the age of just thirty-six she was playing Gran in the popular Warren Mitchell sitcom *Till Death Us Do Part*. Ironically in real life Joan was four years younger than Mitchell – her on-screen son-in-law – and over twenty years younger than his on-screen wife Dandy Nichols. Joan's ability to hide her teeth with her lips, a talent she had utilised since her teens, was once again used for the character who, complete with wig, flowery hat and cover-all coat, bore a striking resemblance to the Gran played by Joan during her days in *More Intimacy at Eight*.

While Joan received acclaim for her role as the gin-loving old lady – who was more than a match for her irascible, foul-mouthed son-in-law – in the mid 1970s she admitted she found the character

'depressing' and 'demoralising' to play. Johnny Speight, the programme's writer, was keen for Joan to have her own spin-off series
as Gran – an idea she politely declined. Despite being a great admirer
of Speight's writing and scripts, which she considered to be 'superb',
her decision was not one she would regret. Norah Holland would
later reveal that Joan felt aspects of the character were too close to
home and that Joan secretly feared that one day she would 'end up
like' the character she was playing.

A more positive aspect to the role was the opportunity to work
with Dandy Nichols, whom Joan considered to be 'quite brilliant',
and it also reunited her with Una Stubbs, playing her granddaughter,
Rita. In total Joan appeared in more than a dozen episodes of the
series and was credited, along with Dandy Nichols and Rita Webb,
with preventing the show from becoming 'two dimensional and far
less lively'. The three ladies were also praised for giving the comedy
'robust reality' [247] and Joan would also guest-star in the 1972 film, *Till
Death*, based on the television series.

In addition to playing hotel proprietor Connie Philpotts (another
nagging-wife-type role mainly opposite Sid James) in *Carry On Girls*,
1973 also saw Joan cast as Miss Tipdale in the low-budget, all-star,
Leslie Phillips farce *Not Now, Darling (*in which she was required to
ride a Lambretta scooter). She again shared the screen with Leslie in
1973 when she played Lady 'Birdie' Mainwaring in the Brian Rix film
comedy, *Don't Just Lie There, Say Something!* Based on the successful
stage farce the film saw Joan receive star billing and despite being
poorly rated it has been frequently repeated in the years since its
release. Television work was also flowing in and as well as the 1973
Carry On Christmas special,[248] Joan also featured in a succession of
guest roles including an appearance in Ronnie Barker's series *Seven
of One* and two roles in *The Goodies*. Despite an accident with a wand
on set she received a glowing review for her appearance in *The Wednesday Wand*, an episode of the popular children's series *Jackanory*,
being described as 'an enchanting twentieth-century fairy who was
clearly Madame Arcati's niece – if not a closer relation'.[249]

By the time *Carry On Dick* was released in 1974 Joan was again
noticeably gaining weight. Although looking magnificent, and obviously feeling at her best in eighteenth-century period finery, her
appearance was a marked contrast to the curvaceous figure she had
been less than a decade earlier in *Carry On Cowboy*. Well corseted

and with a distinctly cheeky 'bogus' French accent, Joan revelled at the opportunity to dress up in yet another 'historical' *Carry On* romp. In between takes she was able to catch up with two of her greatest friends, Hattie Jacques and Kenneth Williams, and exchange curry recipes with Jack Douglas.

Joan's love for the series never wavered and even at this late stage Barbara Windsor remembers 'she bounded on the set like it was her first ever job – she had such enthusiasm for her work'.[250] The film was loosely based on the adventures of the notorious eighteenth-century highwayman Dick Turpin and saw Joan cast as Madame Désirée, the leader of a group of girls who travel the country entertaining with various acts in public houses.

Carry On Dick was the twenty-sixth edition in the series and significant as the final feature film for two of its stalwarts: Sid James and Hattie Jacques. It was also the last entry scripted by Talbot Rothwell. In many ways this parody of the classic story of Dick Turpin marked the beginning of the end of the popular and long-running films.

It was only on the rarest of occasions that Joan spoke on camera about her time spent working on the *Carry On* films. Almost a decade after her final appearance in the series she would admit 'we were like kids at school' and went on to say:

> There was a fantastic atmosphere. Everyone got on with everybody else. There was no star quality... there was nobody with a big head. It was just a jolly good team show and we worked jolly hard.[251]

Of her co-stars Joan remained proud of what was essentially a 'tremendous team' and grateful for the 'great buddies' they had all become. While a number of her co-stars, particularly Kenneth Connor, Bernard Bresslaw and Peter Butterworth, led fairly private lives away from the media spotlight, they were always pleased to reunite for another film – an experience likened by Joan to returning to school after the summer holidays. Between takes laughter was almost guaranteed and in 1993 Peter Rogers would recall the combined comic antics of Joan and Kenneth Connor as 'hysterical'.[252]

While Joan continued to work at a steady rate her mother took the opportunity to revel in her daughter's success when she lunched at Claridges in London with over twenty other mothers of famous faces from British national life. Suitably attired in a suit and large hat, Gladys was joined by, amongst others, Morna Briers (doing a 'sort of double act' with her actor son, Richard Briers), Hilda Hookham (mother of Dame Margot Fonteyn), Sybil Ray (the 'suntanned fitness fanatic' mother of Andrew and Robin Ray who announced at the event she could still do the splits) and Mrs Mary Heath (the fifty-four-year-old stepmother of Prime Minister, Edward Heath).[253] Also among the 'celebrity mums' was Hattie Jacques' mother, Mary (a slimmer version of Hattie who passed on her striking good looks to her famous daughter), with whom Gladys was good friends.

After experiencing the distinctly 'tight' budgets of the *Carry On* films, the luxury of a supporting role in the Disney film *One of Our Dinosaurs Is Missing* was a rare treat for Joan. Filmed in the autumn of 1974 the film starred Helen Hayes, the legendary American theatre actress of whom Joan became very fond, and Peter Ustinov.[254] Also among the cast of the film, which centred around a secret strip of microfilm being hidden in a dinosaur skeleton in London's Natural History Museum, were Derek Nimmo, Bernard Bresslaw, Roy Kinnear, Natasha Pyne and Amanda Barrie. As Emily, the nanny sidekick of Helen Hayes (as Hettie), Joan gave a vigorous performance and regular television repeats of the film have ensured it remains one of Joan's best-known film roles outside of the *Carry On* series.

Following Joan's notable supporting role in Disney's lavish production came another golden opportunity: a role in a made-for-television film starring Laurence Olivier and Hollywood screen legend Katharine Hepburn. Directed by George Cukor, *Love Among the Ruins* is the story of Jessica Medlicott (Hepburn), an ageing actress being sued for breach of promise by the scheming Alfred Pratt (played by Leigh Lawson). Joan, playing Alfred's mother, Fanny Pratt, is seen in a cameo role being cross-examined in court by Laurence Oliver (playing Sir Arthur Glanville-Jones, Jessica's former lover).

Bruce Copp, who thought Katharine Hepburn to be a screen 'goddess', remembers that Joan was in a 'state of nerves' when she was invited to meet Miss Hepburn on the set in her caravan. Since Joan did not have a caravan of her own Katharine Hepburn insisted that Joan use hers so that she did not have to sit in her heavy period costume all day between takes. When Joan first entered her

American counterpart's caravan she found her lying on the floor reading her script and was greeted with a request to 'come and sit down'. Joan duly obliged by joining Katharine on the floor! Years later Joan would recall how Katharine Hepburn (who died in 2003 at the age of ninety-six) disapproved strongly of her smoking. When asked if she minded Joan smoking in her presence Miss Hepburn replied ('in that famous drawl'), 'No. I just feel sorry for you.' [255]

Although Joan's role in the award-winning production, which was first screened in March 1975, was a relatively small one she regarded it as one of the 'high points' of her entire career. Bruce Copp remembers it as a 'lovely memorable performance in a serious role' and it again proved just how versatile an actress Joan could be. [256]

On the flipside of the coin of Joan's career came her other most notable role of 1975 – as Daphne Barnes in *Carry On Behind*. Filmed in March and April the conditions on the set of the film, which centred upon the antics of a caravan park and an archaeological dig, were somewhat reminiscent of those on *Carry On Camping* seven years earlier. The ground was clearly muddy, the trees bare and it was obviously distinctly cold.

Joan, suitably dressed in a black fur coat but still shivering between takes, conceded that the conditions were marginally better than her experiences on the set of *Carry On Camping* and did her best to kept spirits high. Visiting the set, journalist Hugh Herbert thought that Joan and Bernard Bresslaw 'would be jokers and comforters in any group' as he experienced, first hand, the behind-the-scenes world of the *Carry On*s:

> All the actors and actresses not in the scene are muffled against the raw April air. Talk is desultory at first. Patsy Rowlands varnishes her nails, Bernard Bresslaw does a crossword, Ian Lavender yawns. But the ebullient Bresslaw isn't silent for long, and they are all chatting soon about other locations, other *Carry On*s. Bresslaw: 'There was this bloke came up and asked me for my autograph, you see, and he said, "You know, I've got a very odd hobby. I collect organs." Well, what do you say to that? I said, "What kind of organs?", and he said, "Mine's a cinema organ."'
>
> 'Does it go up and down?' cries Joan Sims, pat on cue.
>
> 'That's what I said. "Does it go up and down?" And he says, "No, I live in a semi, but I've got this friend in Rochdale, and his goes up and down from the cellar."' [257]

The film, written by Dave Freeman following the retirement from the series of Talbot Rothwell in 1974, saw Joan playing Patsy Rowlands' mother (despite just eight months' difference in age) and Bernard Bresslaw's mother-in-law. Somewhat prematurely Joan has suddenly developed from the nagging wife of the series to the nagging matriarch. *Behind* was a rare chance for Joan to play opposite the endearing Peter Butterworth (a superb stalwart of the series in his fourteenth *Carry On* film), as his estranged wife. Their scenes together towards the end of the film when they are reunited after a long absence are especially poignant.

It was clear by now that the series was beginning to run out of steam and the final three 'true' *Carry On* films failed to match the success previously enjoyed by the series. Kenneth Williams pointedly refused to take part in any of the television spin-offs that began in 1969 although the rest of the main team joined in (to some degree or another), not least Joan who featured in starring roles in ten episodes of *Carry On Laughing* in 1975. The thirteen twenty-five-minute episodes, filmed at Elstree Studios, saw various writers being brought in (including Dave Freeman and Barry Cryer) to try and boost the popularity of the series but, despite some valiant performances by the actors involved, *Carry On Laughing* failed to make any real impact and the results of some of the episodes were distinctly mixed. It was, however, fun to see Sid James and Hattie Jacques (as Sir Francis Drake and Queen Elizabeth I) reunited for their final *Carry On* appearance in *Orgy and Bess*, and many episodes gave Joan the chance to satisfy her love of dressing in period costume. Her tongue-in-cheek homage to Angela Baddeley (Mrs Bridges in the television classic *Upstairs, Downstairs*) in *And In My Lady's Chamber* and *Who Needs Kitchener?* was considered a highlight of the series.

As Joan's career continued to progress so too did her friendships, especially with a new generation of actors. Sherrie Hewson, now best known as a mainstay of the *Loose Women* panel and for her roles in a succession of television favourites (from *Coronation Street* to *Benidorm*) joined the *Carry On* team in 1975 as Carol in *Carry On Behind* and also appeared in four episodes of *Carry On Laughing* on television. She was introduced to Joan by Peter Eade who took her to Joan's home in Hurlingham Road, recalled by Sherrie as 'a beautiful, three-storey Edwardian property with memorabilia all over the place. On the walls were posters from all the plays and musicals she'd ever done, plus photos galore of the stars she had worked with from Hattie Jacques and Kenneth Williams to Katharine Hepburn and Laurence Olivier.'[258] Like Joan, Sherrie was a graduate of RADA. The pair quickly became friends and Sherrie lived with Joan at Hurlingham Road for a short time in the mid 1970s where she became privy to the 'glorious' and 'wicked' antics of her older contemporary, not to mention those of Kenneth Williams who was a frequent visitor to Joan's home.

By now Joan's life had taken on a set routine. A *Carry On* film was almost guaranteed to keep her occupied for at least six weeks of the year and there was plenty of other work, especially on television, to keep her busy. A magazine interview with Roger Elliott revealed much about Joan's life at the time.[259] She admitted to being lazy: 'I'm full of good intentions, but never seem to get anything done' – a habit that grew worse with the passage of time and something confirmed by those closest to her. Her personal solitude was flippantly cast aside with the comment 'I'm not the family type' and she revealed that although she loved the countryside she felt 'safe' in London. In this respect she was not unlike Kenneth Williams who fantasised about retiring to the countryside although few of those closest to him could imagine the man born within the sound of 'Bow Bells' ever leaving his beloved London. In her mid forties she may have been single and living alone but, professionally at least, Joan was still very busy and there can be no doubt that her continued success as an actress brought with it a good deal of purpose, personal satisfaction and above all happiness.

6

The Lady Regrets

'… booze filled in the gaps'

FOLLOWING HER FATHER'S DEATH IN 1964, Joan and her mother would invariably spend Christmas Day at Eardley Crescent with Hattie Jacques and her numerous other guests. Hattie was such a brilliant and generous hostess that the guest list was often a long one and would usually include her ex-husband, John Le Mesurier (and his wife Joan), Bruce Copp, Joan and Gladys, and of course Hattie's two sons, Robin and Kim. David Kernan was another guest and would recall these joyous times to the author:

> Christmases with Joan were always a treat. At least three Christmas days were spent with the wondrous Hattie Jacques, an ample angel with a heart of gold. Food and booze in abundance, music, fun and games… On one occasion there was an LP of the Andrews Sisters playing on the gramophone so Hattie found an old discarded wig for me, and joined Joan and I as we mimed 'Chattanooga Choo Choo'.[260]

It was during this annual event that Bruce Copp often encountered Gladys Sims. Memory can sometimes be selective, yet Bruce's memories of Joan's mother remain strong and clear. Now a sprightly ninety-four-year-old, Bruce thought Gladys to be 'an appalling woman – and obviously very unhappy in her own relationships'. He went on to further explain his thoughts on the woman who so greatly influenced Joan's life:

> I loathed her and I've never used that word to describe anyone I've ever met. I don't want to upset anyone, especially the family, but I think the truth should be told.

> She was a burden at Christmas time and nothing was ever good
> enough for her – her chair would be in the wrong place, or she would
> be sat in a draught. She really was a bloody nuisance.

Fully aware of how fragile Joan could be, and how heavily influenced she was by Gladys, Bruce remembers the practical (not to mention emotional) effect she could have upon her daughter: 'One phone call from her mother would turn Joanie to the bottle for the rest of the day. She just couldn't get away from her.' [261]

Joan Le Mesurier saw a lot of Joan during Hattie's lifetime and never more so than at Christmastime. She was well aware of how much Joan depended upon Hattie on a daily basis: 'Hattie was like a mother and a sister to her really and she [Joan] loved being there with Hattie.' Although she usually only saw Gladys on an annual basis Joan Le Mesurier was struck by the difference in their relationship and admits that Hattie gave her the impression that Gladys was 'a little bit of a tartar'.[262]

Gladys was undoubtedly a massively dominant influence in Joan's life. She was the first person mentioned by Sir Tom Courtenay when he recalled his former neighbour in 2013:

> I just have this memory of sadness of her relationship with her
> mother and the weight and the burden of it. She seemed to be
> dominant in a way that was not welcome... I remember Joan was
> quite upset about her mother... she was resentful of her and felt
> guilty about feeling that way. I do remember Joan complaining to
> me. I think she tried to like her mother, but she couldn't.

Sir Tom remembers Joan describing her mother as 'very mean-spirited, discouraging and not helpful', and having met Gladys on several occasions he could well believe what Joan was saying. His own memories of Gladys centre around a lady who struck him to be 'rather straight-laced and tight about the face... not a lot of fun – in fact not any fun at all!' [263]

Director Nicholas Ferguson, who got to know Joan well in the early 1980s, remembered his friend's complex personality and the influence of her parents:

> She was quite a nervous person, quite, quite sensitive really. I think
> psychologically there was unhappiness... and I'm sure the parents
> were a part of that and perhaps controlled her.[264]

Inevitably during her widowhood, and as Joan's boyfriends began to dwindle, Gladys became a frequent visitor to Hurlingham Road. Such visits would usually be prolonged and often made Joan very unhappy. Despite the regular presence of her mother, Sir Tom Courtenay's impression of Joan was that of a solitary person: 'I always felt that she was lonely.'[265]

In the early 1970s, while her son was completing his A-levels, Eleanor Fazan briefly lived with Joan at her home in Fulham. Almost forty years later she would recall that it was not easy living with someone who was often drunk and that Joan's conversations often became 'repetitive'. During these times of heavy drinking, despite the company of one of her closest friends, Joan's 'slight anger' towards the world in general would emerge and she became adept at 'imagining things' that were not necessarily true. Although as Eleanor recalls Joan was still able to relax and be happy with family and close friends, at times, usually when she was alone, 'booze filled in the gaps'.[266]

It was during this time that Eleanor encountered Joan at her most bizarre, as a result of far too much alcohol. After discussing Joan's situation with her friend Barry Humphries (the Australian-born entertainer best known as Dame Edna Everage), Eleanor asked Barry – a recovered alcoholic – if he would come back to Joan's house to speak to her. Aware that Joan had been to see a drink counsellor earlier in the day Barry warned Eleanor that Joan would inevitably be drunk when they returned to Hurlingham Road.

What greeted Eleanor and Barry upon their return is a sight which remains imprinted in the former's mind forty years later. As Barry predicted Joan was indeed intoxicated and was lying in front of a lit gas fire in a bikini, deep in her own fantasy world. This painful memory of Joan is worth revealing since it provides a rare, private insight into how much Joan was drinking at the time and how affected her behaviour was by her addiction.

Joan Le Mesurier spoke briefly with Joan about her drinking habits and realised that Joan did indeed have a 'drink problem':

> She was very bad and did confess to me once that she was on 'anti-booze' and if you have any alcohol you get violently ill and this was the only thing that protected her. That was what Tony [Hancock] used as well and you can't drink, you just can't because you throw up all over the place but nobody makes you take it. It's up to you to have the willpower to take it.[267]

On the other hand, despite living with Joan, a young Sherrie Hewson was quite unaware of how serious Joan's drinking had become as she would recall in her autobiography:

> As she went upstairs to bed, Joan always used to ask me to be a sweetie and bring her some water. Every night, I would dutifully take a cut-glass jug of water to her. Propped up by big, plumped-up pillows, she'd be as snug as a bug. I'd pour her a glass of water, then sit and talk for a while. I loved this time with Joan. It wasn't until many years later that I found out that the water was in fact vodka and I shouldn't have been giving it to her – by then she had an implant fitted to stop herself from drinking. I felt so guilty.[268]

Others were also led to believe that Joan had something 'fitted' to help her stop drinking and that her frequent visits to health farms (particularly Grayshott Hall) were taken in an attempt to curb excessive drinking.

Apart from Eleanor Fazan only Pat and Bill Clayfield were privy to the full effects alcohol had on Joan. Although Pat was jokingly annoyed that Joan never suffered from hangovers ('The awful thing was she never got a hangover – I never forgave her for it!') and was never 'moody', she admits her friend was not immune to the more immediate effects of alcoholic poisoning.[269] Pat clearly remembers attending to Joan at times when she was at her lowest ebb following heavy drinking sessions. Invariably Joan would take to the floor where Pat often discovered her vomiting into a bowl. It was an image far removed from their earlier days when the pair had innocently made cocktails and 'discovered' vodka. During their Jermyn Street years Pat and Joan had 'hilarious' times with each other – and times of nursing each other through problems.[270] Now the hilarity had vanished and the nursing was one-sided.

Joan's drinking bouts appeared to have a familiar pattern. For anywhere up to five days she would cut herself off from the outside world and – in the days before answering machines and caller identification – could only be contacted by very close friends via telephone with a coded signal.[271] During these times she simply 'couldn't handle other people'.

Unlike many heavy drinkers Joan was very honest about her habit and when Pat Clayfield would question, 'Are you drinking a lot?' Joan would invariably reply, 'Yes, but I'm so depressed.'[272] Joan's 'private benders' were often followed by a great deal of remorse and self-hatred, particularly when she had abstained from alcohol for a significant amount of time.

As Joan became increasingly reliant upon her career as the sole focus of her life, so too did she become reliant upon alcohol to numb her personal loneliness. Eleanor Fazan felt that her friend simply could not cope with many of the realities of life and that both acting and alcohol provided Joan with an escape: 'She needed it... she couldn't bear too much reality.'[273]

The sadness in Joan's private life, which had been noticed as far back as the late 1960s by some colleagues, manifested itself in several ways but was rarely displayed publicly. Generally speaking, as confirmed by friends, Joan never drank when she was working. Although a number of colleagues within the industry were aware of (or at least suspected) that she had her fair share of private demons, Joan was always a consummate professional and would remain so until the end of her life, as Nicholas Ferguson remembers: 'She never let anybody down either in filming or in the studio *ever* to my knowledge – she came from that period where people just didn't let you down. She was, as they say, an old trouper.'[274] It was during periods of unemployment when she spent most of her time alone that that loneliness led her to seek solace in alcohol. This in turn led her to feeling ashamed and resentful of her own actions. Increased drinking also led to further weight gain which did nothing to help her already battered self-esteem and confidence. A vicious circle had developed in Joan's life, and certainly in the long term her drinking habit did nothing to improve her health or indeed her figure. Lord Rix, who knew Joan from her earliest days, realised the impact Joan's drinking had on her life and observed sadly: 'Alas, she was (or seemed to be) unhappy in her private life which led to her early death.'[275]

*

Having worked with Joan during the filming of *Carry On Dick* in April 1974 and finally again for three episodes of *Carry On Laughing* the following year, Sid James had kept busy on television, starring in his popular sitcom *Bless This House* alongside Diana Coupland, Sally Geeson and Robin Stewart. Sid was performing at the Sunderland Empire Theatre in a season of *The Mating Game* in April 1976 when he collapsed on stage and died shortly afterwards. He was sixty-two years old.

Sid's death hit Joan deeply. She adored her co-star, loved his old-fashioned protectiveness of the fairer sex, and considered him to be a 'darling man'. Over the years his reputation and fidelity to his final wife (former actress Valerie Ashton) would frequently be questioned by the media, much to Joan's annoyance, yet her admiration for the South-African-born actor never wavered.

Despite the shock of Sid's sudden death, just days after his demise filming began on *Carry On England*. The twenty-eighth entry in the series saw Joan as Private Jennifer Ffoukes-Sharpe, a role which brought her little pleasure. Without Sid James, Kenneth Williams, Charles Hawtrey or Barbara Windsor it was left to Joan, Kenneth Connor, Peter Butterworth and Jack Douglas to represent the old guard. Sadly both Joan and Peter merely featured in supporting roles and the film (which famously had to be 'toned down' for the censor) flopped at the box office. Also missing were such stalwarts of the series as Hattie Jacques (by now uninsurable for film work due to her ongoing weight gain and associated health problems), Bernard Bresslaw and Patsy Rowlands.

Although Joan received good billing in the film her role was a minor one and she was given little to do other than lust after Sergeant Major 'Tiger' Bloomer (Windsor Davies) and wrestle Major Carstairs (Peter Butterworth). On the set of *Carry On England* actor Peter Quince remembered Joan 'said they offered the cast a smaller fee, with a percentage [of royalties] – no one accepted'.[276] The issue of royalties (or lack thereof) from the *Carry On*s was one which would haunt the stars of the films throughout their lives.

Aside from realising that the film had none of the 'magic' of previous *Carry On*s Joan was also unhappy with her appearance in an army uniform. Whereas in her childhood Joan had revelled in donning uniforms to take part in Girl Guides and Girls Training Corps she now detested being seen in clothing which did not disguise her increasing waistline.

Joan's weight was indeed once again giving her cause for concern – and even featured in a 1976 newspaper interview. Discussing her continued stage fright she admitted that she ate more when working:

I'm sick with fright just before a television recording. Most actors go off their food, but I become even more hungry. I have what I call a 'comfort' meal. It consists of all the things I wouldn't normally eat – such as chips, sausages, fried eggs and baked beans.[277]

By this stage of her life Joan conceded that she was 'frightened' to weigh herself, and although regular two-week visits to Grayshott were still part of her life the effects of her stays there tended to be short-lived; 'I lose weight then, but I put it all back on as soon as I start to work!'[278] She later admitted to being warned by her doctor in about 1960 that unless she was very 'careful' she would find it 'exceedingly difficult to keep the pounds off'.[279] Left to her own devices Joan tended to both eat too much and drink too much. During one of her holidays with Molly Hornsby it was a sense of personal pride and something of an achievement for Joan that she did not gain weight during her visit – although this was simply because Molly was very careful in the portions she gave Joan.

Although Joan's appetite was always hearty the main cause of her weight gain was her heavy drinking and the effects of this at key stages in her life (the mid 1970s, the early and latter 1980s and the late 1990s) were clear to see. Pat Clayfield confirms her friend's vices:

I would blame the drink [for the weight gain] – although she always had a good appetite and would love Yorkshire pudding on a Sunday... and loved puddings. She really enjoyed her food and we were pleased because it took her mind off drinking.[280]

Having seen many friends and contemporaries struggle with alcohol addiction, Fenella Fielding was well aware how 'terribly difficult' it could be to give up drinking and felt that 'by the end Joan had sort of given up trying to be slimmer – because of the drink'.[281]

In the same year as *Carry On England* Joan also featured in *East Lynne* for BBC2. Among an all star-cast which included Polly James, Leonard Sachs, Christopher Cazenove, Georgina Hale and Annette Crosbie, she was in good company; 'I could hardly have asked for a better cast,' director Barney Colehan told *The Stage*.[282]

The nation spent most of 1977 celebrating the Silver Jubilee of Queen Elizabeth II and it was the first year since 1964 in which Joan had not filmed a *Carry On* film. Instead she returned to the stage (see Chapter 2), appearing at the Chichester Festival Theatre, and played Miss Pratt in six episodes of *Lord Tramp*, a children's series starring

Hugh Lloyd (who also created the series) as a tramp who inherits a title, a fortune and a fifty-room mansion complete with staff.

Having been relegated to a cameo role in *Carry On England*, Joan at least had a more sizeable role in her final *Carry On* appearance as the uptight housekeeper, Mrs Dangle, in the infamously awful *Carry On Emmannuelle*. Joan's twenty-fourth *Carry On* film was her twentieth in a row and would be her last feature film for over a decade.[283] She realised at the time it would be her last – and she was right. In an attempt to keep up with the *Confessions* films, the script was distinctly 'smutty' and Joan later admitted it was 'not at all' to her liking. While Joan was certainly no prude – indeed she relished schoolboy jokes and was well known privately for her sense of humour – she was not a fan of vulgarity and at the end of her life admitted to being 'quite embarrassed' by explicit scenes on television.[284] One of the few funny scenes of *Carry On Emmannuelle* is when Joan recounts her most amorous experience – which involved a wordless scene with Victor Maddern and a range of apparel in a launderette.

Peter Eade had now been Joan's agent for almost thirty years. She relied on him totally, both professionally and personally. When Myles Rudge said in a 2002 documentary that Peter 'organised Joan's whole life for her' it was not an exaggeration.[285] From offers of work and contracts to her finances and personal anxieties, Peter Eade was the first person Joan turned to.

On 25th April 1979 Peter Eade died suddenly from a massive heart attack. Not only had Joan lost her first and only agent but she had also lost a dear and devoted friend. Pat Clayfield remembers the massive impact this unexpected loss would have upon Joan:

> Joan was absolutely devastated when Peter Eade died – possibly even more upset than when her parents died. He was absolutely wonderful and he did keep an eye on the drinking and it was after he died that I think that things really went downhill. She adored him.

Peter was extremely well liked by Joan's inner circle including Pat Clayfield who would often meet him for lunch at a little Italian restaurant and would sometimes be joined by Kenneth Williams. Williams too was devoted to Peter (like Joan and Ronnie Barker he had remained a client of Peter's since the early 1950s) and was distraught following his death. Kenneth would manage to compose himself enough to read at Peter's memorial service in Ropley, Hampshire, where Peter's elderly father lived, but even months after Peter's death the mere sight of his photograph would reduce him to tears.

Increasingly as the 1970s drew to a close Joan became more and more unsettled in her home. She frequently complained of 'hearing noises' (whether the noises were real, imaginary or the result of intoxication we shall never know) and in her autobiography she would blame the increasing violence in the area and three burglaries on her home for her decision to sell up. David Kernan's memories of that time justify Joan's fears.

> My partner and I invited Joanie to join us for lunch. She seemed happy about the idea but Christmas Day dawned and Joan, some-times a shy and private person, called to say she was not up for it. I was somewhat disappointed and peeved by this response and embarrassed her into ordering a cab to bring her to Battersea. We had a good time, the lunch was okay and then it was time for me to run her home. We got to her house in Parsons Green and we were met with a ground-floor window smashed to smithereens. Anything of value was gone. Apparently it was the cab driver. You cannot imagine how badly I felt insisting she came to that lunch.[286]

After this Joan made the decision to move from Hurlingham Road. It was a choice which received mixed opinions among her friends, some of whom thought that financially speaking she could not have sold at a worse time. Pat Clayfield, on the other hand, aware of Joan's increasing fears, readily admits: 'I was glad she pulled out.'[287]

The move from Hurlingham Road to a 1930s two-bedroom flat in Thackeray Street, Kensington, meant a considerable amount of downsizing for Joan and she called upon Hattie to help her declutter some of the clothes and possessions she had amassed over the past sixteen years. The two friends spent hours sorting out Joan's con-siderable wardrobe of clothes into piles: items to keep and items to send to charity. As a result of this downsizing the vast collection of theatre memorabilia remembered by Sherrie Hewson did not feature in Joan's new home.

A short walk from the ever bustling Kensington High Street, Thackeray Street is a pleasant and exclusive spot in central London. Given its close proximity to one of the capital's best-known shopping areas it is a relatively quiet location but it lacked the greenery and space of Joan's former home.

Director and artist Nicholas Ferguson remembers Joan's flat during her first days there as sparsely decorated and almost 'minimal' in its appearance:

> The flat absolutely made no impression on me at all and I'm very visual. It was as if all her personality was in her (and her shoes!) rather than in the set she was living in. It was like a cell in a sense – she just lived there, existed there. I don't think there was any love for the place. It was minimal – but in a sad way. As I remember it was completely stark and lacking any of her personality at all.

The one section of Joan's flat that did reflect some of her personality, Nicholas remembers, was the second bedroom where Joan kept her vast collection of footwear:

> She loved shoes and had a room full of them in her last flat… the flat was very undecorated apart from this mad room with the shoes – they were literally all over the floor and on shelves and things.[288]

There was a home-maker in Joan. Polaroid photographs show her flat to be simple, tidy and bright. Pat Clayfield remembers Joan's cream-and-white home filled with 'lovely pictures and china'.[289] Eleanor Fazan has similar memories of a home filled with 'nice china, lovely plates, paintings and so forth – it was cosy'.[290] An inventory of Joan's flat following her death showed that she owned many fine pieces of furniture, ornaments, china and glassware, as indicated from the small selection of the inventory featured in Appendix B.

The inventory did not specifically list a framed photo of Hattie Jacques and a photograph of Joan meeting the Queen, and two of her most beloved possessions – her 'tit boxes' which took pride of place on top of her mantelpiece. These simple wooden boxes were a gift from Ronnie Barker sent to Joan in 1967 after they had worked together on television in the revue show *Before the Fringe*. It was during the production that Joan had reduced Barker (and other members of the cast and crew) to hysterics when she mentioned a wildlife programme she had heard on the radio.

> It was hosted by this elderly, military type, who said his favourite birds were tits, and he then went on to describe how he had built 'tit' boxes and put them around his garden. There were different-sized boxes for different-sized tits: big tits, medium tits, small tits…[291]

Such was the hilarity of the story, relayed by Joan with superb comic timing, that several weeks later Ronnie took it upon himself to send his friend and colleague her first tit box – containing a painted ping-pong-ball 'tit' complete with a small pink nipple made out of clay. The 'tit' was carefully placed in a small, polished, wooden box with the letters TRESEP (the name of the makers of the gramophone head) engraved on the top. It was accompanied by a letter from 'TRESEP' (Tit Research Establishment Society Experimental Project) informing Joan that she had been awarded their annual prize. Several months later another identical box was delivered to Joan, this time containing a lifetime achievement award from TRESEP – their prestigious golden tit box and a letter stating that since she now had a pair of 'tits' she would be able to show them 'as a pair, to all and sundry'.[292] Joan would recall the full story behind the boxes in her autobiography along with copies of the letters which accompanied them. By 2000 it was noted that the 'tits' were slightly deflated and one of the plasticine 'nipples' had disintegrated, but the boxes remained treasured possessions and a great source of amusement until her death.

Amid the mixed emotions at this period in Joan's life came one of her most notable television performances, as Amelia Elizabeth Dyer in 'Suffer Little Children', an episode of *Lady Killers*, screened for the first time on 31st August 1980. The series, introduced by Robert Morley (clearly reading from an 'idiot' board) and produced by Pieter Rogers,[293] ran over two series and each episode featured a notable murder case involving a woman.

Amelia Elizabeth Dyer is now regarded as the most prolific 'baby farm'[294] murderer and is believed to have killed over 400 children over a period of two decades. Nicholas Ferguson directed Joan in this sinister role and they quickly became friends and saw each other socially. Along with Pieter Rogers he realised almost immediately that Joan was a 'brilliant, underestimated actress' and was suitably impressed with her technical perfection and sheer acting range:

> During the barrister's long speech the camera was on Joan and what she was able to do was quite rare during the five-minute take on just her. The close-up was her reacting to what he said – she did this wonderful performance which was quite extraordinary – she was able to pull it off and it was technically very clever and emotionally very clever.

She just had star quality and it almost looked effortless but I know she was nervous about things and that she was probably still drinking when I knew her. Secretly we suspected that she had a little hip flask. Certainly the drinking never affected her performance. As long as you turned up and did the show no one cared about drinking. It was quite normal.

She certainly seduced the crew – it could be fifty people – everyone thought she was wonderful. She had that sort of glow around her.[295]

Coming as it did so soon after the death of Peter Eade, Joan's appearance in *Lady Killers* was a difficult one but ultimately proved to be extremely rewarding, as she herself would recall:

I was at my fattest and my lowest, and it was a very gruelling part to play. Parts are apt to take me over a little, and this was a horrific part. But I was thrilled to be able to make people churn in their stomachs, to make them feel sorry for me, as opposed to sitting there going ha-ha, isn't she funny.[296]

In a rare moment of self-praise Joan admitted years later that it was 'one of the few pieces I'm proud of'.[297] The role should have allowed Joan to move into the bracket of serious character actress since it demonstrated beyond all doubt that she was more than just a comic talent. Over the next five years she was given a handful of opportunities in serious dramas but on the whole was still regarded by casting directors (and indeed the public) as a comedy actress.

Joan Le Mesurier saw the production and was 'frightfully impressed with Joan's sinister baby face'[298] while Pat Clayfield remembers being extremely emotional after watching her friend's performance, particularly as Joan's character came down the prison stairs after being found guilty. Pat was also aware that the production may not have had a big enough audience for the role to significantly impact on Joan's career: 'I don't think enough people saw her in *Lady Killers* and grasped how good she was, so it was sad. After that she should have been doing major parts.'[299]

Despite her versatility as an actress Joan had long since realised that she had often been pigeonholed by casting directors and producers. As early as 1964 she aired her thoughts on being typecast:

Once you have been in a revue, people seem to think you are only capable of playing burlesque parts, and it is awfully difficult to get something different.[300]

Later that year, almost reiterating the thoughts of Anthony Asquith, she also conceded that her physical appearance impacted upon the roles she was offered: 'I've been told my "bun face" fits the comedy parts better than anything else.'[301]

*

In February 1980 Hattie Jacques suffered a crushing blow when her devoted mother Mary died suddenly at the age of eighty.[302] The bereavement marked a significant and obvious decline in Hattie's own health – her ballooning weight and chain smoking led to increasing breathing difficulties during the summer of 1980 and she was forbidden by her doctors to travel abroad. Instead the indomitable actress packed herself – and a group of friends – off on a visit to Ireland where she admitted to her long-time friend and lodger Bruce Copp, 'I'm not going to live long.'[303] Her last screen appearance came at the end of April 1980 when she appeared in Eric Sykes' 'silent' television comedy 'short' *Rhubarb Rhubarb*, playing a short-sighted and short-tempered Nanny. Walking with some difficulty (and in one scene having to perilously hang on to the side of a moving golf buggy in order to stop herself toppling out) she was among an all-star cast including Jimmy Edwards, Beryl Reid and Roy Kinnear. Despite her failing health she remained devoted to her charitable work until the very end of her life.

At the beginning of October Hattie was briefly admitted to hospital because of a 'shortness of breath'.[304] Ever the professional she somehow managed to persuade her doctors to allow her to go home. On 6th October 1980 Hattie Jacques was found dead in her bed at her home in Eardley Crescent by her youngest son, Jake. Hattie's sudden death from a heart attack in her sleep was a massive blow for her family and friends as recalled over thirty years later by Joan Le Mesurier:

> When Hattie died it was a terrible, terrible shock… We were staying in London when the phone rang and it was Jake – John's son – telling us that his mother had died. Then we phoned round to anyone who knew her and Joanie [Sims] was heartbroken. When I think of all the people that knew Hattie, apart from very close family, I think Joan suffered the most from losing her.[305]

Joan did indeed suffer greatly following Hattie's death at the relatively early age of fifty-eight. She was certainly far too distraught to attend her friend's funeral. Totally bereft in the immediate wake of the unexpected loss of her closest friend, Joan was again reliant on others to come to her aid. Joan Le Mesurier remembers the day of Hattie's death and how the family managed to 'rescue' Joan in her grief:

> John [Le Mesurier] went to get Joan from her flat and brought her over to the house and she stayed all day and the next night because she didn't want to be alone. The four of us [Joan, John and Joan Le Mesurier and Jake Le Mesurier] had a kind of wake and talked about Hattie and what she had meant to us. It was a case of 'let's go and get her'. She was quite helpless really in lots of ways – even when it came to things like shopping and running her flat.[306]

Along with the Le Mesurier family, Joan was joined at Eardley Crescent by many other old friends, including Bruce Copp who had the sense to check Hattie's fridge ('It was bulging as usual!' remembers Joan Le Mesurier) and feed the many guests at the house.

Bruce Copp remembers visiting Joan at her home immediately after Hattie's funeral service and finding her 'in a state of collapse and drunk... sitting on the floor sobbing'.[307] Along with David Kernan, Bruce rescued Joan 'from her gin-soaked grief' and took her to Earl's Court where, 'as per Hattie's instructions, everyone got "very pissed", shared their memories of Hattie and shed laughter and tears in equal amounts'.[308]

Grief has a way of uniting families and friends and this was certainly the case following Hattie's death, at least for a short period of time. Aware of how much Joan had relied upon Hattie and how happy she had been in her company, John and Joan Le Mesurier tried to bridge the gap.

> After Hattie's death we kind of took her under our wing – the family – and she used to come down to Ramsgate a lot. She loved it down there because she could be who she was and we used to have some wonderful times and she was very happy and that went on for quite a while.[309]

Away from London and in the company of good friends Joan was able to relax, enjoy time larking about in the Le Mesuriers' paddling pool and tuck in to summer barbeques. It was a chance to remember Hattie and take stock of the future. For Joan Le Mesurier these were also happy days as the family united, and she admits that everyone adored the 'fun' of Joan's company. Equally, Joan Le Mesurier was well aware of how 'fragile' Joan was and how much she depended upon and 'adored' Hattie; and while initially Joan had enjoyed escaping from London to spend time with the Le Mesuriers, the happy arrangement was not sustainable:

> Both of them were similar in so many ways except that Hattie was the mother of all mothers – the mother hen – whereas Joanie was a little girl. Hattie was her rod and staff and when she died it went deep. I tried to take the place for a while but I think Joan got frightened of coming down. I think she just went into her little hideaway flat and that was it.[310]

Hattie's death impacted on Joan in a variety of ways.[311] Routines and rituals which had been upheld for years vanished overnight. In times of need Joan could no longer pick up the telephone and heed Hattie's words of wisdom. She no longer had the huge support that Hattie had provided for two decades, and without it she was lost. Perhaps the most difficult time immediately after Hattie's death was Christmas 1980. Throughout the 1970s Joan (and Gladys) had invariably been Hattie's guests. Now this joyous time of year – made all the more riotous by the combined antics of Hattie, Joan and Kenneth Williams (who also joined them on a number of occasions) – would become bittersweet: a time of memories of the past.

In her autobiography Joan wrote that Hattie's household became like a second home to her and she loved the 'normality' of family life she experienced there. Although at times this normality made Joan painfully aware of what her own life 'lacked' and as a result 'cut through her like a knife', the safe haven provided by Hattie was essential to Joan. Joining Hattie and her family and friends at Eardley Crescent gave Joan buoyancy. She was always happiest in company – and more importantly was able to curb her consumption of alcohol in such situations. Hattie's death and the loss of this safe haven was just one more reason for Joan to sit at home – alone – and open a bottle. Twenty years after the death of her adored closest friend, Joan would sadly admit, 'I still miss her.'[312]

Within months of Hattie's death a further bereavement would hit Joan. After suffering a series of strokes Gladys had moved into St John's Nursing Home in South Croydon, Surrey. Here she was close to her sister and brother-in-law who were frequent visitors.

Bedridden and unwell, Gladys was also visited by Joan, often accompanied by Pat and Bill Clayfield. It was only Joan's constant work commitments at the time which prevented her from spending more time with her mother at this final stage of her life, something she would regret.

A sudden telephone call from the nursing home warned Joan that Gladys was quickly declining and Bill Clayfield drove Joan to South Croydon. Bill later related to his wife that when he and Joan arrived at the nursing home a ringing noise was summoning staff to Gladys's room. She had passed away at the very moment Joan arrived.[313]

Gladys Sims died on 21st January 1981, five days after her eighty-fifth birthday.[314]

Although naturally 'very upset' following the death of her beloved mother, Pat Clayfield confirms that Joan 'handled it very well'.[315] Upon their return to London, Bill Clayfield suggested Joan stay the night so that he and Pat could keep an eye on her, since they knew she was likely to start drinking again – something they didn't want her to do especially as she was about to start work again. Having inevitably outlived many of her contemporaries, Gladys Sims's funeral was a small, low-key affair with the Clayfields providing refreshments for some of the guests after the service. Kenneth Williams wrote about Joan's bereavement in his autobiographical book, *Back Drops*:

> Joan Sims rang. 'My mother's just died,' she said, 'and the undertaker's bill says I get ten per cent discount if I pay promptly. There's scant regard for the bereaved these days. And Southend Council have written an illiterate piece asking when the furniture in the house is to be disposed of. It's a bit much, you know.'[316]

Many of those who knew Gladys have spoken of her dominant and often negative influence over Joan. Her niece, Yvonne Doyle, remembers sadly that 'Auntie Glad never seemed a very happy person. She was always moaning about Joan and worried about her drinking. My mother tried to assure her things would be okay.'[317] Throughout her life Joan had been very close to her parents and following John Sims's death in 1964 Gladys had become an even larger figure in Joan's life.

Joan Le Mesurier felt that Joan was 'under the thumb of her mother' and that ultimately her parents 'took the guts out of her' by preventing her from finding happiness in a relationship.[318] Bruce Copp, whose disdain for Gladys was heartfelt, feels that Joan could have had an even more successful career without the interference of her mother. He felt that Gladys was 'domineering' and 'ruined Joan's life' and that much of the unhappiness Joan experienced was 'mainly due to her mother... she criticised her all the time'.[319]

While Joan admitted that her mother was never especially happy with her choice of roles (particularly when it came to the *Carry On* films), it also struck Bruce that ironically Gladys 'revelled in Joan's success – but never told her'.[320] It was perhaps because of her deep-seated snobbery that Gladys was able to take great pleasure in her daughter's stardom but very little pride in her achievements as an actress.

Joan's two closest surviving friends do have some fond memories of Gladys. Eleanor Fazan thought Joan's mother to be 'a nice woman who adored Joan although she found it hard to understand her as an artist, or even as a person'.[321] Pat Clayfield was well aware that Gladys was 'a snob – with nothing to be snobbish about' and admits that when she first met Gladys their relationship was somewhat strained, especially since Gladys wasn't entirely sure how suitable a flatmate Pat would be for her only daughter. By the time of Gladys's death those days had long since passed, especially as Gladys's temperament mellowed somewhat with old age; and Pat remembers, 'Towards the end I really got on well with Mummy Sims.'[322]

A touching afterword to the complex relationship Joan shared with her mother is contained in a note written by Gladys to Joan on the back of a telephone slip. This was kept by Joan and presumably discovered after her mother's death. Dated 7th April 1972, with Gladys's address (11 Thurston Road) also written at the top of the note, it reads:

My dear Joan,

Thank you dear for everything you have done for me to make my life happy. You have been so very kind and I can never thank you enough.

I am not 'depressed' nor have I had a 'Scotch' I just know that I do not feel as well as I would like, but time marches on. Only hope you will find someone kind to you as you have been to me.

God Bless,

Mother xxxx

Almost six years later the letter was re-dated, in another pen, 18th January 1978 and at the same time Gladys added to the note, 'Now it's 1978 and I'm 82.' At this point Gladys also chose to underline five key words and added a further two 'kisses' at the end of the note.[323]

There is no knowing how Joan felt when she read Gladys's note. The fact that she chose to keep it until her own death surely indicates its importance. It can be seen as ironic that Gladys belatedly hoped that Joan would find someone to make her happy, given that she had been such a dominant influence in Joan's life (particularly when it came to boyfriends and potential suitors). Joan was well aware that her mother suffered from bouts of depression and these appear to have continued into old age. As hinted upon in the note, like her daughter, Gladys may have also occasionally found solace in alcohol during such times.

Above all, the note illustrates Gladys's deep gratitude and love for her daughter, and despite her often negative influence on Joan's life perhaps this is how she should be remembered. Joan summed up their relationship in her autobiography:

> Despite the occasional upsurge of friction there was a very deep bond between us, and I missed her dreadfully. I still do, and even after all these years after her death find myself waking up in the morning and thinking, I must phone Mum and tell her about – and then with a sudden wrench I realise that I can't.[324]

Coming as it did just months after Hattie's sudden death, Joan Le Mesurier regarded Gladys's passing as 'a double blow' but the string of bereavements did not end there.[325] Not long after the death of Gladys came yet another loss: the death of Joan's accountant, J. C. Wilson, who had taken care of her financial dealings since the 1950s. As with Peter Eade, he was another significant figure in Joan's everyday life and his practical assistance was almost essential to her. Eleanor Fazan remembers Joan being 'petrified' of paperwork and in particular anything surrounding income tax returns, and as a result she was 'always dependent on other people to sort out such things… in this respect, as with so many other things in life, she enjoyed having everything done for her'.[326]

It was not in Joan's nature to burden her friends with her personal demons. Although many of her colleagues were aware that her private life, at times, was often unhappy, only those closest to her knew of the true depths of her depression; yet in many ways they were powerless to help. Increasingly, rather than relying on others for company or seeking counselling, Joan would continue to lock herself away and continue to find solace in a bottle of alcohol.

Joan never admitted to being an addict. When questioned whether she thought she was an alcoholic at the end of her life by journalist Deborah Ross, Joan replied, 'Well, that's what they say I am, dear. Actually, I don't think I am...' [327] It is possible to describe Joan as a 'functional' alcoholic since her heavy drinking did not particularly affect her work or obligations and many who encountered her were completely unaware that she had a drink problem. As her drinking increased so too would her body's immunity to the effects of alcohol (although it would still lead to organ damage and alcoholic dependence). A classic symptom of functional alcoholism is denial and avoiding seeking the help of professionals. This was clearly evident in Joan's case. Her dependence on alcohol could also explain Joan's reluctance to become involved in long-running television series. Several offers of long-term television work (which would also have provided a welcome regular income) were turned down, as Pat Clayfield explains: 'I remember Joan saying "I can't be playing anything too long" – she just felt she couldn't do it.' [328]

Joan would sum up her relationship with alcohol and the drink problem which plagued her for so long in her autobiography:

> Drink became my friend, and although I'd try to control it, in times of loneliness – there was no partner with whom to share the joys, frustrations and trivia at the end of the day in my empty flat – I'd go on my own private little bender. As far as I was concerned at the time this was an entirely personal matter between me and my liver. [329]

Her fondness for the bottle meanwhile had already made the headlines of a Sunday-morning tabloid newspaper in 1979 when, unbeknown to Joan, her conversation with John Troke over tea at a London hotel was secretly recorded and subsequently featured in a two-page newspaper spread under the banner 'My Battle With the Booze – By Carry On Star'. Troke had known Joan for years having taken care of a great deal of publicity for the *Carry Ons*. He had also accompanied Joan on her South American trip in 1966. Joan's sense of betrayal – having known and trusted Troke for so long – was immense. She admitted to being deeply upset by the articles as was Gladys, who was staying with Joan at the time and subsequently 'bore the initial brunt' of her anger.[330] The next week a follow-up article entitled 'Loneliness of the Carry On Star' added salt to Joan's wounds and, although she claimed to have calmed down by the time of Troke's second feature, it goes without saying that she became increasingly wary about discussing her inner feelings. Throughout her career Joan found interviews (and in particular television interviews) to be a massive ordeal. It would become extremely difficult for her to muster the courage needed to sit down and discuss her life and career and over the course of the next two decades she agreed to talk to just a handful of journalists.

Sometimes only very dear friends can be brutally honest and it was left to Pat Clayfield to discuss Joan's burgeoning weight – something she knew brought Joan a great deal of personal torment. Seeing Joan in a dark auburn wig in character for her appearances in *Born and Bred* brought a familiar figure to Pat's mind, causing her to ask: 'I know you love Hattie, Joan, but do you *really* want to look like her?'[331] The combined effects of Joan's recent bereavements had again led to a heavy increase in her drinking and in her television appearances around this time (*Worzel Gummidge*, etc.) she looked distinctly bloated. By now Joan's life was spiralling out of control and her actions and choices once again had a clear knock-on effect: her private grief and depression led to heavy drinking which in turn led to an increase in her weight and consequently further anxiety over her appearance.

Ever since they had first worked together in 1964, Kenneth Williams and Barbara Windsor would meet up every three or four months for lunch or drinks and kept in regular contact over the telephone. On the set of the *Carry On*s Barbara had only ever seen Joan drink one or two glasses of wine with lunch but via Williams was aware that Joan was drinking heavily and that her spirits were sinking low. Barbara remembers a particular telephone call from Kenneth when he had found Joan in a 'terrible, terrible state and almost suicidal'. It was left to Kenneth to rescue Joan from her solitude. Taking her to an Italian restaurant for £5 a head and spending time with her was all that was needed to lift Joan's morale and by the end of their time together she was 'okay' enough to be left on her own.[332]

In the summer of 1979 Barbara was thrilled to be cast as Saucy Nancy in *Worzel Gummidge* – a series she had loved watching. Aware that Joan had also featured in the popular children's programme (playing the snobbish Mrs Bloomsbury-Barton), an added bonus to the offer was the opportunity to catch up with her former *Carry On* co-star and on the first day on location Barbara remembers asking members of the crew 'Where's Joanie?' A hushed silence followed and it was only later that Barbara was taken to one side and quietly told that Joan had been 'written out of the series' because of 'a drink problem'.[333] This incident occurred not long after Peter Eade's death so it is not entirely surprising that Joan was not in a fit state to work.

Una Stubbs, the likeable, evergreen actress and dancer best known for her film work with Sir Cliff Richard in the early 1960s and more recently as Mrs Hudson in television's *Sherlock*, worked with Joan 'on quite a few productions', including *The Dick Emery Show*. When Joan was cast as Gran in the Johnny Speight sitcom *Till Death Us Do Part*, she played Una's grandmother (despite being just seven years Stubbs's senior in real life) and they were reunited several years later in *Worzel Gummidge*, in which Una co-starred as Aunt Sally. As a result of their professional association over the course of almost two decades Una had more of an insight into Joan's real personality than many of her other colleagues. While she found her to be 'brilliant and in real life very jolly and witty and lovely to be around', Una would also admit 'one always felt that there was a secret sadness'.[334]

While Joan had continued working during 1980, even managing of course to give one of her finest performances in *Lady Killers*, by the following year there was a telling and uncharacteristic gap in her credits.[335] The deaths of Peter Eade, Hattie Jacques, Gladys and J. C. Wilson within the space of less than two years were too massive a toll for Joan to bear. Work, which had always been her salvation and driving force, was now a second priority as she had to take charge of her health and state of mind.

*

Banstead Hospital opened in 1877 as the third lunatic asylum for the county of Middlesex. It was under the general control of the Middlesex justices of the peace until 1889 when, on the establishment of the London County Council, it passed into their hands. In 1948 the

TOP LEFT: Joan's mother, Gladys Marie Sims (nee Ladbrook), c. 1915
TOP RIGHT: Joan's father, John Henry Sims, during active service in World War I
BOTTOM LEFT: The stationmaster's daughter. Joan as a toddler c. 1931
BOTTOM RIGHT: A rare photograph of Joan with her parents in the early 1930s

"It was such a glorious day… we swam in our pants and bra. It shocked my granny when she saw the photos!" Joan swimming in the Thames with PARADA chums Pat Clayfield, Brian Matthew and Derek Royle
(Photos courtesy of Pat Clayfield)

TOP: Joan during her days in rep after graduating from RADA in 1950
BOTTOM LEFT: John Sims at the time of his retirement in 1952
BOTTOM RIGHT: Gladys Sims in 1959

An early studio portrait of Joan. A lifelong smoker, in later years she refused to be photographed holding a cigarette in case it influenced young fans to take up the habit.

TOP: Joan in the mid 1950s as her career on stage, screen and television was
rapidly taking off (Photo courtesy of Pat Clayfield)

CENTRE: Passport photographs of Gladys Sims in the early 1970s. Her influence
over Joan lasted until her death in January 1981.

BOTTOM: *Intimacy at 8.30.* Joan with colleagues (left to right) Aud Johansen,
Eleanor Fazan, Digby Wolfe, Joan Heal and Paula Hinton
(Photo courtesy of Eleanor Fazan OBE)

TOP LEFT: Joan with the cast of *Our House*: Norman Rossington, Ina de la Haye, Frank Pettingell, Frederick Peisley, Leigh Maddison, Trader Faulkner, Hattie Jacques and Charles Hawtrey

TOP RIGHT: Antony Baird, the Scottish-born actor who became Joan's live-in boyfriend (Photo copyright © Rex Features. Reproduced with permission)

BOTTOM: With Charles Hawtrey, Kenneth Williams, Hattie Jacques, Sid James, Jim Dale and Barbara Windsor during the filming of *Carry On Again Doctor* in the spring of 1969 (Photo copyright © Rex Features. Reproduced with permission)

TOP: Christmas in the early 1970s. Joan in high spirits miming 'Chattanooga Choo Choo' with Hattie Jacques and David Kernan
CENTRE & BOTTOM: A rare public appearance: Joan taking part in a 1977 cricket match

TOP LEFT: "I know you love Hattie, Joan, but do you *really* want to look like her?"
Joan as Molly Peglar on the set of *Born and Bred*

TOP RIGHT: Joan on the set of *Cockles* in 1983. Her dramatic weight loss followed a two-month stay in Banstead Hospital.

BOTTOM LEFT: Joan deseeding a tomato during Christmastime in the early 1980s
(Photo courtesy of Pat Clayfield)

BOTTOM RIGHT: Joan with Pat Clayfield (and Pat's stepmother, Pegs)
(Photo courtesy of Pat Clayfield)

Carrying on abroad: with colleagues including Peter Jones during her 1988
Middle and Far East tour of *Bedroom Farce*

TOP: Joan's bedroom in Thackeray Street, complete with the teddy bear that was with her during her final days in hospital (Photos courtesy of Pat Clayfield)

CENTRE: Treasured possessions: Teddy and the tit boxes (Photo: Author's collection)

BOTTOM: Light, neat and airy – the reception room of Joan's flat where she spent much of her time during the last years of her life (Photo courtesy of Pat Clayfield)

Joan on holiday in Portugal in the late 1990s with Pat and Bill Clayfield
(top left photograph, far right) (Photos courtesy of Pat Clayfield)

TOP: A fitting swansong. Joan on the set of *The Last of the Blonde Bombshells* in November 1999 with Dame Judi Dench and Sir Ian Holm

BOTTOM: Ladies who lunch – a snapshot taken by Thelma Ruby at her home in February 2000. Clockwise from left: Eleanor Fazan OBE, Helen Cotterill, Joan, Jennifer Gosney, Bridget Armstrong, Daphne Goddard, Patricia Lancaster and Dilys Laye (Photo courtesy of Eleanor Fazan OBE)

hospital came under the South West Metropolitan Hospital Board and the Banstead Hospital Management Committee, which lasted until 1974. With the reorganisation of the National Health Service the hospital came under the management of the North West Thames Regional Health Authority and the North East Health District until 1982 when it then became part of the Victoria District Health Authority and finally the Riverside Health Authority in 1985 prior to its closure in 1986.

In the spring of 1982, under the direction of her doctor and at her lowest ebb, both physically and mentally, Joan was admitted to this grim Victorian institution where she would remain as a patient for about two months.

Joan's decision to admit herself to Banstead took many of her closest friends by surprise. She was not sectioned by a medical prac-titioner or in any way forced to enter the hospital but once there would not be discharged until she was deemed well enough by her doctors.

It is impossible to exaggerate the emotions Joan would have gone through during her time in the hospital – from being strip-searched upon entering the building to her encounters with the other patients. It was not a place for the faint hearted. For a shy, sensitive lady who had been brought up in a genteel upper-middle-class household, the grim realities of Banstead must have been almost unbearable. Having seen 'winos and vagrants' wandering the streets of London, particularly during her latter days in Hurlingham Road, Joan would later admit that joining them in Banstead was an experience she would never forget. Indeed Joan found her time there to be 'frightening' and she was 'absolutely petrified' of some of the other patients.[336] After spending some time being assessed (behind heavy dark glasses in an attempt to mask her identity) Joan was placed on a ward where she would encounter a number of 'odd bods' including a German woman who abruptly woke Joan in the middle of the night shouting '*Zigarette? Zigarette!*' The Falklands War began during Joan's time in Banstead and she would remember the reaction of the other patients to this news – from patients cowering in the corners of rooms to others screaming through the corridors.[337] A briefly 'touching' moment came one day when Joan was taken by the hand and led around the garden by a young man who took a shine to her, but on the whole her time in the institution was unpleasant to say the least.

Hospital life, with its constant noise and unbending routine, is rarely conducive with rest and relaxation and Joan spent her days making raffia mats in what she would later describe as an almost dreamlike state.

Pat and Bill Clayfield were among a select few who were privy to the fact that Joan had been admitted to Banstead. Thirty years later Pat's memories of the former lunatic asylum remain raw and painful: 'I didn't like it at all – neither did Bill – and we did everything we could to try and get her out of there.'[338]

In her autobiography, written almost twenty years after her stay in Banstead, Joan summed up her time there in just over one page, admitting that it was not an episode on which she wanted to 'dwell'. During her period of hospitalisation Joan of course remained sober and in the process lost a considerable amount of weight. Despite her 'dreamlike state' Joan's stay in Banstead must inevitably have allowed a great deal of time for reflection – not only on her life in general but also on her career and the path it had taken.

In 1988 Joan reflected on her string of losses she suffered between 1979 and 1981 and remembered this phase as the most difficult period of her life: 'It was a terrible time. I am an only child and my father had died some years earlier. It seemed like everyone I cared about had gone.'[339]

Personal bereavements also coincided with the demise of the *Carry On* series which had meant so much to Joan during the past twenty years of her life. While Joan freely admitted that she thoroughly enjoyed working on the *Carry On* films, it is also quite possible that she chose to stay with the series for so long out of a sense of insecurity.

Many of Joan's friends, colleagues and fans agree that she never reached her full potential as an actress perhaps because of her loyalty to Gerald Thomas and Peter Rogers. Having reached the pinnacle of comedy success, Joan should have been able to ride the crest of a wave professionally speaking – but on the whole it was not to be. Her public saw her as a comedienne and that was it.

While remembering her friend as a 'wonderfully observant' actress, Eleanor Fazan feels that Joan's fame as a comedienne limited her chances of becoming a serious actress.[340] There is no question that Joan had the ability to be a very good dramatic player, as illustrated by her roles in *Lady Killers* and (at the end of her career)

The Last of the Blonde Bombshells. Her ability to play pathos within comedy was also one of her strongest talents – arguably something which was never fully utilised. Joan's wonderful expressive hazel-brown eyes could show such depth of emotion and it is a pity she was never allowed to fully express this as an actress.

In an ideal world, Joan should have been given the opportunity to shine in Alan Bennett's television monologues of the 1980s and 1990s (as was her near contemporary in age, Patricia Routledge – best known as Hyacinth Bucket in television's *Keeping Up Appearances*). Joan's lack of interest in playing more serious roles was long standing and perhaps twofold. In life generally Joan hated anything too serious, depressing or morbid (and as a result disliked the role of Gran in *Till Death Us Do Part*) but more importantly playing such parts did not allow her the joy of escaping her own personal unhappiness. It was only really at the end of her career, when her private life became much more content, that Joan began to consider a wider range of parts.

Like many comedy actresses of her era Joan suffered somewhat from being typecast. Joan Le Mesurier saw all too clearly how Hattie Jacques had been pigeonholed into playing 'funny fat ladies' and admits: 'A lot of producers back then didn't have foresight – typecasting was everything.'[341] Barbara Windsor, aware of Joan's significant body of work on stage long before her *Carry On* days, feels that perhaps Joan was 'sucked into that [*Carry On*] image', saying, 'Only people in the business remember theatre work.'[342]

Nicholas Parsons saw Joan develop from her earliest days but realised her comic abilities also held her back as an actress: 'She was never given the chance to do serious roles which was a shame because she had such sophisticated timing… A lot of people think when you go into comedy you've lost the ability to be a serious actor.'[343]

Writer Bob Larbey was also well placed to comment on Joan's career. Having worked with Joan on several occasions, both he and his wife became good friends of Joan's. He fully agreed with the sentiments of many of Joan's other colleagues: 'I always felt it a pity that she did not get to play more serious roles because she had the talent to do it.' Joan's lack of confidence was one of Bob's 'sad' memories of his friend: 'She was never truly convinced of her own considerable talent when it was plain for everyone who worked with her to see.'[344]

Joe Grossi, who worked with Joan in children's television at the end of the 1980s, is sure Joan's full talent was never truly exploited:

> She could have done more straight roles – like Bernie Bresslaw (I saw him do Shakespeare in Regent's Park).The costume-drama turns she did in her last years merely scratched the surface of her talent. I always felt she could have done most straight drama, given the chance, and shine. Pinter, Beckett, Shakespeare – why not? [345]

Pat Clayfield was also well aware that Joan's career had been limited. It was a topic occasionally discussed by the two friends:

> I hoped they would suddenly realise how talented Joan was [after *Lady Killers*]. She would have loved to have done something more serious. The trouble is they wouldn't take her seriously – so she wasn't offered the parts.
>   She'd say if she walked on a stage people would say, 'Oh, it's Joan Sims,' and they'd all laugh. Once or twice she said, 'They don't think I'm capable of doing it' [serious parts] which of course wasn't true – especially after *Lady Killers*. She really could do it.[346]

Joan's appearances in the theatre in the 1970s did indeed often result in audiences roaring with laughter as soon as she appeared on stage. Although Joan was able to continue in character – and the audience would eventually settle down – it was clear that she was now so well recognised as a *Carry On* actress that it was difficult for the public to see her as anything else. This overwhelming recognition even resulted in Joan being forced to withdraw from a production of *Romeo and Juliet* at the Old Vic (in which she was due to play the Nurse) because she knew her very presence on stage would disrupt the entire production.

In later years Sylvia Syms was a close Kensington neighbour of Joan's. Like Joan, Sylvia's film career had taken off in the 1950s with starring roles in *Ice Cold in Alex*, *No Trees in the Street* and *Victim*. She was one of many who thought that Joan's talent was 'never fully appreciated'. Even in her late seventies Syms admitted it was still easier for male actors to gain roles, and that successful actresses such as Dame Maggie Smith, Dame Judi Dench and Dame Eileen Atkins had to be 'fifty times as talented' as their male contemporaries.[347]

While a number of her later credits were lacklustre, at least from the mid 1980s (until the breakdown of her health a decade later) Joan remained very busy as a constant fixture on the small screen, both in several series and as a guest star. Her willingness to take on cameo roles not only ensured she remained visible to the viewing public as a working actress but also provided a source of income. Professional risks are all well and good, but Joan remained a single lady with bills to pay and offers of work were always gladly received. While being more 'particular' in her choice of roles may have led to more worthwhile material it could also have led to professional obscurity. Finding acting roles for any actress in her fifties is no easy feat and Joan was only too aware of her need to keep working.

Towards the end of her life Joan admitted she was slightly disappointed not to have received recognition for her body of work: 'I do sometimes think that perhaps I may have been undervalued.'[348] Honours and accolades for many of her contemporaries began in the 1970s and the list is extensive: Sheila Hancock OBE in 1974 (and CBE 2011), Beryl Reid OBE in 1986 (and a BAFTA Lifetime Achievement Award in 1991), June Whitfield twice honoured with an OBE in 1985 and CBE in 1998 (in addition to a Lifetime Achievement Award at the British Comedy Awards in 1994), Dora Bryan OBE in 1996 and so on.[349]

Pat Clayfield was among many of Joan's friends who agreed with her sentiments. However, when the pair discussed the issue after Barbara Windsor was awarded the MBE in the New Year's Honours 2000, Joan was philosophical about the matter and simply confided to Pat, 'That's life... it's not my scene really.'[350] There is no question among Joan's fans that her lack of a 'gong' was an outrage. In the early 1990s there was even press speculation about why her career had not been formally recognised by the establishment with one journalist writing that it was 'a national scandal that Joan is still waiting for her much-deserved OBE for services to the *double entendre*'.[351] In this respect Joan would not be the first actress (or indeed actor) who was seemingly overlooked. Many of her contemporaries who enjoyed long and busy professional careers on stage, screen and television have failed to be honoured for their contributions to Entertainment and the Arts.

It is equally disappointing that Joan also missed out on critical acclaim from the media. Numerous television and radio tributes have been produced over the past two decades for many of Britain's best-known comedy actresses (including the *Funny Women* series on television in 1997 and Barbara Windsor's *Funny Girls* radio series in

2011), yet Joan has rarely been the subject of these.[352] Perhaps her unwillingness to 'court' the media simply led to Joan being overlooked for gongs such as a Lifetime Achievement Award, something she arguably deserved.

One can only speculate how Joan felt when friends and contemporaries took on roles that were varied, high profile and well paid. Her good friend Elizabeth Spriggs was a prime example of a character actress who had a highly enviable career, particularly from the early 1990s right up until a few weeks before her death in 2008.[353] With roles in productions ranging from *Shine on Harvey Moon* to *Oranges Are Not the Only Fruit* she became a familiar face to screen and television audiences. She also had her fair share of period drama, including outstanding performances in *Middlemarch*, *Sense and Sensibility* and of course *Martin Chuzzlewit* (alongside Joan), as well as more contemporary productions such as *Playing the Field*, *The Sleeper* and *Midsomer Murders*. It seemed that she was never particularly typecast and was able to take on roles in big-budget international films, even if they were occasionally physically demanding (such as her appearance as Mrs Roberts in *Paradise Road*, filmed in Australia in 1997).

Joan herself always remained modest of her talent and believed that her success was partly due to luck rather than ability: 'I don't believe in this job that success is entirely due to talent. It's very much a matter of luck. If I'd not been lucky, I would have probably given up hope after about three years, as I could never have worked in repertory all my life.'[354] This self-effacing quality ran deep – perhaps too much so – and possibly affected her chances of securing more dramatic roles on stage and screen. Yet professional success remained paramount, almost vital, to Joan. As Eleanor Fazan points out, Joan 'had to be a success – she was brought up that way'.[355] Equally she revelled in the trappings of her achievements, never more so than when working on the *Carry On* films. Since Joan always liked having everything done for her she was at her happiest with a chauffeur collecting her to take her to the studios first thing in the morning and then the wardrobe, hair and make-up departments taking over to transform her into character. Even having a script to learn was a joy to Joan since it allowed her to escape into another world. The importance of acting, which became 'her life', and the joy it brought was highlighted in Joan's autobiography:

Acting has given me a freedom that I never really felt when I was just being myself; it may be a cliché of the profession, but I really do feel that I only truly exist when I'm performing. I've been like a sort of Walter Mitty, with the parts I play allowing me to escape from the reality of being a shy, unconfident, self-conscious person. Once I'm out there in front of a camera I've got all the confidence in the world, but switch that camera off and I sink back into my timid self.[356]

7

Jobbing Actress

'A true artist'

JOAN'S RE-EMERGENCE FOLLOWING HER STAY IN BANSTEAD began with her appearances in several television series including *Crown Court* and Dame Thora Hird's popular sitcom *Hallelujah!* Her appearance in the BBC seaside comedy, *Cockles*, filmed in September 1983, saw her play opposite her RADA contemporary James Grout and Norman Rodway. Photographs taken during the production show the dramatic weight loss Joan had experienced during her time in hospital. Indeed it was clear that she was slimmer than she had been for more than a decade. Although tanned, smiling broadly and, as always, immaculately groomed, Joan looked tired and drawn. She was obviously still very unwell. Nevertheless she threw herself into her work, realising that while she remained busy with acting roles she was less likely to take up drinking again. Over the course of the next decade Joan was rarely idle, taking on a variety of assignments (almost exclusively on television) from guest appearances to lead supporting roles in a succession of series. She had emerged from probably the most difficult period of her life and seemed determined to maintain her highly successful acting career.

Proving that she was back on form, at least as a professional actress, Joan took on the role of Mrs Ashworth in a television adaptation of *Waters of the Moon* in 1983. It was a performance fondly remembered by her co-star Geoffrey Palmer:

> I worked with her first of all in *Waters of the Moon*... it was a studio-bound production; we rehearsed it in the famous Acton rehearsal rooms – now gone. The whole cast used to say 'we'll have two tables

together' in the canteen at lunch and that was really where Joan entertained us. She was an extraordinarily funny and delightful woman.

There was a hugely distinguished cast: Virginia McKenna, Lesley Dunlop, Richard Vernon, Ronnie Pickup, Penny Keith, Phoebe Nicholls, Dilys Laye and we were kind of all at her feet – and she gave a wonderful performance as well!

The role of Mrs Ashworth had previously been played on television in 1968 by Kathleen Harrison but it was Joan who brought an added touch to the role. Geoffrey Palmer remains fulsome in his praise: 'She was an extraordinarily moving, subtle, economical, serious actress… beautifully understated.'

Geoffrey recalls that at the end of the production the entire cast was invited to dinner at Penelope Keith's home. Alas, Joan did not turn up to the event – much to the disappointment of her colleagues – and there was no response when Penelope telephoned Joan's home.

Despite being back at work and providing an excellent supporting role in *Waters of the Moon*, Joan's demons were clearly still not vanquished. Geoffrey Palmer was well aware that Peter Eade's death had greatly affected Joan and feels that she was only able to give so much of herself for a certain length of time:

I can visualise now – we all wanted to be with Joan at lunch or in the studio… it may have been a pressure in the end… Because she was a naturally funny, lovely person, everyone loved her so much and wanted to be around her. She was extraordinary.[357]

Again, as with her performance in *Lady Killers*, Joan's appearance in *Waters of the Moon* should have allowed her to move into the category of a serious character actress with regular, sustained roles in quality productions. Alas, this scenario would have been ideal in a perfect world but, as a single lady and a jobbing actress, Joan was not allowed the luxury of being overly particular about the roles she accepted. While there can be no doubt that the quality of Joan's work (and indeed the productions she appeared in) was generally first rate, she certainly did not approach her work with a 'game plan' or think about the kind of roles she should like to play. Rather, the majority of offers were accepted so long as she was available, with Joan being fully aware that at the end of the day she lived alone and had bills to pay.

The following year Joan was reunited with her friend Sherrie Hewson in the little-seen political satire *Fowl Pest*, based on George Orwell's *Animal Farm*. The cast also included legendary comedy actress Irene Handl and Christine Ozanne, who had made her screen debut in *Carry On Nurse* a quarter of a century earlier. Almost thirty years after *Fowl Pest* first aired on television, actress and writer Sheila Steafel (at one time married to Joan's co-star on several occasions, Harry H. Corbett) would recall the project:

> *Fowl Pest* was the only time I worked with Joan, and it was an age ago! The only thing I remember about the whole experience was that we had to wear the most unfortunate and uncomfortable 'chicken' costumes (hot and unwieldy), and the set was a giant henhouse of some sort, impossible to negotiate! It was a miserable experience for all concerned, and we were all bad-tempered, hated the poor young director who was well out of his depth, and it was a relief when the ghastly day was done.[358]

In the same year Joan would again work with Penelope Keith in the TV play *Hay Fever* and made a guest appearance in *Poor Little Rich Girls*, a classy studio-based sitcom devised by theatre stars and real-life friends Jill Bennett and Maria Aitken and written by Charles Laurence.

Perhaps one of Joan's finest performances of the 1980s was her role as Miss Murgatroyd in *A Murder Is Announced*, filmed in Dorset for BBC television in 1985. This was the third episode of a lavish series of twelve productions (produced between 1984 and 1992) which saw Joan Hickson cast as Agatha Christie's popular sleuth, Miss Marple. For many Hickson became the ultimate Miss Marple and the role brought her worldwide fame in her late seventies as well as an OBE in 1987 and three BAFTA nominations. Hickson of course was no stranger to Joan since the veteran actress had made guest appearances in no less than five *Carry On* films; filming scenes with Joan as the efficient sister in *Carry On Nurse*, drunken Mrs May in *Carry On Constable* in 1960 and the eccentric hotel guest Mrs Dukes in *Carry On Girls* thirteen years later.

On the set of *A Murder Is Announced* Joan was among an all-star cast including Ursula Howells, Samantha Bond (the future Miss Moneypenny in four James Bond films), Simon Shepherd, Ralph Michael, Mary Kerridge, Kevin Whately and Renée Asherson, who thought that both Joan Hickson and Joan Sims were 'marvellous'.[359] Twenty years after they had worked together on *The Big Job*, Joan was reunited with Sylvia Syms, who recalled her contemporary as 'a wonderful actress with great versatility… a kinder person it would be impossible to know'.[360]

Joan's co-star and on-screen partner, Paola Dionisotti – cast as the formidable and forthright Miss Hinchcliffe – found herself 'awe-struck' to be working with Joan, whom she considered to be 'one of the showbiz icons' of her youth. Equally fascinating to Paola was the general direction that Joan's career had taken – 'such a different path' to her own career which has seen her as a notable and award-winning stage actress who spent time with the Royal Shakespeare Company at the end of the 1970s. Nevertheless, despite the vast differences in the two actresses' professional lives, they became friends during the filming of the production. It was clear to Paola that Joan was 'some-one who had been through a lot' particularly 'health wise' and as a mother of a seven-year-old at the time, Joan's life struck Paola as a rather 'solitary' one.[361]

Joan's role as the naïve, childlike Miss Murgatroyd was a com-pelling, serious performance and to Paola it seemed Joan approached her work with 'a very precise professionalism'. Despite this, there was also inevitably frivolity and 'many laughs', thanks mainly to Joan's 'almost compulsive need to provoke laughter'. Ultimately Paola felt Joan's performance to be 'wonderful… so clear and simple' and she considered her co-star to be 'a true artist'.[362]

In the two-part 1985 telemovie *Deceptions*, Joan played house-keeper Mrs Thirkell. Her brisk walk and no-nonsense approach was somewhat reminiscent of her portrayal of Mrs Dangle in *Carry On Emmannuelle*, although in 1985 Joan was still significantly slimmer than she had been in 1978. Adopting a distinctly (slightly exaggerated) Cockney accent, possibly for the benefit of the American audience at whom the production was primarily aimed, Joan was given good billing in the all-star production which was headed by the glamorous Stefanie Powers playing the role of twin sisters who decide to swap lives. It was a typically lavish production of the type so frequently produced in the 1980s. Joan would later admit to being a 'huge fan' of Stefanie Powers, who was probably at the height of her professional success through her role as television detective Jennifer Hart in the long-running series *Hart to Hart* (in which she co-starred with Robert

Wagner) while Miss Powers would recall Joan as 'a nice lady'[363] almost thirty years after the production.

While *Deceptions* was a significant 'international' appearance for Joan, on a personal note it also brought her the chance to work with the 'stunning looking' international screen legend Gina Lollobrigida; and she also shared a scene with Garfield Morgan,[364] the former husband of her old friend and co-star Dilys Laye.

Amidst the constant string of professional engagements of the 1980s were a few more relaxing outings. She was seen as a guest in the 1983 television special *An Audience with Kenneth Williams*, revelling in the anecdotes of her close friend and sitting next to a gregarious, white-haired Betty Marsden. It was also a chance to catch up with many other old chums, including Bernard Bresslaw and Dora Bryan. Five years later she could be seen roaring with laughter when she was a guest at *An Audience with Victoria Wood*.

In 1986 Joan returned to Pinewood Studios and sat with Kenneth Connor (casually smoking a cigarette), Peter Rogers and Barbara Windsor to be interviewed for television's *Movies from the Mansion*. Here she recalled Gerald Thomas tricking her into drinking 'neat' gin in *Carry On Regardless* and 'being out for the count for the rest of the day', 'begged to differ' about the 'size of the parts' in the shower scene of *Carry On Constable*[365] and happily giggled as Barbara Windsor recalled conditions on the set of *Carry On Camping* (and her famous exercise routine).

Joan's guest appearance as Queen Katryca in *Doctor Who* ('The Mysterious Planet') brought her among the most mixed reviews of any of her television appearances. The four episodes in which she appeared, transmitted in the late summer of 1986, were the beginning of the 'Trial of a Time Lord' storyline centring on the Doctor (Colin Baker) being put on trial for his crimes of interference.

As the leader of a group of semi-feral humans (on the planet Earth, which had been renamed Ravalox) Joan's appearance in the popular series was distinctly Boudicca-like and saw her donning a long flame-red wig. It was a robust, almost energetic, performance with Joan leading the Tribe of the Free ('surface dwellers') through a variety of settings – shot on location and in the studio – against a band of technocrats who live below the Earth's surface. The character of Katryca was eventually electrocuted to death ('fried alive') by the robotic Drathro to the relief of many *Doctor Who* fans!

Reviews of Joan's appearance were varied and not always flattering. Some critics thought 'the transition from [*Carry On*] battle-axe to warrior queen [was] a bit of a leap, and she was a less-than-sprightly 56 when she took the part'[366] while others were just relieved that Joan was not as 'miscast' as Beryl Reid who had played Captain Briggs in a 1982 episode of the series. For Joan herself such criticism would not have been as damning as might have been expected. She later admitted to 'hating' her appearance in the series, the appeal of which had 'always been a mystery' to her. Without wishing to offend *Doctor Who* fans Joan would later write that her guest role in the cult classic 'was simply a matter of learning the lines, going in, not bumping into the furniture, and collecting the cheque'.[367]

A return to mainstream television comedy would follow in Joan's next professional engagement, *Farrington of the F.O.*, a sitcom written by Dick Sharples for Yorkshire Television. The studio-based series was centred on Harriet Emily Farrington (played by Angela Thorne) being posted to a 'Latin American "banana republic" as the new British Consul-General'.[368] Joan was cast to co-star as Annie Begley, Harriet's trusted and efficient Vice Consul (Admin). The camaraderie on the set of *Farrington of the F.O.* among the middle-aged cast of television veterans was clear. Angela Thorne held Joan in high esteem and in 1997 would remember the 'endless laughs' they had on set.[369] Over a quarter of a century after they had worked together Angela's memories of Joan remain vivid:

> I worked with Joan on *Farrington of the F.O.* and we became close friends. She was a very funny, dear person and made me laugh a great deal. She was a very witty, intelligent person and had the capacity of seeing the funny side of life.
>
> That she was a brilliant comedienne goes without saying and I learned a great deal about playing high comedy from Joan.
>
> She always looked elegant and dressed beautifully and had wonderful legs![370]

Although it only ran for two series (a total of fourteen episodes), and the rest of the supporting cast had relatively little time to form strong friendships, John Quayle (who played the upper-class Major Percival Willoughby-Gore) would later remember Joan with affection and admitted that 'it was a pleasure to have worked with a highly professional actress with a very lovely personality'.[371]

By the time she began filming *Farrington of the F.O.* Joan had gained a certain amount of weight, yet despite this she appeared to be in good health and spirits. The series, unlike many of her appearances of the 1980s, allowed her to be beautifully dressed and made-up and showed that in her late fifties the prettiness of her youth remained intact.

The spate of work in which Joan was now involved inevitably involved publicity, and in 1987 she not only granted a rare television interview (on *Good Morning Television*) but was also interviewed by David James Smith for *TV Times* in a two-part special covering her 'lonely' childhood, early career and current work.

This rare glimpse into Joan's private world revealed she had been working constantly for three months and that plans to check herself into a 'classy health-farm' to celebrate her fifty-seventh birthday had gone awry after she tripped over a step and sprained her back.[372] There was talk of 'a terrible succession of personal disasters and tragedies' and suspicions of a lingering 'jinx'. Her battle with depression following the death of Peter Eade and Hattie Jacques was touched upon and, without going into great detail, Joan admitted in the interview that recent years had not been easy for her.

Although the interview ended on a positive note, highlighting the fact that Joan was scheduled to appear in several forthcoming television series, the tone of the articles was distinctly melancholic, dwelling on Joan's many insecurities including her childhood, 'strict upbringing', her love life and her looks. Described by James Smith as 'overweight, a sweet woman and a good laugh', the articles were less than flattering for a lady who had spent years being sensitive about her weight. It seems hardly surprising that she would choose to avoid journalists and subsequent interviews for more than a decade.

Joan's appearance on *Good Morning Television* proved to be a major ordeal for her. Although looking relaxed and jolly, she admitted on air that it was only about her second attempt at taking part in a chat show. She was 'terrified' to do it and found the occasion a 'frightening experience'. Notably Joan would not be interviewed for television for more than a decade following her ten-minute appearance on the programme alongside actor Christopher Biggins and Gyles Brandreth (the latter a close friend of Kenneth Williams who also got on well with Joan and 'liked and admired her'[373]).

In the same year when Kenneth Williams, Barbara Windsor, Kenneth Connor and Bernard Bresslaw featured on *Wogan*, Joan was notably absent. The actors had reunited amid speculation that the *Carry On* series was about to be resurrected with a new entry in the series, *Carry On Texas* (later renamed as *Carry On Dallas*). Years later Joan would confess her reason for declining to appear on the popular chat show stemmed purely from her own insecurity regarding her appearance: 'I once wouldn't do *Wogan* because I looked in the mirror and just thought: No.'[374]

Joan's full thoughts on resurrecting the *Carry On* series, nine years after the final film had been released, are not recorded. Since *Carry On Emmannuelle*, various ideas for a new film (aside from *Carry On Texas*) had been suggested including *Carry On Down Under* and *Carry On Nursing*. Suffice to say none came to fruition. Around this time, while recalling the difficult conditions on the set of the *Carry On* films, Joan admitted that she had been 'a lot younger and a lot more resilient' during the series' heyday, perhaps hinting that her enthusiasm for another *Carry On* film had waned.[375]

A guest appearance as Reenie Turpin in the 1987 Christmas Day episode of *Only Fools and Horses* proved to be one of Joan's finest television performances. She positively glowed in her role as Trigger's cheeky, flirtatious aunt, who caught Del Boy's attention by telling him about a hidden legacy of gold (and casting doubts over Rodney's paternity!). The appearance also reunited Joan with David Jason, with whom she had previously worked during *Six Dates with Barker* almost twenty years earlier. Joan's sparkling, seemingly effortless performance once again highlighted her superb comic ability, and the 'happy face' noted by Anthony Asquith so many years earlier had clearly not left her.

Increasingly as the 1980s drew to a close Joan began to become more reclusive, to the concern and sometimes frustration of her friends. Her lifelong reluctance to make public appearances more or less brought to an end her friendship with David Kernan, as he explained to the author from his home in Spain:

> In the 80s our business was hit by the AIDS epidemic. Suddenly I had lost many good friends. I threw myself into putting together numerous Sunday-night galas to raise money. One particular gala, I asked Joan if she would simply make an entrance… nothing more. The sad insecurity hit her once again; she simply said 'no'. It hurt

me. She was adored by the gay brigade and it would have been a perfect way for her to repay some of that adoration.[376]

After this incident David admits sadly that he was 'hurt by her decision not to appear' and saw less and less of Joan. In retrospect he felt that she was 'embarrassed because of her decision' and it marked 'the rather sad ending to a long and happy friendship'.

Happily, despite this sad chapter, David still remembers 'Dear Joan' with affection:

> She was a woman of huge often untapped talent… a witty and adorable person. But like a lot of actors there was the deeper, sadder side. I was so happy to be her friend… for the most part.[377]

Although John and Joan Le Mesurier had tried their best to keep an eye on Joan following Hattie's death in 1980, this was another friendship that 'slowly faded off'. John Le Mesurier famously 'conked out' in November 1983, and as the years passed Joan Le Mesurier found that Joan became increasingly 'frightened to leave her nice little flat. It was so hard to try and drag her out of the safety of her flat. It became hard work in the end.'[378]

While saddened that their friendship tailed off, happily Joan Le Mesurier was aware that the Clayfields were still a key fixture in Joan's life, 'being very kind, looking after her, guarding her zealously and trying their best to keep her off the booze'.[379]

Bruce Copp, who saw a good deal of Joan during Hattie Jacques' lifetime, also regretted losing touch after the latter's death although he admits that Joan was 'not very good at communication' and probably wouldn't have responded even if he'd sent letters. Bruce himself retired to Spain in 1984 although he continued to visit Britain regularly into his nineties.[380]

Likewise by the late 1980s her earlier close friendship with director Nicholas Ferguson had also faded, as explained to the author:

> I think we sorted of drifted apart partly because of work and partly because I think she was quite needy as well. I didn't have enough to be able to give to her because I was doing other things… I think that's the problem with drink [generally] and her personality – there was neediness. Unless you could go on with it, you'd get over-involved with her. It sounds a bit cruel but if you have to get on with your own work, directing other things, you can't always do as much as you'd like to do or feel you could do. You also feel perhaps that it could be

a sort of trap that I'd fall into and I'd then be in her world. It was quite demanding in a way.

A lot of powerful actresses I've known, like Jill Bennett, were similar [to Joan] – quite needy. So unless you were in 'their' gang you couldn't really be in anyone else's gang. I think that showed her vulnerability.

In the end I probably sort of rejected her because all relationships have to have a good balance… and I feel as lovely as she was for me, sort of growing up in a way and maturing slightly, that I probably felt it was too much of a burden… you could have given in to her and been her full-time best friend.[381]

As some friendships faded so too did Joan's desire to leave her flat. She was very candid about her tendency to shy away from many social events and during her 1988 tour of the Middle East admitted:

I'm not the jolliest of people. My privacy is important to me and I never socialise unless I have to. But then that is true of so many comedians.[382]

A decade later she would reiterate her thoughts on the subject, confirming that she would often decline invitations (by saying she wasn't free) because she was too shy to go on her own. Being a single lady placed added pressure on Joan, and she would admit to feeling 'vulnerable' and 'exposed' at parties: 'Life would have been a lot easier if I wasn't on my own.'[383]

As a close, lifelong friend of Joan's, Pat Clayfield knew exactly how 'Timkins' would avoid invitations:

If she had been invited to some big party she would often ring up and ask to come over. We of course would say 'yes'. Then she could genuinely say, 'No, sorry, I'm going somewhere else.' This showed how she worked and what a lovely person she was – she didn't want to tell a blatant lie but she would make it so that in her heart it felt as if she wasn't telling a squib because she genuinely had somewhere else to go.[384]

In later life Joan firmly believed that her largely solitary childhood led to many of her insecurities:

Because of not having had that much contact with other human beings, I've suffered from fears and nerves and painful shyness all my life. Loneliness, in itself, is one of the most terrible things to suffer from. In your heart of hearts you want friends but your body language is all wrong and you come across as unfriendly.[385]

While none of her friends or colleagues has ever agreed with Joan's assessment of her body language and how it may have been interpreted, many, including Geoffrey Palmer, were aware that she was fundamentally a shy lady:

> I think she was very much a shy person... I think she fits in with a lot of people who are shy but have an ability to be the centre of the party but underneath there was an awful cliché... a hurt, vulnerable, desperately lonely person. It's extraordinary that someone who can be that effusive, that extrovert, that outgoing, that giving can be a little lost soul inside.[386]

Fenella Fielding, who had last worked with Joan in 1966, remembers that despite increasing shyness her former co-star remained unchanged in later years: 'I would see her later on – now and again. She came to see a play I was in and was very sweet;'[387] and Pat Clayfield confirms:

> Half her charm was that she remained Joan. I have to be honest – I don't think Joan had an evil or horrid thought in her mind. She was such a lovely person. I don't think anybody knew how kind she was.[388]

Christmas times, previously spent with Hattie Jacques, when Joan would hand out presents 'like a bountiful fairy',[389] were now spent alternately with Norah and 'Dutch' Holland or Pat and Bill Clayfield (and Pat's stepmother, Pegs) as Joan slowly began to adjust to life without the three people she had been closest to. Joan's friendship with Norah Holland was not always an idyllic one and theirs became an increasingly on-off relationship over the years. Norah was evidently a lady of considerable character and could at times be 'rather bossy' in her dealings with Joan.[390] Although Joan would always regard her former stand-in as one of her best friends, she was not always entirely at ease about spending time with her – especially at Christmas. Never one to cause a scene or hurt a friend, Joan would invariably concede and accept Norah's invitations out of fear of upsetting her one-time stand-in. As a result of her strong (some have even said almost domineering) personality, Norah was in some ways not dissimilar to Gladys in that she could, at times, be controlling of Joan. Despite this Joan would still often spend time at Norah's home, particularly in her final years.

It seems ironic that following the death of Gladys, Joan would become slightly dominated again by another strong-willed female in her life, although in fairness Joan had nothing but kind words to say about Norah when she wrote about her in *High Spirits*; and their closeness, as is evident from their 'knicker' encounter in *Carry On Don't Lose Your Head*, cannot be doubted.

It was perhaps part of Joan's nature and personality that she needed 'strong-minded' people in her life. The list of such characters is fairly extensive: her mother, Hattie Jacques, Norah Holland, Peter Eade and so on. When Joan was unable to take control of her own life she relied upon family and friends to take charge. At times this could be extremely successful and suited her perfectly. Equally there were times when it became a huge source of annoyance. As with all relationships Joan had to take the good with the bad.

While her private life was gradually becoming more and more cocooned Joan's workload in her late fifties was distinctly busy. Following on from two series of *Farrington of the F.O.* , she played Lady Fox-Custard in two series of the BBC children's programme *Simon and the Witch*, based on the series of books by Margaret Stuart Barry, a role which brought her many new fans.

Joe Grossi was asked to audition for the part of Lady Fox-Custard's butler, Hopkins, after being spotted by director David Bell in a comedy revue called *Knightmare Kabaret* at the Latchmere Theatre in Battersea. A year earlier he had been in an advert with (Sir) David Jason but genuinely thought the opportunity to work with Joan Sims was an even 'bigger thrill'. Although not nervous about auditioning for the part of Lady Fox-Custard's hired help, Joe recalls the chance to act alongside Joan 'was an even bigger incentive' to 'work his socks off'.

Joe's memories of his much-admired co-star remain clear a quarter of a century after their times together:

> She was, I think, very nervous about not knowing her words well enough. After one rehearsal session on the second series, she stayed a little longer after our lunch (at the East Acton Hilton i.e. the BBC rehearsal rooms' top-floor café). She burst into tears when talking to David about how the pressure of filming all the scenes, one after another, on the Thursday and the Friday was too much for her because of the sheer quantity of text.

Children's television works on small budgets and the scenes at Horty Hall were all rehearsed and shot in a compact way, so that the set could be struck and a new set built. It meant she had scene after scene to shoot: with all the main and supporting characters, plus a few set-piece scenes where there was a houseful.

My reaction to this was to volunteer to stay on after lunch that day and the following day to help her learn her words. I was so upset for her that I blurted out that I felt it a privilege to work with her and to be able to watch her work. And I meant every word I said to her.

A few weeks later, when we shot a jogging scene in a Beaconsfield street (series two), she and I sat in the back of a grips truck, so that she was away from the public gaze. She asked to go through all the words in the scene (including Sally's). Having got it right, she sighed. Then she said that on the *Carry On* films, she and Kenny and the others would just go through their words, over and over. She was very wistful and clearly missed the camaraderie of those days – and missed a time when she worked more regularly and was therefore better at learning her words. It was a special Joanie moment.

On the set of *Simon and the Witch* Joan became friends with the respected stage actress Elizabeth Spriggs, whom she would later work with again on television in the mid 1990s and on radio in 2000. Just eight months Joan's senior, Elizabeth began her career in repertory theatre in her twenties before gaining prominence in the late 1960s as an acclaimed member of the Royal Shakespeare Company, under the direction of Sir Peter Hall. Joe Grossi shared his thoughts on the working relationship of these two great actresses of stage and screen with the author in 2013:

Joan was slightly in awe of Liz because Liz always turned up to rehearsal perfectly in character (as Joanie did) but also word perfect: infallibly word perfect (certainly putting me to shame!). Luckily for Joan, she and Liz only had comparatively few scenes together. But because of the one-or-two-takes shooting schedule, both Liz and Joanie were at most of the rehearsals together, so they could see and hear each other work. The BBC rehearsal rooms are big open spaces and, as I remember it, most of us just sat round waiting our turn.

The series also brought Joan into frequent contact with child actors, including Nicola Stapleton (who would later become familiar as a cast member of television's *Bad Girls* and as Mandy Salter in *EastEnders*), Hugh Pollard (as Simon) and Naomie Harris – who went on to become a leading lady in films such as *28 Days Later* (2002),

Pirates of the Caribbean: Dead Man's Chest (2006) and *At World's End* (2007) and most prominently *Skyfall* (as Miss Eve Moneypenny). By her own admission, Joan was not a particularly maternal person; and to Joe Grossi, at least, 'She was not great with the children though she tried to be sweet.' This was in contrast to Elizabeth Spriggs (who had a daughter Wendy from the first of her three marriages) who appeared to be much more 'comfortable' around her young co-stars.

On the set of the production Joe was able to learn a great deal from Joan about acting for the camera:

> There used to be big Sony CRT monitors and, even when I was not in the scene, I would watch Joanie's mid shots (MS) and medium close ups (MCU). She used her face so economically, never gurning or over-egging it, although she could 'ooh!' with the best of 'em. When the second series of *Simon and the Witch* went out, it was preceded by a re-run, twice a week, of the first series. Comparing my performance in the first to the second series, I can see that I learned a few things from Joan. She told me a trick that she learned at the Rank Charm School: when you face an actor in a two-shot, always look at the eye nearer the camera. I endeavour to do this always.

Recalling his co-star in 2013 Joe was clearly fond of the veteran actress:

> I really, really liked her. I wanted to befriend her but I thought it would be smarmy to try and be her mate: I thought she might think I just wanted to be a friend because she was famous.[391]

Having seen Joan as Lady Fox-Custard on twenty television screens in a shop in Kensington High Street, Derek Nimmo asked her to take part in a Middle East tour of his production of Alan Ayckbourn's *Bedroom Farce*. The chance of an all-expenses-paid trip appealed to Joan although she was filled with self-doubt about her ability to take part in the production and worried about the amount of flying required to fulfil the tour. Finally after much deliberation Joan agreed to Nimmo's offer but even then called upon the help of her actress friend, Polly James, to help her pack and prepare for the journey.

The company's first stop was a four-star hotel in Dubai and from there they moved to Bahrain, Muscat and Al Ain. By 29th February 1988 the company had travelled on to Singapore, where Joan was a guest at the Shangri-La Hotel. Staying in room 1232, she clearly relished her time at the hotel – and over thirty receipts for room service and the minibar in her room show just how much. In addition to taking full advantage of the hotel's facilities, including a drug store (chemist), hairdresser and the pool (where she ordered glasses of white wine), Joan was drinking consistently (and at times fairly heavily) during her stay at the hotel. Sometimes with company, and sometimes alone, the receipts show that as well as the occasional hot beverage and French pastry, among Joan's favourite tipples were cognac, white wine and local beer. Part of the attraction of room service (and the minibar) may have been the cost, since among the receipts is a letter which temptingly states: 'All alcoholic drinks ordered will be subject to 50% discount with the exception of wines and champagne.' [392] Small wonder then that Joan chose to drink more cognac than wine since it ultimately worked out to be cheaper!

The receipts from Joan's time in Singapore, carefully stored in a large hotel envelope and signed by Joan, provide possibly the only evidence of her alcohol consumption. Admittedly she was partly on holiday – and it is well known that many actors head straight for a bar following a performance on stage – yet it can clearly be seen that her drinking habit (although not particularly excessive during this period of work) was sustained and regular. It can safely be assumed that at the times when she was not working Joan would have been drinking far more.

From 29th February until 10th March Joan spent over $1,100 (Singapore dollars) on the hotel's minibar, hairdresser and additional services. [393] She was well known for occasional extravagances and this was one such occasion when she clearly decided to throw caution to the wind.

The tour of *Bedroom Farce* allowed Joan to see a variety of countries and she was especially thrilled to visit Cairo and the pyramids with Peter Jones and his wife, American actress Jeri Sauvinet. In between shows there were outings with other cast members which she revelled in, especially when they involved spending time in or on the water. Swimming remained one of her great pleasures and she took to the water whenever she could. Inevitably, despite the numerous exotic locations in which they performed, Joan was still recognised for her work in the *Carry On* films and constantly questioned by audience members after her performances about the films and her well-known co-stars.

Evidence of Joan's increased drinking also came through her weight gain during the latter half of the 1980s. Having emerged from Banstead Hospital in 1982 looking dramatically slimmer than she had been for years, by 1988 Joan was distinctly plump. As with her weight gain in the mid 1970s her growing corpulence was the direct result of too much alcohol. Joe Grossi, working with Joan at the time, remembers that she was 'modest [and] conscious of being overweight'. Her weight gain now tended to centre around her midriff and what she described as her 'Buddha belly'.[394] In her 1987 TV-AM interview Joan looked back on footage of herself in *Carry On Constable* and quipped, 'I had a waist then.'[395]

*

Amid a spate of professional engagements – making 1988 one of the busiest years of her professional life – came the deaths of two of her closest friends and colleagues. On 15th April it was announced that Kenneth Williams had died suddenly at his London home, his body being discovered by his elderly mother, Louisa (Louie), who lived in an adjoining flat to her only son.

In his final years Kenneth aged noticeably and although only sixty-two at the time of his death he looked a decade older (ironically Louie would outlive her son by more than three years, dying in 1991 in her ninetieth year). Joan, like many of those close to Kenneth, had been aware of his failing health and the fact that he professed to be in near constant pain, particularly in the last few years of his life. He had indeed been plagued with digestive problems for most of his adult life and it was later revealed that he was suffering from a large, deep-seated stomach ulcer. Joan was also aware that her old chum was due to go into hospital for 'quite a serious bowel operation' and that he was 'very frightened about going under the surgeon's knife'.[396] His aversion to growing old was well known and he frequently announced that he had no desire to live past the age of sixty-five.

Barbara Windsor was also a close friend of Kenneth's and was one of a small number of invited guests at his private funeral in Finchley, north-west London. She joined Maggie Smith (created a Dame two years later), Stanley Baxter, Gordon Jackson and his wife Rona Anderson; and realised then that, although she knew all of

Kenneth's closest friends, 'none of us had been out together with Kenny' since he 'liked to keep us compartmentalised, it seemed'.[397]

Joan, of course, was a notable absentee at the funeral. Having not attended Hattie's funeral eight years earlier she had no desire to face the ordeal of another close friend's final farewell. She felt his death keenly and was quite devastated by the news. It was the end of another era in her life and she would admit lovingly, 'I never felt more closely attuned to another performer than I did to Kenny.'[398]

Kenneth left forty-three volumes of diary which were masterfully edited by Russell Davies and published in 1993. They shed little light on the thirty-year friendship he enjoyed with Joan. Based on the edited diaries alone Joan comes across as being something of a thorn in Williams' side, a prudish, domineering, shrew of a woman, and it would appear the diaries have been the basis for how Joan was subsequently portrayed on screen, particularly by Chrissie Cotterill in *Cor! Blimey*. Their differences at Pinewood Studios during the filming of the *Carry On*s were duly recorded, notably with Kenneth calling Joan a 'stupid cow' during *Carry On Don't Lose Your Head*, but there is no real hint as to their closeness and the countless laughs they enjoyed over the years.

Barely six months after Kenneth's death another friend and *Carry On* co-star, Charles Hawtrey, also died. After making a final *Carry On* appearance in 1972, Hawtrey's last years were spent living in a three-storey terrace house in Deal, Kent, surrounded by masses of furniture, clutter and feline friends. He was well known by locals and increasingly disliked because of his drunken behaviour and rudeness to anyone brave enough to approach him for an autograph. Gradually many of the local landlords barred him from entering their premises and he became increasingly reclusive, often ordering taxis to collect groceries or alcohol for him. After the *Carry On*s he made a handful of appearances on stage, the last in pantomime in the winter of 1979-80, and made a fleeting appearance in Eric Sykes' television remake of his classic 'silent' comedy, *The Plank*, in 1979. Five years later he made headlines after being rescued from a fire at his home and photographed semi-naked and minus his toupee being helped by a fireman.[399] Amazingly – and out of the blue – he was to make a final television appearance just a year before his death in the children's television series, *Super Gran*, playing the Duke of Claridge.[400] Looking sprightly and seemingly in good health he was remembered by his co-star, Gudrun Ure, as 'so funny and a true professional. He had a very special quality and was a joy to work with and witness.' [401]

Joan was one of the few people to keep in touch with her former co-star, whom she described as 'notoriously eccentric'. Likewise, according to Kenneth Williams, Joan was also quite unique in that she was able to interpret perfectly Hawtrey's bizarre way of speaking ('telegraphese'). In 2000 Joan would recall the latter years of her friendship with Charlie:

> We kept in close touch, though, after he had retired... and his convo-
> luted telephone calls became a regular feature of Sunday afternoon...
> Poor Charlie was a very lonely and very mixed-up little man.

Within the acting profession Charlie's fondness for alcohol was well known; indeed it was often written into the scripts of *Carry On* films that he would be inebriated (as in *Carry On At Your Convenience* and *Carry On Abroad*). He had been drinking heavily since the early 1960s and in his fifties was faced with the difficult task of caring for his elderly mother who was by then suffering from dementia. She was often at Pinewood Studios with him while he was filming, and despite the burden of her final illness he was distraught when she died. Increasingly bitter, particularly regarding Peter Rogers and the lack of royalties from the *Carry On* films, Charlie's reliance on alcohol grew with the passage of time. He lived long enough to see the *Carry On* films released onto video cassette (VHS) which only served to increase his anger towards the film series which brought him worldwide fame, if not wealth.

In the late summer of 1988 Charlie, worse for wear after another drinking session, fell and fractured his leg in the doorway of a local pub. After being admitted to hospital it was discovered he was suffering from chronic arterial disease in both legs, the result of years of heavy smoking. He was told that his life could only be saved if he underwent an operation to amputate both of his legs. Barbara Windsor, who was especially fond of Hawtrey and remembered him as her 'favourite of the *Carry On* regulars', wrote about her co-star's final days in her autobiography:

> He may have been a bit of an oddball, Charlie, but he was a brave
> one. When he was dying and his doctors told him they would have
> to amputate his legs, he lit a fag and said: 'No. I want to die with my
> boots on.' And that's what he did. [402]

Having refused the life-saving operation, Charles Hawtrey died at a Deal nursing home on 27th October 1988, aged seventy-three. Just nine people attended his funeral, including a vicar, organist and undertakers.[403] Joan of course was not one of them, although it was reported that she sent a floral tribute to the service. Interestingly at the time of his death Hawtrey was relatively wealthy, leaving an estate valued at more than £160,000.

The release of the *Carry On* films for the home cinema audience brought little pleasure to the surviving stars of the series. Barbara Windsor remembers that Kenneth Williams 'was appalled that the *Carry On*s were screened on television and thought they should have been reserved for the big screen. The big screen gives an unobtainable quality whereas television is different...'[404] Apart from the loss of kudos from the films being screened on television, the issue of royalties was also a sore point for many of the actors involved. Since all of the actors involved in the films had been paid a one-off flat fee they were unable to claim residual fees when the rights to the films were later sold. Consequently, despite seemingly never-ending repeat screenings of the films on television (not to mention their release on VHS and later DVD), none of the actors have received a share of the enormous profits earned by Peter Rogers in his latter years.

Peter Rogers always stood by his claim that very early on in the life of the series all of the starring actors had been given the option to share the profits of the film by taking a percentage if they worked for a smaller initial fee. Apparently none of the actors chose to take up this option, preferring instead to have a guaranteed one-off payment for their work in the films. Joan was paid £2,500 for each of the *Carry On* films in which she starred although for some of the films she was paid on a basic daily rate.[405] This set amount did not change over the two decades in which she worked for Gerald Thomas and Peter Rogers and was given as a single payment without any subsequent royalties. Throughout the lifespan of the series the male stars of the films (Sid James, Kenneth Williams and Charles Hawtrey) were always paid more than their female counterparts (Joan Sims, Hattie Jacques and Barbara Windsor). In her autobiography Joan wrote that she was not aware that any actor had been offered a share of the profits and felt sure that Peter Eade, her agent at the time, would have informed her of such an offer. Laurena Dewar, Peter's trusted assistant, was also unaware that any such offer had ever been made by Rogers.

As a result of the constant screening of the films many imagined that Joan was well off although this was far from the case, as Nicholas Ferguson remembers:

> She never had much money because they were paid so badly. She used to get very upset with taxi drivers when she gave a small tip and then they looked at her and said, 'You're so fucking rich and that's all you can give me!' and she was terribly upset about that and she told me they were always saying that to her because she wasn't like that at all – she was generous and was not mean, she just didn't have any money.[406]

Joe Grossi, who was working with Joan at the time when the films were released for home viewing, would remember, 'Joan always struck me as a little heartbroken; she felt robbed by Peter Rogers who famously paid the men more than the women and did not pay any royalties.'[407]

While Joan admitted that the *Carry On* films allowed her to not only buy her own home but also a home for her parents in their latter years and that during the *Carry On* years she 'wasn't exactly staring poverty in the face', the subject of royalties was one which would cast a cloud over the continued success of the series for Joan and many of her co-stars.[408]

Joan's steady stream of television work in the mid to late 1980s, for which she was well paid, meant that she could at least be 'comfortable' but comparatively speaking 'she certainly never felt well off'.[409] Whilst Eleanor Fazan admits that the *Carry On*s were a 'wonderful experience' for Joan, she is also aware that the issue of royalties resulted in all those involved 'turning against' the films which had brought them so much success and personal fame.[410] It was certainly an issue which would hang over Joan, particularly during her final years as the films enjoyed a further renaissance.

The amount of work Joan managed to secure from the mid 1980s until the mid 1990s did allow her some luxuries including holidays with Pat and Bill Clayfield at their villa in Portugal and a make-over for her Kensington home. By 1993 Joan had lived in her cosy flat for more than a decade and the late spring of that year saw her splash out on numerous improvements. She spent over £1,000 decorating and repairing her bathroom and kitchen and at the same time she also had new carpets fitted throughout the flat, where she would increasingly spend much of her time.[411]

Despite her financial woes, there was plenty of work available for Joan as the decade progressed and she remained grateful for the opportunity to appear in some of television's finest productions. Victoria Wood, who recalls Joan as 'lovely to work with', was an actress and comedienne held in very high esteem by Joan.[412] A guest appearance in Victoria's 1989 series both thrilled Joan and at the same time made her extremely conscious of being 'word perfect', especially since her lines were written by Victoria herself. One of Joan's more bizarre appearances came in the autumn of the same year when she featured as a psychic medium in the Morrissey music video, *Ouija Board, Ouija Board*. Clad in a Margaret Rutherford-style tweed cape and brown wig, Joan was required to wield strings of garlic, lip-synch to the song and dance around a wood. Notably the video also featured award-winning actress Kathy Burke – who would later achieve fame as Perry in *Kevin and Perry Go Large* and as Linda La Hughes in three series of *Gimme Gimme Gimme* (1999-2001). Sadly Joan's appearance did not help *Ouija Board, Ouija Board* which was Morrissey's first single not to reach the (British) top 10. Its highest recorded position in the charts was at No. 18.

The release of the *Carry On* films onto video cassette (VHS) combined with Joan's prolific work-rate in the late 1980s meant that by the time she reached her late fifties she was one of the best known and most familiar actresses of her generation. Her appearances in several children's series at the time likewise brought her a new generation of fans and this inevitably led to increased public recognition. Joan remained philosophical about fame and its disadvantages:

> Sometimes it's fun to be noticed but it does have its drawbacks. I mean, I can't go out to buy a loaf of bread looking like the back of a bus in case I am recognised.[413]

In 1990 Joan was cast as housekeeper Mrs Fiona Wembley in the BBC sitcom *On the Up*. The series was headed by former child star and *Minder* actor Dennis Waterman playing Tony Carpenter, a rough-and-ready Cockney businessman/chauffeur coming to terms with new-found wealth and coping with the temper tantrums of his well-bred wife (played by Judy Buxton) and his rebellious teenage daughter (Vanessa Hadaway). Other cast members included Sam Kelly as Sam, Tony's best friend and chauffeur, Jenna Russell, and (for the first couple of episodes of the series) Joan's old friend Dora Bryan.[414] It was Joan's first role in a long-running sitcom since *Farrington of the F.O.* and again brought her back into the public domain of regular television viewing.

In his autobiography, *ReMinder*, Dennis Waterman wrote about Joan's lack of confidence prior to the studio recordings (in front of a live audience) of *On the Up*: 'She'd sit quaking in the make-up room, convinced she was useless and that it would be better for everybody if she went home.' Dennis thought Joan was 'without question the best thing in *On the Up*' although it was impossible to convince her of this, despite the fact that she managed to 'steal every scene'.[415]

The series provided Joan with her first ever catchphrase, 'Just the one!' as her character frequently reached for the sherry bottle. It remains well-remembered in households across the world and was oft repeated to Joan (especially by cab drivers) in the last decade of her life.

During the first series Mrs Wembley revealed her true identity, confiding in her friends that her real name was Miss Haywood and that she had never married after her fiancé had been killed on active service. This truly touching scene (almost a mini monologue) showed that Joan was still an actress capable of turning on a sixpence, moving from broad comedy to heartfelt pathos at the drop of a hat. It must also be said that the emotion behind the scene – as Joan sat with a single tear in her eye – was not entirely due to the lines that she had to deliver.

Joan's co-star Sam Kelly (whose own career as a comedy actor stemmed back to the 1960s) had worked with Joan on two *Carry On* films in the 1970s. Of his *Carry On* experiences he admitted with candour, 'The films have never meant anything to me – a few days' work, that's all.' His memories of Joan were, however, entirely different and he remembered her with great affection as 'a lovely, lovely lady':

> In my opinion a terrific, natural and truthful actress whose career was wrecked by those *Carry On* films, for which they were paid peanuts. None of those actors stood a chance after that sort of exposure. Joan, I think, was the best of them. Despite being hilarious very often, she had a low opinion of herself and died far too early. Loved her and her talent. One thing she told me – when she was a

little girl she'd put on her best frock and dance on the platform for the train passengers passing through the station where her dad was the stationmaster. It all started early!

Sam, who also held Kenneth Connor in high opinion and felt that his career, too, had been limited by the *Carry On* series, also recalled Joan's on-set antics, via Twitter, in 2012:

She often 'corpsed' so much during the audience recordings that the show had to be stopped to redo her mascara.

Joan was indeed famous for her hearty and unstoppable laugh – seen to full effect on screen in the latter stages of *Carry On Abroad* when she is in bed with Sid James as their hotel collapses around them. Her laughter was certainly quite contagious and can also be heard in an oft-repeated 'blooper' from an episode of *Sykes*, from the early 1970s, where Joan again 'corpses' in front of Eric Sykes and Hattie Jacques. Away from the camera she could be reduced to uncontrollable giggles very easily and friends confirm it didn't take a great deal to 'tickle' Joan's funny bone, particularly when it came to jokes of a 'lavatorial' nature!

The first series of *On the Up* was screened on BBC1 on 21st September 1990. A further two series, screened in 1991 and 1992, would follow. By now Joan had gained a considerable amount of weight and although immaculately dressed, coiffed and made up, her physical appearance was a marked contrast to the pleasantly plump character she had been just four years earlier in *Farrington of the F.O.*

In 2004, over a decade after the final series of *On the Up* had originally aired, Judy Buxton, little changed since her days of playing Ruth Carpenter, recalled Joan with fondness and described her as 'a lovely, lovely lady but very shy and nervous'.[416] She went on to say how Joan had consistently declined requests for interviews from various sources, including Michael Parkinson. Eight years later Miss Buxton was contacted again and via email shared with the author her further memories of Joan:

I remember her with great affection and it was a great privilege to work with her on *On the Up*.

She was a joy to be around and I remember all the laughs we had at rehearsals – in fact we hardly ever stopped laughing. When she laughed she literally cried with laughter which made one laugh even more!

She used to get quite nervous on the recording days and hated it if she fluffed her lines but of course the studio audience loved it!

I remember she told me she hated doing television interviews and would avoid them if she could – so she appeared quite shy from that point of view.

She was a gorgeous lady and a National Treasure![417]

Amid the success and happiness of Joan's work in *On the Up* came an unexpected blast from the past when the *Carry On* series was resurrected fourteen years after the last feature film had been released. Keen that as many of the original players as possible take part, Joan was contacted by Gerald Thomas and offered the role of the Queen of Spain in *Carry On Columbus* (with the suggestion that Frankie Howerd play the role of the King of Spain).[418] Despite his insistence that a *Carry On* film 'wouldn't be the same' without her, Joan declined the role. Barbara Windsor[419] was also approached to star in the film as she would recall in her 2000 autobiography:

I hadn't made a *Carry On* movie for seventeen years, and the thought of pulling up at the gates at Pinewood again and being greeted by people I knew and loved really appealed to me. I made a cup of tea and settled down to see what my part was like. It didn't take me long to find out: it was not just bad, it was appalling... I phoned Bernie Bresslaw, whose name was also on the script.

'It's not a good script, Bar,' he said. 'Dick was a good *Carry On*, and I loved doing it. I'd rather remember that as my last *Carry On* film.'

Shortly after Barbara's phone call to Bernard Bresslaw, with whom she had recently co-starred on stage in Blackpool in a successful run of *Wot a Carry On in Blackpool*, came another phone call – this time from Joan.

'Hello Barbara, it's Joanie.' It was Joan Sims who I knew, like me, wanted to do another movie.

'I know, darling,' I said. 'It's about the film. Not very good is it?'

'I think it's awful,' said Joan. 'I'm going to have to say no to Gerald.' I could sense a little anxiety in her voice; I think she was a bit frightened of telling him she was not accepting the part.[420]

Despite rewrites of the script and a surprising plea from Peter Rogers offering more money, Barbara kept to her original decision and did not take part in the film.

Following their telephone discussion regarding *Carry On Columbus* Barbara recalls that she and Joan 'became "chinas" [china plates = mates] over the telephone' for some time, although as was often the case with Joan, this arrangement did not sustain itself.

As it turned out the role suggested for Joan was taken on, somewhat apprehensively, by June Whitfield and the Frankie Howerd role was played by Leslie Phillips. This at least gave hardened *Carry On* fans some joy as it reunited June and Leslie thirty-three years after they had co-starred as young lovers in *Carry On Nurse*. Other veteran actors who were persuaded to appear included Jim Dale (who valiantly took on the lead role as Columbus, twenty-three years after his role in *Carry On Again, Doctor*), Bernard Cribbins,[421] Jack Douglas, Jon Pertwee and Peter Gilmore.

Both Joan and Barbara were of the same opinion when they eventually watched *Carry On Columbus*, which bombed at the box office. In her typically honest way, twenty years after the film's release, Barbara remembers thinking 'it was awful'[422] and remains 'thankful' that 'Columbus's vulgar voyage sank without trace'.[423]

8

National Treasure

'She was a survivor…'

THE 1990s – THE LAST FULL DECADE of Joan's life – happily brought her into contact with numerous old friends and colleagues including George Cole, Sir Donald Sinden, Leslie Phillips and June Whitfield. During the course of the nineties Joan threw herself into some of her finest performances and gained a whole new generation of fans. On the other hand it would also see many difficult times for Joan as her physical and mental reserves would be tested to the limit by a series of accidents and a subsequent re-emergence of the severe depression she had suffered in the early 1980s.

Having become an old-age pensioner in May 1990 Joan would inevitably slowly witness the passing of many dear friends and colleagues: Frankie Howerd in 1992, Gerald Thomas, Bernard Bresslaw and Kenneth Connor in 1993, Terry Scott in 1994, Beryl Reid in 1996, Betty Marsden and Joan Hickson in 1998 and Betty Box in 1999. The list was seemingly endless.[424] For a lady who found death and 'anything morbid' difficult to cope with, such consistent bereavements were increasingly hard to bear. It was certainly no exaggeration when she later admitted to feeling like an endangered species.

Despite reaching an age when most people start to slow down there was no let-up in Joan's work rate. Her role in *One Foot in the Algarve* (a feature-length Christmas episode of the hugely popular television series *One Foot in the Grave*), however, turned out to be something of a personal disappointment. She had optimistically hoped the role would see her jet off to sunny Portugal but instead her role as a passenger on an aeroplane, opposite Richard Wilson,

Annette Crosbie and Doreen Mantle, was shot in a television studio. Equally disappointing was the brevity of Joan's appearance. Dressed in a sleeveless summer dress, with reading spectacles perched on the end of her nose, Joan had just two lines in the production and was seen on screen for less than two minutes. It was in many ways a return to the classic cameo appearances she had been so famous for in the 1950s.

Happily, other assignments were more substantial and in the same year Joan was busy again on the small screen filming six episodes of the children's series *Smokescreen*, adopting a north-country accent for her role as Mrs Nash. At the same time she received a handwritten letter asking her to 'consider' the role of Madge in the BBC sitcom *As Time Goes By*. The sitcom, which first aired in 1992, starred Dame Judi Dench (as Jean) and Geoffrey Palmer (as Lionel) as lovers reunited after a thirty-eight-year separation and was hugely successful both at home and abroad. Joan duly accepted the role as Geoffrey Palmer's lively stepmother and in her first appearance in the series was seen wearing a Stetson whilst driving a pink Cadillac (which proved to be a great real-life thrill for Joan).

After working together in 1983 Geoffrey Palmer had briefly encountered Joan again four years later at the casting call of a sitcom from which she subsequently withdrew. For Geoffrey, working with Joan once more was a delightful experience and again he adored her company.

> It was a huge pleasure working with her again in *As Time Goes By* – she was just a lovely person to be with. I remember her telling me a lovely story about Tyrone Power going back to her flat... one listened to this amazingly touching story from this middle-aged woman who was just telling it in the simplest possible way and you were kind of 'there'. She had an extraordinary ability to hold your attention – in whatever she was talking about.

Dame Judi Dench, working with Joan for the first time, was delighted to be in the presence of a comedy 'legend', writing to the author in 1997:

> The whole cast of *As Time Goes By* have greatly enjoyed working with Joan Sims, especially the younger members since Joan is something of a legend from the *Carry On* films. Joan is a very kind, warm person, always cheerful, and we are great friends.[425]

In 2013 Dame Judi would reiterate her fondness for her legendary colleague:

> Joan was the most adorable person, with a great sense of humour. I wish I had known her better. My funniest memory of her is when we were filming *As Time Goes By*. We were on location and the two of us were at the top of a hill, waiting for the next shot to be set up. We both wanted to go to the loo, which of course was impossible. I think we made sure that shot was done in one take![426]

Jauntily dressed, invariably in leggings, flat boots, loose-fitting blouses and waistcoats (in an attempt to disguise her now very prominent 'Buddha belly'), Joan relished her role as Madge. *As Time Goes By* would ultimately gain Joan a new generation of fans and she was relieved in time that she became as well recognised for her part in the sitcom as she was for her work in the *Carry On* films. Without a doubt the role of Madge was one of the finest in Joan's latter career and certainly one which brought her a great deal of personal pleasure.

When cast as Lettice Deveral in the all-star romantic drama *A Village Affair* (based on the novel by Joanna Trollope) Joan felt the role would be another ideal way to relinquish the lingering shadows of the *Carry On* series. With most of the major parts of her first scene 'in the can', Joan was required to ride a bicycle through a wooded area towards the camera as part of her approach shot. During the rehearsal process Joan was thrown from the bicycle after the front wheel hit something in the ground. Falling with considerable force it was later revealed that she had fractured a rib as a result of the accident.

By the time Joan began filming *A Village Affair* she was in her mid sixties; overweight, diabetic, suffering from a long-standing back problem and at times already uncertain on her feet. In retrospect it is easy to question the decision to ask her to ride a bicycle over uneven terrain during one of her scenes. Geoffrey Palmer, whose son was a camera operator on the production, felt that Joan – ever the professional – would simply have responded to the request by saying 'I'll have a go' without undue concern for her physical well-being.[427]

Joan's injury was the start of a long decline in her general physical and mental health and Pat Clayfield remembers the months after the accident as 'a very painful, uncomfortable time' for Joan.[428] Unable to complete her work on the TV film, Joan was subsequently replaced in the production by septuagenarian actress Rosalie Crutchley, who enjoyed a fifty-year career on screen as one of Britain's most distinctive character players.

Under the advice of Equity (the Actor's Union) Joan attempted to seek compensation for her injury. The subsequent legal battle proved to be a long, drawn-out affair which left Joan even more depressed than the injury itself (which restricted her ability to work for some time afterwards).

In her autobiography Joan wrote that she eventually burnt all of the paperwork relating to her legal battle. However, a couple of letters survived this 'cull' and provide evidence of the work Joan missed out on as a result of her accident – not to mention the substantial loss of earnings and potential repeat fees. The correspondence shows that Joan was due to start recording another television programme, *Cat's Eyes*, less than a week after her accident and due to her injuries 'reluctantly' had to be recast.[429] By the summer of 1996 the case was still ongoing and Joan was advised by her solicitors to accept an amount in compensation which would cover her loss of earnings for *A Village Affair* plus her loss of earnings (and subsequent repeat fees) for *Cat's Eyes*.[430] The letters show that while Joan was earning thousands of pounds for her acting appearances she was also paying 40% tax in addition to her agent's commission fee.

Joan had hoped that *Cat's Eyes* – an educational children's programme for BBC television – would have provided her with substantial repeat fees and a pension for her old age. Figures from the paperwork left behind show that it could potentially have provided substantial and regular residuals for Joan, but since there was no way of knowing exactly how much she could have earned she was forced to settle for a relatively modest amount in compensation.

A moment of sheer delight came for Joan when she reunited with Elizabeth Spriggs, six years after their work together in *Simon and the Witch*, on the set of the BBC costume drama *Martin Chuzzlewit*. Elizabeth would count Joan as one of her 'closest friends' and admitted they had 'endless fun when working together'.[431] For both ladies it was a happy assignment. Joan's cameo role of Betsy Prigg, the day-nurse in Charles Dickens' classic novel, was a consolation prize in many ways since she had been considered for the larger role of Sarah Gamp, which was subsequently played by Spriggs. In retrospect Joan was somewhat relieved by missing out on a starring role in the production especially since the part of Sarah Gamp involved many difficult lines and 'peculiar phrases' which Joan doubted she could handle, given she was still recovering from her accident. The role was probably the least glamorous in Joan's entire career. Luckily she had admitted years earlier, 'I enjoy character work, it is much more demanding than a glamorous role and more fun.'[432] With blacked-out, yellowing teeth, dirt under her fingernails and a costume consisting of 'a bundle of rags' she admitted that the production's make-up department 'really went to town' on her.[433] It was in this state that she encountered an elderly fan who peered into the window of her caravan between takes. Complimenting Joan on her roles in the *Carry On* films and various other productions, he ended the conversation by saying, 'Sad we have to get old, isn't it?'[434] It was a less abrasive remark than 'Mind you, you're all dead now' – a line often said to Barbara Windsor in recent years by fans discussing the *Carry On* series.[435]

Rated 'one of the most delightful, beautifully-written sitcoms in ITV history... a perfect balance of comedy and pathos' by *The Mirror*, *My Good Friend*, written by Bob Larbey, was a happy affair which briefly took Joan's mind off the anxiety surrounding her injury and legal fight. Her role as Miss 'Pickles' Byron in two episodes of the genteel sitcom reunited her with George Cole, with whom she had of course worked a couple of times before during the course of both their long careers (*Will Any Gentleman?* way back in 1953 and *That Old Black Magic* on television in 1967). While Joan went on to achieve worldwide recognition through her work in the *Carry On* series, Cole would become a television star in middle age as the lovable spiv Arthur Daley in ten series of the popular television series *Minder*. Both in their youth and in later life Cole would describe Joan as 'absolute heaven to work with'[436] and perhaps not surprisingly Joan would later make a third appearance in the series when her character was seen to be suffering the effects of early-stage senile dementia. Again the role proved Joan's versatility and she was incredibly believable and touching as the lonely spinster, particularly when her character admitted to the realisation that she was gradually losing her mind.

Prior to filming her further appearances in *As Time Goes By*, Joan travelled to Grayshott Hall Health and Fitness Centre to undergo a full medical assessment for insurance purposes on 15th September 1994. The report shows that by the age of sixty-four Joan was suffering from 'mild, maturity onset, non insulin dependant diabetes' (type 2 diabetes). This was 'completely' controlled by the drug glibenclamide.

Joan's height was given as five feet and four inches. Both her blood pressure (150/80) and pulse rate (68 per minute) were normal as were her blood tests. Her general health was deemed to be good and the report confirmed that she had never been refused medical insurance. Joan's injury following her 1994 accident was listed on the report as a fractured nineth left rib (now completely healed) and it also revealed that she had undergone a hysterectomy (including the removal of an ovarian cyst) in 1992. Joan's weight, always a sore point for her, was listed as thirteen stone and six pounds, showing that she was approximately three stone overweight for her height.[437]

Joan's work on *As Time Goes By* saw her on location and in the television studio, usually for four to six days at a time. Just four days after her medical examination she was recording another appearance in the fourth series of the programme, screened in the spring of 1995.

Geoffrey had known of Joan's 1994 accident and the difficulties she faced after it. Spending further time with Joan reinforced not only his affection for her but also his awareness of the sadness in her life:

> She was a wonderful, wonderful companion, a wonderful actress and wonderful person to be with – but there was a huge underlying sadness that one became more and more aware of.[438]

Almost inevitably as the 1990s progressed there were times of remembrance and reflection for friends and colleagues who had since passed away. When Comic Heritage decided to honour Hattie Jacques with a blue plaque at her former home at 67 Eardley Crescent, Earls Court, they hoped that Joan could be called upon to unveil the plaque or at least to attend the event. Joan Le Mesurier was also invited to the event and recalls speaking to Joan over the telephone about taking part in it:

> I begged her to do it and said, 'Joanie you'd be so proud of yourself if you did it. You'll feel as if you've got over a hurdle.' And she said,

'I'll come, I'll come,' and at the last minute she said, 'I can't.' I said I'll come and get you by taxi, I'll be right by your side and we'll take you home again, we'll be right round you. She was so shy at showing her feelings and very sensitive.[439]

Needless to say Joan did not attend the event and it was left to Eric Sykes and Clive Dunn to unveil Hattie's plaque on 5th November 1995. It was just one in a series of events in which Joan declined to take part.

Joan's appearance in *The Canterville Ghost*, a Hallmark telemovie filmed in the bitterly cold winter of 1995, was to be the last time she worked with Leslie Phillips and Sir Donald Sinden. Cast as housekeeper Mrs Umney (with Sinden playing her husband, the resident Canterville Hall chauffeur) it was the first time she had worked with Donald Sinden since they both appeared in *Twice Round the Daffodils* in 1962 and almost forty years after they had danced together in *The Captain's Table*. Sir Donald regarded Joan with 'abject admiration' as a 'wonderfully professional actress who could do almost anything'.[440] Leslie Phillips had remained close to Joan over the years and was well aware of her personal demons: 'She had a slight weakness for the booze and never found anyone she wanted to marry. I fear she was quite unhappy beneath all the jollity.'[441]

The storyline, based on the Oscar Wilde classic story, involved an American family moving to Canterville Hall and the resident ghost, played by Sir Patrick Stewart (best known as Captain Jean-Luc Picard in *Star Trek: The Next Generation*), being befriended by 'Ginny' Otis (American leading actress Neve Campbell). Despite her dramatic accident a year earlier, Joan appeared to be in good form during the production and at one point could even be seen gamely trotting after the 'whirling dervish' Otis boys (Ciarán Fitzgerald and Raymond Pickard) as they excitedly ran through the haunted residence.

In the autumn of 1996 Joan changed her agent and for the remainder of her career was exclusively represented by Richard Hatton, the former actor who set up his own theatrical agency in 1954.[442] Among Hatton's other clients were such well-known names as Leo McKern (with whom Joan would become friends at the end of her life), Wendy Craig and Michael Crawford. Like Peter Eade, Richard deliberately kept his client list relatively small and 'select', thus ensuring each one of them received the very best of his attention. Handwritten notes from Joan to Richard show that she valued his professional opinion and would ask for his thoughts on certain offers of work made to her during her final years. The two became good friends and under Richard's management Joan felt she was in safe hands and that her career 'took on a distinct new lease of life'.[443]

By now along with Frank Middlemass she was a regular member of the cast of *As Time Goes By* and the off-screen chemistry between the actors was clearly reflected on film. Dame Judi Dench, well known for her tactile nature and mothering instincts to actors and crew on set, was clearly delighted to be working with Joan while the series' writer, Bob Larbey (who had previously worked with Joan in several series of *On the Up*), was very pleased to be reunited with her again during her guest appearances in his latest work. Both Bob and his wife were friends of Joan and he would remember her as 'a very fine comedy actress, with an impeccable sense of timing and a wonderfully expressive face'. He was also aware of Joan's darker side:

> Personal memories are always warm ones. Joan was a lovely lady, always fun to work with, who was always popular with her peers. I remember Geoffrey Palmer saying that he'd like to take her home and put her on his mantelpiece! For all her sense of fun there was, I think, an underlying sadness which seemed to stem from her earlier private life. This is no more than a theory on my part you understand.[444]

Following Joan's death Frank Middlemass would continue to appear in *As Time Goes By* until 2005 (with the absence of his on-screen wife explained in a variety of ways). Like Joan, he never married and spent forty years living in the 'spare room' of his close friend Geoffrey Toone until the latter's death in 2005. It was, as Frank was keen to point out, a purely platonic friendship. A working actor into his mid eighties, his final stage appearance was as Canon Chasuble in a tour of *The Importance of Being Earnest* in 2004. It was at this time that he would remembered his co-star as a 'sweet and lovely lady', if somewhat shy.[445]

Among a handful of guest appearances on television in the mid 1990s was Joan's role as Harriet Coverly, one of a pair of swindling sisters whose recipe for bread-and-butter pudding is coveted by Detective Inspector Crabbe (Richard Griffiths), in *Pie in the Sky*. It was the first and last time Joan would work with Griffiths, the portly

Hartlepool-born actor well known for his countless roles on stage, screen and television, and as well as finding Joan 'a gracious and charming lady' he later admitted he 'respected her talent and experience'.[446] Notably, her role in the popular series was also a rare occasion when Joan was required to drive a car on camera. In the following year – all pink rouge and feather boa – Joan played a vivacious wheelchair-bound character in a guest role in Patricia Routledge's popular series *Hetty Wainthropp Investigates*.

Work on radio continued to provide Joan with some of her finest roles and she 'played a marvellous cameo as Mrs Pusey, a superficial, prattling widow of an age which had been advanced by several decades as more information became available' in *Hotel du Lac* for BBC Radio 4 in the summer of 1996.[447] Around the same time she worked on a radio version of *101 Dalmatians* (with an all-star cast including Patricia Hodge, Brenda Blethyn, Polly James and Nicky Henson) and was reunited with June Whitfield (starring as Miss Marple) in the BBC radio adaptation of *4.50 From Paddington* in which she played the sleuth's friend Elspeth McGillicuddy who witnesses a murder aboard a train only to be ignored by the police when she reports the crime.

Although Joan's physical injuries from *A Village Affair* healed relatively quickly, the legal case which dragged on for over two years left her mentally drained and immensely anxious. In the spring of 1997 a further physical blow came when, following a fall at her flat, Joan fractured her spine and spent four weeks in the Chelsea and Westminster Hospital in London. This latest accident caused Joan to sink into a severe bout of depression which at times would almost overwhelm her over the course of the next two years.

An enforced period of physical inactivity would follow Joan's stay in hospital and it allowed her perhaps a little too much time to once again reflect on her life, both professionally and personally. From the mid 1990s Joan saw the careers of some of her closest colleagues take on a new lease of life. From 1992 June Whitfield starred as Mother in the exceptionally popular comedy series *Absolutely Fabulous*, a role she would reprise on regular occasions over the next twenty years. It brought her a new generation of fans and would lead to a series of high-profile appearances on stage and in film and television (almost inevitably she would join the cast of *Last of the Summer Wine* in 2001, making over forty appearances in the long running series).

Likewise, when Barbara Windsor joined the cast of *EastEnders* in 1994 her initial appearance saw viewing figures reach 27.5 million. It must have seemed ironic to Joan that a combination of ill health, caused through her accidents, and bouts of depression, and perhaps her own persistent reluctance to take on a role in a long-running series, prevented her from achieving similar professional success at a time when it was arguably due to her.

Not surprisingly, given her most recent accident, professionally speaking 1997 was one of the quietest years of Joan's life. Less than a handful of acting roles were accepted. They included another guest appearance in *As Time Goes By*, the role of Aunt Hattie in the James Fleet comedy series *Spark*, and a terrifying 'live' television appearance in *Noel's House Party* (playing the Fairy Queen); and she resurrected her 1990 role as Mrs White in *Cluedo* to provide the voice of the cook in the video game of the series, based on the ever-popular board game. Small wonder that her friend and colleague Leslie Phillips would comment 'Joan is not in good shape I'm afraid' in the same year.[448]

Taking advantage of this relatively quiet time in her professional life Joan accepted the offer to holiday with Pat and Bill Clayfield at their villa in Portugal. It was the perfect chance to rest and recuperate and Pat remembers Joan had 'a marvellous time because there was no one to bother her and nothing to worry about'. The only time Joan was really recognised during her stay was during a visit to the local bank where Bill Clayfield had driven her to collect some money. A group of English tourists gathered to wait for Joan outside the bank and asked Bill if he was 'Mr Sims'. He politely replied that he was not married to Joan and that she was on a private holiday. When Joan eventually walked out of the bank her first words to Bill were, 'Okay darling, I'm ready to go!' The group of tourists raised knowing eyebrows at Bill – wrongly assuming that he was in fact married to Joan – and wished Joan a happy holiday, followed by '...and you too Mr Sims!'[449]

During her time in Portugal Joan was able to completely relax. She made a huge impression on everyone she met there and as always managed to light up whenever she was in company. Following an evening meal in a local restaurant Joan even caught the attention of a group of special-needs children, one of whom stood staring at her as music played in the background. To the delight of the child Joan took him by the hand and gently danced with him, seemingly quite oblivious to the attention she may have attracted. She remained an excellent swimmer in her sixties and relished spending time in the pool as well as enjoying many laughs and generally 'arsing about' with the Clayfields and their circle of close friends. Richard Hatton for one noticed an improvement in Joan's general well-being after her Portuguese jaunt, as Pat Clayfield explains:

> I remember Richard [Hatton] saying, 'Jeepers, when she came back she was a different person,' and Bill said, 'I know. We should have kept her out longer than two weeks.'[450]

With her mobility and ease of movement already affected by an ongoing back problem which had troubled her from the late 1980s, Joan's latest accident further restricted her ability to take on certain acting roles. She was therefore relieved at the end of 1997 when she received the script of a television dramatisation of William Makepeace Thackeray's *Vanity Fair* and word that she was being considered for the part of Miss Crawley. Having met with the director, Mark Munden, Joan was extremely optimistic that she would indeed gain the part in the lavish costume drama. Her spirits were left totally deflated when word came in the New Year that the part had been given to Miriam Margolyes. The depression caused through fracturing her spine was only compounded by this latest setback, and the familiar cycle of locking herself away with only the company of a bottle manifested itself once again.

In April 1998, on what would have been Sid James's eighty-fifth birthday, the *Carry On* series celebrated its fortieth anniversary with a reunion of surviving actors and crew at Pinewood Studios. Not surprisingly (and to the huge disappointment of *Carry On* fans) Joan did not appear at the event where she alone should surely have taken centre stage. Her numerous colleagues were also disappointed by her absence at the event. Alan Curtis, a supporting actor in *Carry On Henry* and *Carry On Abroad*, commented later that year: 'It's very sad. She really has become agoraphobic and doesn't like going out at all nowadays. I saw her some time ago on stage and she did like the fact that she could get home before the pubs emptied, thus avoiding crowds of people.'[451] In addition to Peter Rogers, over twenty actors attended the event with Barbara Windsor, Leslie Phillips, June Whitfield and Jack Douglas unveiling Comic Heritage Plaques in memory of Kenneth Williams, Charles Hawtrey, Hattie Jacques and Sid James.[452]

Several months later, after much persuasion and much personal anguish about her appearance and whether she would be able to give sensible answers to the questions she would be asked, Joan did relent and returned to the studios to be interviewed on camera for the Carlton Television documentary, *What's A Carry On?* Looking fit and relaxed – her face somewhat leaner than in other recent appearances and with an uncharacteristic reddish tint to her hair – she shared some of her memories of *Carry On Cowboy*, *Don't Lose Your Head* and *Up the Khyber*. Points of discussion included her 'favourite' scene in *Carry On Cowboy* and the 'decline' in her appearance by the time she featured in *Carry On England*. Joan also revealed her thoughts on recent stories regarding Sid James and his alleged infidelities.

A year before the documentary Peter Rogers had paid tribute to the leading lady of so many of his films:

> Joan Sims started in the *Carry On*s as a pin-up teenager and ended up as a matron. The transition, of course, was gradual and she took it in her stride. Such is her professionalism. Actually, she can play anything and is a pleasure to work with. I think I have had more laughs with Joan Sims off the set than any other member of the cast. She has had a lot of sadness in her life and she has overcome it. It is always a pleasure for me to see her on television in shows other than the *Carry On*s.[453]

Joan's return to Pinewood would be an emotional one. Peter Rogers and Audrey Skinner, his long-time assistant, were there to greet her and a banner with the words 'Welcome Home Joan!' was erected in her honour. Ultimately going back to Pinewood proved to be an excellent tonic for Joan. She would later admit that many memories came 'flooding back'. Happily they were all positive ones and the visit became the inspiration she needed to begin work on her long-awaited autobiography.[454] Significantly *What's A Carry On?* was only Joan's second (and final) television appearance in what had been yet another difficult year.

When Joan returned to television screens for what turned out to be her final appearance in *As Time Goes By* at the end of 1998 there was a noticeable and significant change in her posture. At the age of sixty-eight, *anno domini* and the effects of her fractured spine had now left Joan looking smaller in height and slightly stooped. Now using a walking stick between takes and clearly in some degree of pain, the physical change in Joan was noted by Geoffrey Palmer: 'The comparatively youthful ebullience had gone a bit. She was still lovable and fun and everyone loved her... but she had slowed down and ironed out a bit.' [455] Nevertheless Joan continued to sparkle as the effervescent Madge Hardcastle and, dressed in a loose-fitting multi-coloured blouse, joined a group of OAPs in an enthusiastic rendition of the 'YMCA' dance. Her sheer presence managed, quite simply, to light up the screen and the fun and jollity which had endured throughout her career and her numerous performances continued in the role of Madge. Although concerned about her failing health, Joan managed, in typical fashion, to disguise her inner anxieties and maintain a reputation for utmost professionalism.

Privately the change in Joan's posture had been something of a concern for a number of years and seems likely to have started following the back injury she mentioned in her 1987 *TV Times* interview. Both Pat and Bill Clayfield were fully aware of the problem with Joan's 'funny' back; as Pat remembered in 2012, 'She became stooped and more hunched... Bill would say *sit up Joanie* and she'd say *I can't*.' Her successive falls and subsequent periods of inactivity in the late 1990s only served to aggravate the problem and she became increasingly careful in her movements, particularly when walking on wood floors or tiles.

At the end of what had been an '*annus horribilis*' Joan took the unusual step of granting her first major interview in a decade which was published in the *Daily Mail* on Boxing Day 1998. Under the banner of 'the hidden loneliness behind her success' Joan discussed with Lester Middlehurst her current financial predicament, her childhood, failed romances and relationship with Kenneth Williams.

Those closest to Joan were surprised that she agreed to be interviewed, especially since 'she did keep herself very much to herself' when it came to dealings with the press.[456] They were also slightly aghast when Joan was quoted as saying:

> I don't mind admitting that I'm in a bit of a muddle, financially. I'm hanging on in there but I'm afraid the next article about me will probably be headlined 'Joan Sims goes bankrupt'.

Joan claimed not to have worked for 'two years' which of course was an exaggeration. Although she was not rich (despite her prolific acting career) it is fair to say that her financial plight was not quite as dire as she painted. Pat Clayfield, Joan's closest friend at this point in her life, reveals: 'Peter Eade set everything up so fantastically [financially]. Half the trouble was she didn't realise what she had... She wasn't really broke.'[457] Monetary worries, however, did cause Joan an extreme amount of anxiety, particularly at times when she was physically unable to work.

Amazingly, the article ended in an extremely positive way. Never self-pitying, Joan admitted, 'I'm a great fighter. At the moment I feel so alive that I can't wait to start delivering the goods again.'[458]

Even before the publication of the *Daily Mail* interview, many of Joan's friends and contemporaries were now aware of her plight. Sylvia Syms, herself deprived of royalties for many of her early films,[459] admitted that Joan's later life was 'hard' not only because of problems with her health but also because of economic hardship. Sylvia was also well aware that even at the very end of her life Joan's fan mail 'reached the ceiling'[460] of her flat – a touching testament to her popularity but also something which caused her added expense (around this time the glossy photographs previously sent out to fans were replaced with more economical photo 'cards', with pre-printed signatures, as the demand for Joan's autograph increased).

*

In the final years of her life Joan rarely left her home and filled her days by sitting in a special high-backed chair watching television 'for hours'[461] and consuming, by her own admission, 'gallons' of diet Coca-Cola.[462] Her home became a safe haven and in this respect she was not dissimilar to Kenneth Williams (although she had none of Williams' neuroses about visitors and the use of facilities). Without hobbies or any real interests outside of work, the issue of how Joan spent her time baffled many of her friends, including Nicholas Ferguson:

> I think they [Joan and Kenneth Williams] forgot that you could have a life on your own sitting in your flat with some nice things around you or listen to some music. I don't know what she did with herself on her own.[463]

Eleanor Fazan felt that on the whole the last years of Joan's life were 'reclusive and rather sad' although even in her twenties Joan had tended to be slightly reclusive in that she wasn't 'adventurous' when it came to the glitzy social circuit she could have been part of.[464] However, it could be argued that, contrary to popular belief, Joan was not a recluse or agoraphobic in the accepted sense of the words during her final years – she simply chose to be very selective about where she went and with whom she spent time.

Sunday afternoons spent with the Clayfields were a regular feature and would remain so until the very end of her life. Bill Clayfield would collect Joan from Thackeray Street and she would often spend the night at their beautiful apartment in Hammersmith. In later years, as Joan's mobility became restricted, the Clayfields even had their guest bathroom specially adapted for Joan's frequent overnight visits. Here she could be completely relaxed – and pampered – and with her hearty appetite could relish good old-fashioned cooking such as Pat's Sunday roast or meat and mushroom pie with onions 'and a nice crust!' Even when Joan was going through 'really, really difficult times', the Clayfield's home provided a retreat. Very occasionally, despite their best efforts, Pat and Bill would find Joan worse for wear and not wanting to get out of bed or leave her home. At these very desperate times Pat Clayfield admits poignantly that the situation was heartbreaking for all concerned; 'It wasn't like *my* Joan.'[465]

Other invitations to be entertained were now almost always refused and in the final years of Joan's life she became 'increasingly difficult to winkle out' of the security of her flat.[466] One of the last times she left her London home for a social engagement was to attend a birthday party for Ronnie Barker. Once more she was reliant on someone else (in this case Eleanor Fazan) to not only accompany her to the event, but also to drive her there and back.[467] Jimmy Perry recalled the occasion in his autobiography. It was the first time he and Joan had encountered one another since their time together at RADA fifty years earlier and in Jimmy's view 'time had not been kind' to the girl he once knew.[468]

Having reacquainted on the set of *The Last of the Blonde Bombshells*, Joan accepted another invitation, this time to a luncheon party, given by actress Thelma Ruby in February 2000.[469] Accompanied by the ever-loyal Eleanor 'Fiz' Fazan, Joan was in the company of several old friends including Dilys Laye and Patricia Lancaster as well as actress Helen Cotterill, Jennifer Gosney,[470] actress and professional hatmaker Bridget Armstrong and the late actress Daphne Goddard. It was an enjoyable afternoon with Joan taking centre stage at the head of the table. Over a decade later Thelma Ruby, still a professional working actress in her late eighties, recalled that Joan was 'hilarious' when trying on Bridget Armstrong's hat![471] Even in her seventieth year the Essex girl evidently still loved dressing up and entertaining an audience, even in a small social environment. She was remembered by her hostess as 'very funny and delightful'.[472] Photographs of the occasion, one of the last times Joan was entertained, show her to be a picture of beaming good health and happiness.

On a day-to-day basis tasks such as shopping became increasingly difficult with the passage of time, not only because of her restricted mobility but because of a consistent amount of public recognition – something that never failed to take her by surprise (particularly after an attack of Bell's palsy, see Chapter 9, when she considered that her looks changed somewhat). By the late 1990s Joan was well known and familiar to a new generation of television viewers as Madge in *As Time Goes By*. The success of the series was a double-edged sword for Joan since it resulted in many fans approaching her in public – something she had always dealt with politely but had never particularly enjoyed and grew to dislike even more as her health declined. She hated being recognised, for example, when popping into her local Marks and Spencer, so the job of food shopping was often left to her cleaner. This was, in many ways, rather typical of Joan, who had always enjoyed being looked after and having things done for her.

A frequent visitor to Joan's flat from the late 1990s was her cousin Yvonne (or Evie as she was always known to Joan) who worked in the city and often popped along to Thackeray Street to have lunch with her famous relation. Very close friends such as Eleanor Fazan would also be invited to the flat, usually on a night, where Joan would happily order a Chinese takeaway which could be delivered to her door. Despite being diagnosed with diabetes in her sixties, her eating habits remained largely unchanged ('She never really bothered with the diabetic things – she was a bit of a rascal,' confesses Pat Clayfield). Eventually she all but gave up cooking for herself and was convinced that pre-prepared meals would provide all the sustenance and nutritional value that she would need. In one of her final interviews when the subject of cooking was raised she answered truthfully, 'I can't be bothered any more… It's all M&S [Marks & Spencer], pop-in-the-oven stuff. I can recommend M&S moussaka, and their smoked salmon, of course.'[473] Her interest in cooking, which had been listed in the 1980 edition of *Who's Who in the Theatre* as one of her hobbies, had started to wane as far back as the 1970s when she had a 'modern kitchen' full of 'cordon bleu gadgets' but admitted 'you're still lucky if you get a boiled egg'.[474] The 'natural homemaker', once capable of preparing the best of simple English cooking, was now perfectly content to sit down with a ready-meal for one.

Despite a gradual 'winding down' of many everyday tasks Joan remained conscious of maintaining her immaculate appearance until the end of her life and she enjoyed dressing as 'a star'.[475] Regular visits at home from her hairdresser were a key feature, as were manicures and a keen interest in clothes and fashion. Above all Joan's main concern was her work, and her desire to pursue new roles never left her. Professionally and personally Nicholas Parsons summed up Joan by saying: 'She was a survivor and kept working to the end… she brought so much happiness to so many lives.'[476]

9

Time Overdrawn

'Everyone who knew her is going to remember her forever'

THE NUMEROUS SETBACKS OF THE LATE 1990s seemed to force Joan's hand in many ways and as a result she finally sought the help of a professional counsellor. It had been nearly twenty years since her gruesome stay in Banstead Hospital and attitudes and treatments for depression had come a long way in the meantime. It says much for Joan's courage and fortitude that she was able to seek – and accept – such help.

By 1998 Joan was receiving medication and counselling to treat her depression, undergoing hydrotherapy for the continued problems with her back and also receiving treatment for her ongoing addiction to alcohol. Although at the time she considered her life to be in something of a 'mess' it was a relief to her friends to see that Joan was taking a proactive approach to her problems. She had always been quite honest about her bouts of depression, and never more so than in her autobiography when she candidly wrote:

> There is nothing to be ashamed about in suffering from depression. It is perfectly curable – and in my case was in due course cured.[477]

In February 1999 an attack of Bell's palsy would very nearly derail Joan on the path to recovery. While relaxing with a cup of tea and a cigarette after answering yet another batch of fan mail, Joan noticed a 'curious sensation' in her face. It wasn't until the following morning when she looked in the bathroom mirror that Joan realised something had gone terribly wrong. With the left side of her face 'collapsed', her left eye lower than the right and half of her mouth 'gaping open', Joan initially assumed she had suffered a stroke. A hasty trip to the accident and emergency department of the Chelsea and Westminster Hospital revealed the true cause of her temporary disfigurement. Sent home with steroids and an eye patch, Joan's appearance would soon return to normal but the return trip home in a taxi was enough to leave her completely despondent. Realising that her latest setback would significantly reduce her chances of getting work on television, Joan asked the taxi driver to stop at the nearest off-licence and asked him to go in and get two bottles of Cuvée Napa – her 'old favourite'. Despite not having had a drink for over six months Joan then proceeded to sink into an alcoholic depression – later admitting that she had rarely felt so low.

Joan was well known for locking herself away during her darkest periods and drinking herself into a stupor. In many ways this latest episode was a return to the very dark times she had lived through in the early 1980s. Thankfully within a few days Joan had come to her senses and contacted the counsellor who had helped her through her latest bout of depression. It was then decided that Joan should be admitted to hospital to 'detox' and receive 24-hour care and rehabilitation.

Several days later when Joan received word that she could be admitted for treatment her mindset had suddenly changed. Far from accepting the help of others (and she had often relied upon friends to assist her in many aspects of her life), Joan decided to take charge of her own destiny and make a 'fresh start'. At this point she admitted to being 'sick to death of lurching back and forward... leaning on somebody else's shoulders' and was adamant that she would not be admitted into hospital again.[478] As she approached her seventieth birthday Joan had come to the conclusion that the only way to solve her problems was on her own and this is exactly what she proceeded to do.

Friends were amazed at Joan's new-found positivity and independence. Her first task was to abolish any trace of alcohol from her flat and destroy any correspondence relating to her 1994 accident and the subsequent legal proceedings which had weighed so heavily upon her mind.[479] From this point onwards Joan managed to abstain from drinking alcohol – a combination of self-discipline and medical necessity since she later admitted that her high levels of medication did not mix well with the demon drink and that it now made her feel 'hot and uncomfortable'.[480] Diet Coca-Cola and the occasional cup of tea became Joan's main 'tipples' at the final stage of her life.

Bristow, a new radio series in which she played a tea lady, saw Joan reunited with Liz Fraser – almost forty years after their appearances together in *Doctor in Love* and *Carry On Regardless*. The role provided Joan with a significant boost in self-confidence and at the same time she began work on her long-awaited autobiography, ably assisted by writer Sean Magee.

Prior to completing her autobiography Joan had spent eleven days in November 1999 filming what would turn out to be a fitting swansong to her fifty-year career. Her role as Betty, a feisty pianist, in the BBC/HBO television film *The Last of the Blonde Bombshells* proved to be one of Joan's most significant roles – both personally and professionally. The plot of the 'sentimentally cast' production centred on a 1940s all-girl band getting back together to perform at a school dance. Written by Alan Plater, the well-known Jarrow-born dramatist who produced more than two hundred scripts for theatre, film, television and radio, and produced by Su Armstrong, *The Last of the Blonde Bombshells* was screened in the late summer of 2000. It showed, beyond all doubt, that Joan was an excellent character actress more than capable of holding her own among the all-star cast which included Dame Judi Dench, Sir Ian Holm, Olympia Dukakis, Leslie Caron and Billie Whitelaw.

Also among the illustrious line-up of actors was June Whitfield who would recall working with Joan for the final time – forty years after they had first worked together in *Carry On Nurse* – in her 2000 autobiography:

> It was also good to see Joan again, and in such good form. She has had a marvellous career, and was a stalwart of the *Carry On*s. I was in four, but Joan was in twenty-four and was one of the main reasons for their success.[481]

June recalled her co-star further in 2012 as 'a brilliant actress' and someone she 'admired greatly'. Her overriding memory was that Joan was a 'great giggler'. It was a view shared by so many of Joan's friends and contemporaries.[482]

Joan's role in *The Last of the Blonde Bombshells* was her first television appearance in more than twelve months. She had noticeably gained further weight and was walking with some degree of difficulty, using for the first time on screen the walking stick she had used privately for some time.[483] Nevertheless Joan – as always – looked immaculately groomed. With her hair perfectly styled she dressed in loose-fitting blouses and overshirts, teamed with neckscarves in jaunty leopard-print designs, while large, bold jewellery helped complete her look as the band's straight-talking leader.

Gillies MacKinnon, the Scottish-born film director, was the man behind the all-star production and remembers the assignment with fondness:

> This was a film which required a cast of older actors and I was simply presented with the contenders by the casting director and the suggestions looked great to me. When Joan's name came up I immediately thought she was absolutely right. The decision was painless. The thing I recall about these older and seasoned actors is that, however difficult it may have been, how effortless it seemed to them. Even the difficult training of having to learn to mime their instruments caused no fuss. Their approach was totally calm and professional.
>
> It was 15 years ago when I worked with Joan. I remember the first time she came to meet me in the office of some ex-army barracks where prep was happening. For some reason it was night time and she had come in a taxi. She seemed quite shy, didn't say a lot, but seemed terribly sympathetic and likeable. There was no question that she would be given the role of band leader and I made sure she knew that as soon as we met. I had been told she lived alone and was quite lonely. I don't know about that, but she was a real delight from start to finish and people adored her. I seem to recall she told me they were paid peanuts on the *Carry On* films.
>
> When you make a film there is a constant pressure and I find everyone else remembers what happened more than I do, but I do recall Joan on stage, addressing Judi Dench and the other band members, making quite a speech. At one point she said something like '…because, whatever happens you certainly cunt…'
>
> She stopped, frozen to the spot with her arms aloft and her eyes wide as the four-letter word which was meant to have come out 'can't' hung in the air for long seconds. I finally shouted 'Cut!' and everyone breathed again, and laughed their heads off.

The final shot of Joan in *The Last of the Blonde Bombshells* (and the last glimpse audiences would have of Joan Sims in an acting role) saw her in a side profile shot playing the piano as Dame Cleo Laine's character of Gwen sang '(Ah, The Apple Trees) When The World

Was Young'. For Joan's fans it is a touching, almost melancholic moment. Deep in concentration, there would be no trace of the 'happy face' Anthony Asquith had seen so many years previously. After half a century largely spent in comic roles it was ironic that Joan's final moments on camera would show her in repose.

The film went on to receive critical acclaim, both at home and overseas. Dame Judi Dench would receive a BAFTA Award (for Best Actress) and a Golden Globe Award (for Best Actress in a Mini Series or Motion Picture Made For Television) in addition to numerous other nominations for her role as Elizabeth.[484] The production also received an Emmy Award Nomination for Outstanding Cast in a mini-series, movie or a special.

Joan had spent eleven days working on *The Last of the Blonde Bombshells* with her first scenes in the film being recorded on location at Hastings Pier. The location, in the middle of winter, brought with it a fair share of problems. The conditions for Joan must have been slightly reminiscent of her *Carry On* days and she would later recall:

> There were no loos and the easiest way to transport me to the nearest ones, near the pier entrance, was to shove me in a wheelchair. Of course it was pouring with rain, absolutely pouring, and I had this old mac thrown over me and a plastic hat. I must have looked like 'Penny For The Guy'.[485]

It was only after the production had wrapped that Joan revealed she had fallen out of her caravan in yet another accident. Determined not to lose out on the best role she had secured in years, Joan carried on filming as she later revealed:

> I kept absolutely schtum about it and I was in agony and I thought I had pleurisy. I couldn't sleep in my bed. I got up at 3am one morning and had to sit up the rest of the night in a chair. After I finished my 11 days which I was scheduled for I went to the hospital because I couldn't stand it any longer and I had also gone down with a chest infection. They said: 'You've re-fractured your spine.'[486]

In a further interview she made the brave but perhaps unwise decision to discuss her multitude of health problems ('diabetes, arthritis, back pain and blood pressure') and the prescription drugs needed to combat them. Her daily tablets were neatly organised in dosette boxes with each day labelled. During one newspaper interview she made light of her situation: 'This sweet little box is my daily supply. I've already downed thirteen tablets this morning, darling… I'm a regular pharmacist.'[487]

In her honesty Joan perhaps forgot how easy it is for actors to become 'uninsurable' for film and television work. In later years, for example, Hattie Jacques was dropped from the *Carry On* series because of health problems (which effectively ended her film career at the age of fifty-two)[488] while Joan's near contemporary and fellow comedy actress, Pat Coombs, would also find work restricted in later years because of health problems. Pat, or Patty as she was known to friends, admitted to the author that she and her friend Peggy Mount had a 'pipe dream' of bringing their popular television series, *You're Only Young Twice*, up to date in 1999 but conceded: 'The insurance on us *both* would go through the ceiling.'[489]

Sadly Joan's health problems were now a dominant feature in her life. Catastrophe would fall in January 2000 when, while staying with friends in Dorset, she fell off a patio and found herself lying on her back 'half wrapped around a bush'.[490] Joan was subsequently placed on a stretcher by paramedics, lifted over the garden wall and transferred to the Conquest Hospital in Hastings. She had fractured her hip and spent two weeks at the hospital following hip replacement surgery. Ironically at around the same time she cancelled by telephone her membership to a private health fund she had joined in July 1985 (at a cost of £49.88 per month). Her reasoning behind this decision seems not to have been financial but simply because the fund did not cover many of the problems she was now suffering from, including 'diverticulosis, toe trouble, diabetes, anxiety/depression or conditions aggravated by alcohol'.[491]

Despite yet another accident Joan remained on a high as the result of her role in *The Last of the Blonde Bombshells*. She made a good recovery from surgery and with the news of her forthcoming autobiography she was suddenly 'in vogue' again. Her brilliant performance as Betty delighted not only her fans but also friends and colleagues. Barbara Windsor for one was 'thrilled' at Joan's involvement in the production and even wished she'd been offered a role in the film. After watching her former co-star on television, Barbara also thought at that point Joan was 'alright health wise'.[492]

Joan decided to avoid any *Carry On* clichés in the title of her memoirs, instead opting to 'borrow' the title of *High Spirits* from one of her favourite revues of the 1950s. Commissioned by Partridge, a division of Transworld Publishers, the book was ghostwritten by Sean Magee; 'She couldn't have done it on her own,' admits Eleanor Fazan.[493] It provided the first major insight into Joan's life and career and was met with eager anticipation by Joan's countless fans.

Letters in Joan's private collection show that she travelled to Transworld Publishers' offices in Ealing in 1999 and was later invited to join their autumn sales conference in Bournemouth in September of that year.[494] Joan did indeed travel to the conference where she talked to about eighty people, including many of the publisher's sales team. She clearly charmed her audience as a further letter indicates: 'Thank you *very* much for your brilliant performance at our sales conference in Bournemouth last week. I hope you enjoyed yourself as much as we all did!' [495]

Released to coincide with Joan's seventieth birthday in May 2000, *High Spirits* was well received and had the added bonus of considerably topping up Joan's bank account. While recent reports regarding her dwindling finances were slightly exaggerated, her substantial deal with Transworld at least gave monetary security at the end of her life and Pat Clayfield was able to assure the author quite unequivocally that 'Joan did *not* die penniless'.[496] Sadly Joan did not live long enough to reap the financial benefits of the paperback edition of the book, which was released in 2001.

Reviews of the book were very favourable. Roger Lewis[497] wrote one for *The Spectator* which he later sent to Joan along with a hand-drawn caricature of her holding a cocktail glass and cigarette (in a holder) underneath the caption 'Ding-Dong!', made famous by Leslie Phillips.

The Daily Telegraph meanwhile hailed Joan a 'national treasure' and Hugh Massingberd's review of 'our Joanie's' book labelled it 'good humoured, honest, straightforward, unpretentious, matter-of-fact, warm, generous... and at times unaffectedly moving'.[498]

The success of Joan's autobiography even prompted the possibility of her writing a cookbook, as confirmed by Pat Clayfield and private correspondence from the archives of Richard Hatton. Since Joan's interest in cooking had long since waned, the irony of this proposed venture was not lost on Bill Clayfield, who raised a knowing eyebrow when Joan discussed the possibility. The proposal certainly caused much self-deprecating laughter from Joan herself.

With the release of her autobiography Joan emerged from her self-induced seclusion to give a series of television and radio inter-views to help publicise the book. She even agreed to undertake a couple of signing sessions in local bookstores, giving *Carry On* fans the very rare opportunity to meet one of the last surviving icons of the series. A less high-profile appearance took place one Saturday afternoon in the summer of 2000 at a church fete in Hammersmith when she also signed copies of the book; 'She went there, she sat, she was charming, talked to everybody... boy did it go down well and nobody has ever forgotten it – everybody loved it!' recalled Pat Clayfield.[499]

According to the Bible we are each allotted three score years and ten. On 9th May 2000 Joan Sims reached that Biblical milestone when she celebrated her seventieth birthday. By this time she had completely recovered from her hip replacement operation and was looking forward to new work projects. Photographs of Joan taken by Neville Elder in her flat to mark the occasion showed that she had lost none of her prettiness and her unlined face defied her years. Dressed in powder blue with a co-ordinating scarf loosely placed around her neck and carefully chosen accessories, Joan appeared totally relaxed and it was clear to see that she was relishing her new-found contentment.

*

Amid the joy of *The Last of the Blonde Bombshells* and *High Spirits* came a storm cloud whipped up by the popular press which threatened to sabotage Joan's new-found happiness. In retrospect it resulted in one of her most difficult encounters with the press during her fifty-year career. It was almost as if in publishing her memoirs Joan had opened the gates to her private world – and private thoughts – which had been securely locked for so long.

The storm had certainly been brewing for at least a couple of years and began with the opening of Terry Johnson's play *Cleo, Camping, Emmanuelle and Dick* at the National Theatre in 1998. The production centred on the love affair between Sid James and Barbara Windsor which took place around 1973. After meeting with Terry Johnson, who wrote and directed the play, Barbara gave her full support to the venture – to the astonishment of many – and even attended the play's opening night.

Two years after the play's debut it was adapted for television as *Cor, Blimey!* (again directed by Terry Johnson) with Barbara Windsor featuring in a cameo role (as herself in the final stages of the film) as well as being a consultant on the film. The two stars of the play – Geoffrey Hutchings and Samantha Spiro (as Sid James and Barbara Windsor) – reprised their roles for the television production and were joined by Adam Godley (as Kenneth Williams), Hugh Walters (as Charles Hawtrey) and Chrissie Cotterill as Joan.[500]

The television adaptation aired for the first time on ITV in April 2000. Although Joan did not see the stage play, as a confirmed 'telly addict' she did watch the small-screen production which she subsequently described as 'unspeakably awful'.[501] Jack Douglas, by then in his early seventies and living happily in semi-retirement on the Isle of Wight, was interviewed by the *Daily Star* newspaper and branded the production as 'disgusting'. As the unofficial elder statesman and spokesperson for the *Carry On* series he went on to say:

> The *Carry On*s were family entertainment, but came over in this as homosexual, obscene, debauched and filthy.

Jack was especially upset about the on-screen portrayal of Kenneth Williams as a 'raving homosexual' and references in the film to 'bums and piles'. Equally upsetting to Douglas was Barbara Windsor's involvement in the production: 'I have the greatest respect for Barbara as an actress, but I'm at a loss to see how she went along with this programme… It's as if I never knew her.'[502]

The play and subsequent TV film left Joan 'fuming' and 'so bitterly upset'.[503] Her main concern centred on Valerie James, Sid's widow, and his children for whom she had immense sympathy.[504] Behind closed doors Joan expressed her anger to close friends about the whole situation although she did later 'repent' about some of the things she had said.[505] In her autobiography Joan wrote carefully that she felt Barbara could have been 'a little more circumspect when revealing her relationship with Sid' while ultimately admitting that the affair (and Barbara's handling of it) was none of her business.[506] During her 1998 interview for *What's A Carry On?* Joan would describe the intense interest in Sid's private life as 'quite unnecessary' and her voice almost broke when she urged that Sid's memory (and his family) should be 'left alone'.

Following an interview with *The Stage*, when Joan went on to further describe *Cor, Blimey!* as 'sleazy and horrid',[507] an article appeared in the *Daily Telegraph* which fuelled speculation regarding Joan's relationship with Barbara Windsor. Joan was quoted as saying:

> I loathed it, I have to say. Utterly, utterly tasteless and quite horrible. I don't know why Barbara had to rake it all up. I think the nice thing would have been that, on Sid's demise, it was all forgotten. I don't kiss and tell at all just because you hurt so many people. I haven't discussed it with Barbara and I don't want to. I just did not like it. She condoned it totally – of course she did.[508]

It would appear that the article was intended to spark a rift between 'the two great ladies of the *Carry On* films' and was ultimately deeply upsetting to Joan. Even Joan's description of Barbara as a 'tough cookie' was picked up on by the press, although arguably Joan had intended this to be a compliment to Barbara's professionalism and tenacity.[509]

Barbara Windsor clearly remembers Joan phoning her up – in tears – to apologise about what had been written. Her old co-star was totally sympathetic: 'The thing is Joanie wasn't used to press interviews… I knew what they could be like because by then I'd been in *EastEnders* for a while and was used to the press but Joan had only ever done the occasional interview for posh magazines.'[510] Those closest to Joan reiterate the fact that it was not in her nature to ever intentionally upset anyone, least of all Barbara, despite her heartfelt anger over *Cor, Blimey!*

Thankfully before the story turned into a disaster, which could easily have been labelled 'Carry On Feuding' by the press, both ladies were able to nip it in the bud.

During an interview with Sheila Johnstone, Joan discussed the play, the press and her relationship with Barbara Windsor:

> I talked to Barbara about it last night, in fact, and said, 'I get the feeling that they're wanting to make a little spat between thee and me,' and she said, 'So do I.' But I can assure everybody, and put their minds at rest, that we've ironed it out.[511]

Over the issue of a possible 'rift', Barbara confirms this was never an issue:

How could you not be friends with someone like Joan? She was a wonderful lady – always laughing and with an amazing giggle! I loved her – she was such a jolly, jolly person and in fact she was loved very much by everyone who knew her.

Barbara's affection and admiration for Joan is unquestionable. She admits that 'some of the best moments in the *Carry On*s were with Joan' and in particular loved Joan's appearance in *Carry On Up the Khyber*, a performance she considers 'magnificent'. To this day Barbara remains 'eternally grateful' for Joan's assistance in helping her master a French accent – something Barbara was required to adopt for her role as the maid in *The Boyfriend*. Although Barbara already knew that Joan was adept at a variety of accents she was still slightly amazed when Joan asked, 'Which part of France?' Likewise, when it came to doing an Irish accent Joan would ask, 'North or south?'[512]

The last time the two ladies would speak to each other was in the early autumn of 2000 when Joan rang Barbara for advice on where to buy a wig. Without any real justification, Joan had become concerned that her own hair was beginning to thin and sought the assistance of Barbara, who had worn wigs or hairpieces for most of her adult life. Barbara remembers Joan being worried about the cost of a wig made from real hair, but assured her old 'china' that a synthetic wig would look just as good and told her of a place in Notting Hill where she could buy one at a reasonable price.[513]

Interviews and publicity aside, Joan's biggest thrill was that she felt able to work again. Buoyed by the release of her autobiography and her role in *The Last of the Blonde Bombshells*, Joan remained optimistic about her future and the opportunity to continue her career. In one of her final interviews to promote her book she shared her thoughts on how she wanted to 'carry on':

I've been deprived of work because I've been physically unable to do it, but I'm now working on a pilot show for Radio 4. Really, I've lived to work all my life and see no reason to stop now.[514]

Dogged Persistence, a play for BBC Radio 4, turned out to be Joan's last major work as an actress. Recorded in the late summer of 2000, and specially written for Joan and Elizabeth Spriggs ('two of the great stalwarts of British acting'), it featured Joan as a widow who has to take on her husband's snappy dog, with Spriggs playing a dog

174

trainer. The afternoon play, produced by Cherry Cookson, also featured one of Joan's old RADA chums, James Grout. It was both fitting and pleasing that Joan would be reunited with Elizabeth Spriggs – who became friends with her during their time working together on *Simon and the Witch* in 1987/88 and had kept in touch ever since – for this final acting role.

*

After several busy months promoting her autobiography on television and radio and granting a handful of interviews with newspaper journalists, Joan quietly entered the Chelsea and Westminster Hospital in London in November 2000 for what was considered a 'routine' colon operation. She had been suffering from diverticulitis, a digestive disease of the lower bowel, for some time and this condition now required surgery. Unlike her late, lamented friend, Kenneth Williams, who thirteen years earlier had been terrified to face the surgeon's knife, Joan had no fears or undue concern regarding the operation.

The operation itself, which involved the removal of a small section of Joan's colon, was indeed routine and had been a planned procedure. Despite her underlying health problems Joan came through the surgery without incident and was not expected to remain in hospital for very long. Her cousin Yvonne remembered, 'She was so good and so well the day after the operation.'[515] Within a few days, although still in intensive care, she was walking around and 'lively, full of beans and looking well' and strong enough to invite Pat Clayfield to lunch with her (courtesy of a charity set up by Sir Elton John).[516] The Clayfields, convinced that Joan was going to be fine, even optimistically planned another holiday to Portugal for the three of them, to help Joan convalesce.

Eleanor Fazan also confirms that Joan was 'up and about and walking' after the operation but while still in hospital suffered a sudden and massive collapse.[517] Thereafter her health never fully recovered and she would remain hospitalised for the next seven months, initially in an induced coma to try to aid her recovery. For a lot of her time in hospital Joan was, surprisingly, in a public ward, although often shielded from view. Here, at least during her conscious periods, she had some degree of company and stimulation.

There were even brief moments of comic relief as Joan had to cope with another patient breaking wind constantly which caused her much laughter, but made others on the ward complain bitterly. Joan confided in Pat Clayfield, 'No one around here seems to have a sense of humour!'[518] It was just the kind of schoolboy antic guaranteed to tickle Joan's funny bone.

Joan's final illness proved to be a long, drawn-out affair and Eleanor Fazan admitted that the months following her operation were 'horrific' with Joan often slipping in and out of consciousness.

> I was told by the nurses to speak to her when she was unconscious but of course I wasn't sure if she could hear me. The nurses assured me that she could. When I next saw Joan and she was awake I asked if she remembered hearing anything of what I had said and she replied 'no' so I've had very little faith in the theory that unconscious people can hear things ever since.[519]

Joan's cousin Yvonne visited almost every day during her lunch breaks from work. On one occasion she remembers Joan sitting up in bed looking well and sprightly and enjoying a salmon sandwich, but on the whole Joan was usually unconscious when Yvonne visited.[520] Richard Hatton, Joan's agent, also visited and was accompanied on a couple of occasions by his wife, Elizabeth, who recalls holding an unconscious Joan's hand and talking to her at her bedside.[521]

Pat Clayfield was luckier and managed to talk to Joan on numerous occasions during the final weeks of her life. By the time Joan celebrated her seventy-first birthday in hospital on 9th May her health appeared at last to be improving. Pat Clayfield, holidaying in Portugal (with her husband and stepmother), rang her old friend and ended the conversation full of hope for the future:

> I rang Joan on her birthday and we thought she was going to get out and join us. The next thing we knew she rang me and said, 'I know things are not good Pat… something's wrong – can you come back?' We returned to London immediately.

Upon her return to London, Pat collected Joan's beloved teddy bear from her bedroom in Thackeray Street and took it into the hospital. Pat would later recall that when Joan woke and saw her old toy she briefly thought that she was back home in her own bed. The bear would remain with Joan until the end of her life and then with Pat.

Realising at this point that she was seriously ill, Joan thought about the need to write a will and discussed the idea with Pat. Joan requested that Pat bring her 'a shorthand notebook, two pencils, a pencil sharpener and a rubber' and announced that she was indeed going to write a will. On this subject Pat recalls:

> I would go in and ask, 'How are you getting on?' and she would say, 'I haven't started it yet Pat,' and I said, 'Well, probably there is no need, you won't need a will yet anyway for years… but you ought to think about it Joanie.' [522]

In the end Joan never did write a will and would die intestate. Under Probate, her estate was granted to her cousin Yvonne Doyle. The Probate document confirmed 'that the gross value of the said estate in the United Kingdom does not exceed £210,000 and the net value of such estate does not exceed £100,000'.[523] This amount did not of course include subsequent royalties and residuals earned from repeat fees from Joan's latter television appearances and the paperback edition of her autobiography. Heartbreakingly, at the very end of her life Joan did write a 'last, little note' to her 'Darling Pat'. Most of the writing was sadly illegible but the note did mention wanting 'to do lots of things' but 'not being able'.[524]

In the final period of her life Joan was visited by a handful of close friends but news of her long illness was mercifully kept out of the public domain, a testament to the loyalty and discretion of her friends and family and the professionalism of her agent, Richard Hatton. Even old colleagues and acquaintances such as Barbara Windsor and Oscar-winning costume designer Julie Harris (who in later years would occasionally speak to Joan on the telephone, not least because they shared the same cleaning lady, see Chapter 5) were unaware that for months Joan was seriously ill in hospital. Likewise, letters from Peter Rogers following Joan's death confirm that he too was unaware of her long period of ill health and hospitalisation. Offers of work continued to reach Richard Hatton's office during 2001 which he subsequently had to turn down, without revealing the true reason why.

The ever-loyal Eleanor Fazan, Norah Holland and Pat Clayfield remained vigilant visitors until the very end and her old friend and colleague Dilys Laye would call to read at Joan's bedside.

Around the 22nd of June 2001 Joan again slipped into a coma, from which she only briefly regained consciousness three days later.

During this time she was visited by a local priest who said the Lord's Prayer at Joan's bedside in the presence of Pat Clayfield and Joan's cousin, Yvonne. Pat admitted that Joan 'never went to church and never really discussed religion although she sometimes used to say her prayers' so the presence of a priest at her hospital bedside was slightly ironic.[525]

Even at the final stage of her life Joan's strength of spirit endured – impressing not only those closest to her but also hospital staff. In the end it was Norah Holland[526] who sat patiently holding Joan's hand as she breathed her last. She would recall her friend's final moments in a 2002 television documentary revealing that in the last minutes of Joan's life, as her breathing became laboured, she spoke to her old friend – convinced that Joan could hear her despite her comatose state. To the apparent amazement of Joan's doctors Norah told Joan to go and 'find' her old friends Hattie, Kenny and 'my Dutch' (Norah's late husband, Leslie Holland) as she gradually began to weaken.

Joan Sims died on 27th June 2001.

*

While there can be no doubt that Joan received the best level of care during her final illness, the exact cause of the 'collapse' she suffered, and never recovered from, remained something of a mystery – at least during her time in hospital. Pat Clayfield tried her best to find answers but not being a blood relative was limited in the information she could ascertain from hospital staff and remained somewhat frustrated by their vagueness.

Joan's cousin Yvonne felt the main problem was connected to Joan's chest. As a lifelong smoker, by the time she entered hospital she was suffering from chronic obstructive airways disease and 'constantly needed her chest clearing'.[527] The only real assurance given to both Yvonne and Pat was that Joan was not suffering from cancer. In 2013 Yvonne confided to the author the full details of Joan's long illness and death. Her memories of that time are raw and deeply personal and therefore remain private.

In the end it was only after Joan's death that an explanation for her long decline was given. Unbeknown to those closest to her, Joan was suffering from liver failure (as well as diverticular disease) and this was given as the primary cause of her death.[528] If, in Joan's words, her long-standing addiction to alcohol had been a matter between herself and her liver, it would ultimately prove to be her greatest downfall.

*

The news of the death of the 'Queen' of the *Carry On* series was announced by Richard Hatton on 28th June, ironically on the same day as the death of another comedy legend, the American actor Jack Lemmon (1925-2001). Although it was apparent from her auto-biography – and recent appearances on television – that Joan's health was declining, her death was nevertheless a shock to her many fans and even to colleagues who had not been aware of her condition. Precise details of the passing of the nation's favourite character comedienne were not forthcoming – nor would they be. A spokes-person for her agent stated simply and discreetly that she died having been ill for 'several months'.

Although Joan's death was largely overshadowed in the media by that of Jack Lemmon (indeed one television news announcement of her passing lasted a mere thirty-five seconds), media tributes quickly came pouring in for the actress who was truly loved by the public at large.

Patrick Janson-Smith, from Headline Publishers, remembered Joan fondly in one newspaper obituary:

> She was a really delightful woman, but quite a private person, living alone in a small rented flat in Kensington. She was not a great hoarder and did not have lots of memorabilia to remind her of her successes. When she was writing her book it was quite a job to coax the story out of her, but when she came to our sales conference she was an immediate hit. There was this instant warm glow of recognition shared by everyone there, from the ages of 21 to 70. She was a national treasure.

A touching tribute came from Barbara Windsor, by this stage busy again on the set of *EastEnders*:

> To me she was the last of the great Carry Ons. She was there from the beginning. Her talent was wonderful, she could do any accent, dialect, she could dance, sing, play dowdy and glam. We laughed all the time and giggled a lot. I will sorely miss her.

Joan's agent, Richard Hatton, who died in 2007 six years after Joan, also spoke warmly of his late client:

> I worked with her for the last five years and I got to know her very well. It is wonderful to be able to say that she really did have all the qualities her fans would have wished. She really did have a great sense of humour, a sympathetic and endearing personality, terrific talents and unfailing consideration for others. Everyone who knew her is going to remember her forever.[529]

Scriptwriter Dave Freeman wrote to the author on 28th June 2001:

> Sadly, today they reported that Joan Sims died. Almost the last of the old team, I first worked with her on radio in 1956 together with Ken Connor in a show called *The Floggits*. A very nice lady and a first-rate actress.[530]

Audrey Skinner, long-time personal assistant to Peter Rogers, was informed of Joan's death via telephone by Richard Hatton and passed on the news. Both Peter and Audrey would write to Richard expressing not only their sadness at Joan's death but also the impact it had on *Carry On* fans who had telephoned Pinewood Studios when the news was released.[531]

A more recent colleague, Gillies MacKinnon, had been delighted to work with Joan in *The Last of the Blonde Bombshells* and remembered her with fondness:

> More than anything else I remember feeling very warmly towards Joan and sad when I heard she died.[532]

Geoffrey Palmer, Joan's co-star in several productions, was also deeply saddened by Joan's death and echoed the sentiments of many when he admitted: 'I was deeply fond of her and one was very sad when she went.'[533]

A funeral service of praise and thanksgiving for the life of Joan Sims was held at Putney Vale Crematorium, on 5th July 2001. The service, conducted by the Reverend Dr Roger Curl, included two hymns, a tribute read by Robin Sewell and a reading by Keith Smith.[534]

Prayers followed before a second reading by Joan's lifelong friend and frequent co-star Dilys Laye:

> Everyone suddenly burst out singing:
> And I was filled with such delight

As prisoned birds must find in freedom,
Winging wildly across the white
Orchards and dark-green; on – on – and out of sight
Everyone's voice was suddenly lifted;
And beauty came like the setting sun:
My heart was shaken with tears; and horror
Drifted away... O, but Everyone
Was a bird; and the song was wordless;
The singing will never be done
   – Siegfried Sassoon (1886-1967)

With her impish real-life personality, Dilys was asked to read by Pat 'because she could always make things so joyful'.[535]

Following a private cremation[536] guests met afterwards at the Richmond Hill Hotel. Sadly a notable absentee from the funeral service was Norah Holland.[537]

While Joan's funeral, largely organised by Pat and Bill Clayfield, was an entirely private affair, a more public tribute would follow when a Thanksgiving Service was held in her memory at St Paul's Church, Covent Garden, at 12pm on Monday 22nd October 2001. Her dear friend Ronnie Barker was among the many actors who were present at the church and along with June Whitfield read a combined tribute which recounted the story of Joan's 'Tit Boxes'. It brought the house down. Sadly work commitments prevented a more recent friend, Dame Judi Dench, from attending the event.

Much was also made of Joan's 'lonely' life in many of the newspaper articles reporting her death. One went so far as to label her 'penniless and tormented by loneliness' which caused those closest to Joan a great deal of annoyance and unnecessary upset.[538] Inevitably the 'darker' side of the *Carry On* series would be linked to Joan's life, drawing comparisons to other 'cursed' *Carry On* actors, including Kenneth Williams, Charles Hawtrey and Frankie Howerd.[539] On the whole, however, the tributes were heartfelt and affectionate. She was, quite rightly, labelled the 'Queen' of the *Carry On* series, a witty comic star and an actress who had made millions of people laugh.

The fact that Joan ended her life and career very much in demand was largely overlooked by many newspaper obituaries. Although her work rate remained fairly constant during the last decade of her life, certain health constraints meant that she occasionally had to decline work and she was acutely aware of how dangerous this was to her career. However, following the release of her autobiography and her key role in *The Last of the Blonde Bombshells* Joan was very much in vogue again. Feeling that she was 'wanted' did wonders for Joan's state of mind and arguably at the end of her life and career she left her fans wanting more, something Pat Clayfield (amongst others) felt was 'the nicest way for her to go'. Many of Joan's contemporaries agree that at the end of her life she was happy and content, both personally and professionally. The success of her career was certainly undoubted.

Many journalists naturally commented on Joan's involvement in the *Carry On* series and the 'pittance' she was paid for starring in twenty-four of the films. One report blamed Joan's alleged financial hardships on 'the penny-pinching and sexual discrimination of *Carry On* producer Peter Rogers'.[540] In February 2002 Peter Rogers would hit back at constant criticism that he had exploited the stars of his phenomenally successful series and once again laid the blame very firmly with the agents of the actors involved:

> Joan was wonderful and I adored her… but she and the other actors were secondary to the main star: the *Carry On* title itself. They could all have been very comfortably off if they'd listened to me. Their lives might have been very different if they hadn't gone for quick payoffs instead of investing their talents in the *Carry On*s' success. I paid Joan and the other stars what their agents asked.

Rogers stood by his oft-repeated claim that all of the stars were offered a 'very low basic salary' with a 'percentage of the profits' but this was declined for their 'usual guaranteed regular fee'. In the same interview other *Carry On* stars were also recalled by Peter:

> Kenny [Kenneth Williams] was a strange character who was always moaning. He was usually very serious, but occasionally he'd break out and start showing off. I think he found life boring.

Of Sid James, Rogers would confess 'he wasn't my cup of tea' while admitting that Sid was 'a very good actor and an important member of the *Carry On* family'. His annoyance spilled over to one of the last surviving stars of the series – Barbara Windsor: 'I'm very fond of her, but years later she's still whingeing that I cheated and exploited her.'[541] On this subject Barbara was not alone. Many of the other actors from the films were equally annoyed at not receiving royalties from the series, particularly Joan's friend and colleague Liz

Fraser. Margaret Nolan, who featured in supporting roles in six *Carry On* films from 1965 until 1974, expressed her anger over the issue when contacted by the author in 1998:

> The most ever paid to an actor was £5,000 (Sid James). The producer (Peter Rogers) and director (Gerald Thomas) made the bulk of the costs bill – even at the time of shooting. However, what they received then is nothing on what they have received since. They have both become multi-millionaires and we have received nothing in royalties for the constant reruns on TV and all the videos, compilations etc. that have sold worldwide. I was informed by Equity that on the terminal illness of Charles Hawtrey, Peter Rogers refused any financial assistance to relieve him of his acute poverty (he had contributed so much to their wealth!).[542]

Towards the end of her life Joan had also written to Peter Rogers to ask for financial assistance.[543] Despite being one of the last surviving 'stars' of the series by the time she contacted Rogers, Joan's request was refused, apparently because it would have opened the floodgates from other actors requesting the same thing. Although she did not dwell on the matter it remained a sore subject for Joan: 'I remember that she had bad money problems, and said how maddening it was to sit watching the *Carry On* films on TV, and she never got a penny from their showing,' recalled Thelma Ruby.[544]

Peter Rogers' longevity – he died on 14th April 2009 at the grand old age of ninety-five – meant that he outlived most of the stars of the *Carry On* series. Ironically the man who once said he would 'do anything for my actors except pay them' left £3.5 million in his will to the Cinema and Television Benevolent fund, a charity set up to help actors who have fallen on hard times.[545] Whether Peter Rogers was a saint or a scrooge or quite simply a very astute businessman is surely a matter of opinion – although it will undoubtedly continue to be fiercely debated by *Carry On* fans for years to come.

Thankfully Joan's memory was not blighted by the seemingly never-ending issue of *Carry On* royalties for long. More lasting and appropriate tributes would follow. On 29th September 2002 Barbara Windsor, whose star status through her role in *EastEnders* ensured good press coverage, unveiled a British Comic Heritage blue plaque at Joan's former residence in Esmond Court, Thackeray Street, Kensington. She was joined by a number of other famous faces including Eric Sykes,[546] Liz Fraser, John Inman, Jacki Piper and Anita

Harris. Members of Joan's family and her close friends were also at the event and a celebratory lunch followed the unveiling.

On 17th October 2004 there was a 'Carry On Tribute to Joan Sims' at Pinewood Studios organised by Morris Bright (of Brightside Productions). The event included a screening of highlights from Joan's career at Pinewood and a plaque was unveiled in her memory. A charity auction, including a specially commissioned oil painting of Joan, and a buffet dinner also featured on the day (tickets to which cost £60 each). Leslie Phillips and Peter Rogers presided over the event in addition to special guests including Jack Douglas, Fenella Fielding, Liz Fraser, Madeline Smith and Marianne Stone (Joan's sidekick in *Carry On Screaming* and *Carry On At Your Convenience*, making one of her final public appearances at the age of eighty-two).

In 2005 – on what would have been Joan's seventy-fifth birthday – a blue plaque funded by the Joan Sims Appreciation Society was unveiled by her cousins Audrey and Yvonne at the former Stationmaster's House at Laindon Railway Station to commemorate the years (1930-52) Joan had lived there. Jazz Fox, a professional Frankie Howerd impersonator, was on hand to entertain fans who had gathered at the station[547] and Darren Carey, who had organised the event, described the occasion as 'a magical day with a lovely turnout'.[548] A further tribute came in 2008 as Joan's name appeared on two Royal Mail postage stamps when cinema poster images of *Carry On Cleo* and *Carry On Screaming* were released as 50-pence and 72-pence stamps respectively to celebrate the fiftieth anniversary of the start of the *Carry On* series.

*

Over a decade after her death Joan's memory lives on. She clearly touched the lives of so many of her colleagues – not to mention millions of fans around the world. The success of the *Carry On* series alone has ensured that Joan's 'happy face' remains as well known today as it was in her heyday. Her starring roles in twenty-four of the classic comedy films are what she is best remembered for but countless repeats of television favourites such as *Only Fools and Horses*, *On the Up* and *As Time Goes By* have also ensured Joan's immortality as an actress. Her personal legacy on the other hand is one of strength and courage and above all a determination to succeed in a profession she loved.

It is worth remembering that Joan became a star actress in her twenties and remained a star until her death – yet she never rested on her laurels. Every new assignment was approached with extreme professionalism and enthusiasm. Her passion for acting meant that Joan relished each and every role she took on. Almost uniquely she managed to bring something different to each of the innumerable characters she played and in doing so ensured her position as one of Britain's finest actresses.

The final words on Joan are left to Angela Thorne, who perhaps summed up most fittingly how surviving friends and colleagues still feel about the sweet, modest lady, who entertained audiences for over fifty years and seemed impossible not to like. Angela's simple and heartfelt sentiments would surely have brought a tear to Joan's eye, when she wrote: 'I loved her and felt very privileged to know her. I miss her.' [549]

Carry On Credits 1959-78

Nurse (trainee nurse Stella Dawson)
Teacher (Miss Sarah Allcock)
Constable (WPC Gloria Passworthy)
Regardless (Lily Duveen)
Cleo (Calpurnia)
Cowboy (Belle)
Screaming (Mrs Emily Bung)
Don't Lose Your Head (Désirée Dubarry)
Follow That Camel (Zig-Zig)
Doctor (Chloe Gibson)
Up the Khyber (Lady Ruff-Diamond)
Camping (Joan Fussey)
Again Doctor (Mrs Ellen Moore)
Up the Jungle (Lady Evelyn Bagley)
Loving (Miss Esme Crowfoot)
Henry (Queen Marie of Normandy)
At Your Convenience (Mrs Chloe Moore)
Matron (Mrs Tidey)
Abroad (Cora Flange)
Girls (Connie Philpotts)
Dick (Madame Désirée)
Behind (Daphne Barnes)
England (Private Jennifer Ffukes Sharpe)
Emmannuelle (Mrs Dangle)

Theatre Credits

Dates shown indicate when the play opened, and where known the closing dates have also been included.

Chorus girl.

Principal Girl (Arts Theatre, Glasgow).

1950: Made her professional stage debut in repertory in Chorlton-cum-Hardy (nine weeks' work).

Season of four plays (Regent Theatre, Hayes).

1950-51: Pantomime (Salisbury Arts Theatre).

1951: Rep at the Grand Theatre, Luton, for three months (appearing in a number of productions, including *The Cure for Love*).

1951: *Ann Veronica* (Q Theatre, with Joyce Howard).

1951-52: Principal Girl in Peter Potter's pantomime *The Happy Ha'penny* (Glasgow Citizens' Theatre).

Season of revue at the Players' Theatre. (Her London stage debut came at the Players' Theatre and she auditioned for Peter Myers, thus beginning a long working association.)

July 1952: Appearing in *Just Lately* and *The Bells of St Martin's* (An Intimate Revue) at St Martin's Theatre, Cambridge Circus. Cast: Douglas Byng, Hattie Jacques, Roma Milne, Richard Waring, Patricia Kelly, John Rutland, John Cronin and Peter Felgate.

September 1952: ASM in *Grand Guignol*.

31st December 1952: *Intimacy at Eight* (New Lindsey Theatre).

30th March 1953: *High Spirits* (King's Theatre, Edinburgh).

6th April 1953: *High Spirits* (Her Majesty's Theatre, Edinburgh).

13th April 1953: *High Spirits* (King's Theatre, Glasgow).

20th April 1953: *High Spirits* (Royal Court, Liverpool).

27th April 1953: *High Spirits* (Pavilion, Bournemouth).

West End debut in May 1953 in *High Spirits* at the Hippodrome which ran for 125 performances. Cast: Diana Churchill, Cyril Ritchard, Ian Carmichael, Thelma Ruby, Dilys Laye, Leslie Crowther, Patrick Cargill, Marie Bryant, Eleanor Fazan, Ronnie Stevens, Maxwell Coker, Valerie Carton and John Walters.

31st December 1953: *More Intimacy at Eight* (New Lindsey Theatre).

19th April 1954: *Intimacy at 7.45* (Theatre Royal, Brighton).

29th April 1954: (renamed) *Intimacy at 8.30* (Criterion Theatre, London, 552 performances ending on 10th September 1955). Cast: Joan Heal, Dilys Laye, Aud Johansen, Eleanor Fazan, Ronnie Stevens, Digby Wolfe, Geoffrey Hibbert, Ron Moody and Peter Felgate.

30th April 1956: Jubilee in *Man Alive!* (Theatre Royal Brighton).

7th May 1956: *Man Alive!* (Royal Court, Liverpool).

14th May 1956: *Man Alive!* (Opera House, Manchester).

21st May 1956: *Man Alive!* (Grand, Blackpool).

28th May 1956: *Man Alive!* (Theatre Royal, Newcastle).

4th June 1956: *Man Alive!* (Grand, Leeds).

14th June 1956: *Man Alive!* (Aldwych Theatre, London, 84 performances running until 25th August 1956).

3rd March 1958: Lily Thompson in *Breath of Spring* (Theatre Royal, Nottingham).

10th March 1958: *Breath of Spring* (Theatre Royal, Brighton).

17th March 1958: *Breath of Spring* (Grand, Wolverhampton).

26th March 1958: *Breath of Spring* (Cambridge Theatre, London).

8th September 1958: *Breath of Spring* (Duke of York's, succeeded by Sheila Hancock on 16th February 1959).

13th July 1959: Barbara in *Milk and Honey* (Connaught Theatre, Worthing).

12th June 1961: *The Lord Chamberlain Regrets...!* (revue, Theatre Royal, Newcastle).

19th June 1961: *The Lord Chamberlain Regrets...!* (Royal Court, Liverpool).

26th June 1961: *The Lord Chamberlain Regrets...!* (Grand, Leeds).

3rd July 1961: *The Lord Chamberlain Regrets...!* (Opera House, Manchester).

10th July 1961: *The Lord Chamberlain Regrets...!* (Theatre Royal, Brighton).

17th July 1961: *The Lord Chamberlain Regrets...!* (Streatham Hill).

24th July – 8th August 1961: *The Lord Chamberlain Regrets...!* (Hippodrome, Golders Green).

23rd August 1961: *The Lord Chamberlain Regrets...!* (Saville Theatre, ran for 21 performances until 24th February 1962).

30th June 1964: Lavinia in *Don't Ask Me Dad* (State Cinema, Kilburn). This was later renamed *Instant Marriage* and opened at the Piccadilly Theatre on 1st August 1964, running for 366 performances until 19th June 1965. Cast: Bob Grant, Harold Goodwin, Paul Whitsun-Jones, Wallas Eaton, Don McCorkindale, Rex Garner and Stephanie Voss.

19th October 1967 – 20th April 1968: Melanie Sinclair in *Uproar in the House* (Whitehall Theatre). Cast: Brian Rix, Nicholas Parsons, Peter Butterworth and John Louis Mansi.

19th August 1969: Lady Fidget in *The Country Wife* (Theatre Royal, Bath).

16th December 1971 – 12th February 1972: Queenie in *Goodtime Johnny* (Repertory Theatre, Birmingham). Cast: Ronnie Barker, Colette Gleeson, Valerie Griffiths, Eric Flynn, Adrian Lawson,

Malcolm Rennie, John Baddeley, Paul Chapman, John Gill, Adrian James and Felicity Harrison.

24th May 1977: *Order of Appearance* (roles included Queen Anne) at the Chichester Festival.

14th December 1984 – 1985: Sweetcorn, the Vegetable Fairy, in *Jack and the Beanstalk* (Richmond Theatre). Cast: Jimmy Edwards, Kenneth Connor and Suzanne Danielle.

1988: Delia in *Bedroom Farce* (Middle & Far East tour for Derek Nimmo: Inter-Continental Hotel, Dubai; Hilton International Hotel, Bahrain, 30th January – 4th February; Inter-Continental Hotel, Al Ain, 13th February).

Film Credits

1953

Will Any Gentleman...? (as Beryl)
Director: Michael Anderson
Cast: George Cole, Veronica Hurst, Heather Thatcher, Jon Pertwee, James Hayter, William Hartnell, Sidney James, Diana Decker, Jill Melford, Brian Oulton, Peter Butterworth, Lionel Jeffries, Lucy Griffiths, Eleanor Fazan.

Meet Mr Lucifer (as Fairy Queen)
Director: Anthony Pelissier
Cast: Stanley Holloway, Peggy Cummins, Jack Watling, Barbara Murray, Joseph Tomelty, Kay Kendall, Gordon Jackson, Raymond Huntley, Ian Carmichael, Irene Handl, Gladys Henson, Bill Fraser, Dandy Nichols, Geoffrey Keen (voice).

The Square Ring (as Bunty)
Director: Basil Dearden, Michael Relph
Cast: Jack Warner, Robert Beatty, Bill Owen, Sid James, Bill Travers, Maxwell Reed, George Rose, Joan Collins, Kay Kendall, Alfie Bass, Ronald Lewis, Sydney Tafler.

Trouble in Store (as Edna)
Director: John Paddy Carstairs
Cast: Norman Wisdom, Moira Lister, Megs Jenkins, Margaret Rutherford, Jerry Desmonde, Lana Morris, Michael Ward, Joan Ingram, Eddie Leslie, Michael Brennan, Esma Cannon, Ian Wilson.

1954

The Belles of St Trinian's (as Miss Dawn)
Director: Frank Launder
Cast: Alastair Sim, Joyce Grenfell, George Cole, Hermione
    Baddeley, Renée Houston, Betty Ann Davies, Beryl Reid, Irene
    Handl, Mary Merrall, Richard Wattis, Sid James, Arthur
    Howard, Michael Rimmer, Vivienne Martin, Barbara Windsor.

Doctor in the House (as Rigor Mortis)
Director: Ralph Thomas
Cast: Dirk Bogarde, Muriel Pavlow, Kenneth More, Donald Sinden,
    Kay Kendall, James Robertson Justice, Donald Houston,
    Suzanne Cloutier, Geoffrey Keen, Gudrun Ure (as Ann
    Gudrun), Shirley Eaton, Joan Hickson, Brian Oulton, Harry
    Locke, Cyril Chamberlain, Richard Wattis.

What Every Woman Wants (as Doll)
Director: Maurice Elvey
Cast: William Sylvester, Elsie Albiin, Brenda De Banzie, Brian Rix,
    Patric Doonan, Dominic Roche, Joan Hickson, Prunella Scales,
    Douglas Ives.

The Young Lovers (US: *Chance Meeting*) (as Telephone Operator at
    the American Embassy, uncredited)
Director: Anthony Asquith
Cast: Odile Versois, David Knight, David Kossoff, Joseph Tomelty,
    Paul Carpenter, Theodore Bikel, Jill Adams, Robin Estridge,
    George Tabori, Dora Bryan, Betty Marsden, Victor Maddern,
    Percy Herbert.

To Dorothy a Son (US: *Cash on Delivery*) (as Telephone Operator)
Director: Muriel Box
Cast: Shelley Winters, John Gregson, Peggy Cummins, Wilfrid
    Hyde-White, Mona Washbourne, Hal Osmond, Nicholas
    Parsons, Alfie Bass, Charles Hawtrey, Joan Hickson, Marjorie
    Rhodes.

The Sea Shall Not Have Them (as Hilda Tebbitt)
Director: Lewis Gilbert
Cast: Dirk Bogarde, Michael Redgrave, Bonar Colleano, Jack
     Watling, Anthony Steel, Nigel Patrick, James Kenney, Sydney
     Tafler, George Rose.

1955

Doctor at Sea (as Wendy Thomas)
Director: Ralph Thomas
Cast: Dirk Bogarde, Brigitte Bardot, Brenda de Banzie, James
     Robertson Justice, Maurice Denham, Michael Medwin, Hubert
     Gregg, Raymond Huntley, Geoffrey Keen, Jill Adams.

As Long As They're Happy (as Linda)
Director: J. Lee-Thompson
Cast: Jack Buchanan, Brenda de Banzie, Diana Dors, Jean Carson,
     Janette Scott, Susan Stephen, Jerry Wayne, Hugh McDermott.

1956

Lost (US: *Tears for Simon*) (as Ice Cream Seller in the Park,
     uncredited)
Director: Guy Green
Cast: David Farrar, David Knight, Julia Arnall, Anthony Oliver,
     Thora Hird, Eleanor Summerfield, Marjorie Rhodes.

Keep It Clean (as Violet Tarbottom)
Director: David Paltenghi
Cast: Ronald Shiner, James Hayter, Diane Hart, Ursula Howells,
     Jean Cadell, Colin Gordon, Norman Rossington.

The Silken Affair (as Lady Barber)
Director: Roy Kellino
Cast: David Niven, Wilfrid Hyde-White, Geneviève Page, Ronald
     Squire, Beatrice Straight, Howard Marion-Crawford, Dorothy
     Alison.

Too Happy A Face

Stars in Your Eyes (as Walters' secretary)
Director: Maurice Elvey
Cast: Nat Jackley, Pat Kirkwood, Bonar Colleano, Dorothy Squires, Vera Day, Hubert Gregg, Gabrielle Brune.

Dry Rot (as Beth)
Director: Maurice Elvey
Cast: Ronald Shiner, Brian Rix, Sid James, Michael Shepley, Joan Haythorne, Heather Sears, Peggy Mount, Lee Patterson.

1957

Just My Luck (as Phoebe)
Director: John Paddy Carstairs
Cast: Norman Wisdom, Jill Dixon, Leslie Phillips, Margaret Rutherford, Delphi Lawrence.

Davy (as Tea Lady)
Director: Michael Relph
Cast: Harry Secombe, Ron Randell, George Relph, Alexander Knox, Susan Shaw, Bill Owen.

Carry On Admiral (US: *The Ship Was Loaded*) (as Mary)
Director: Val Guest (also wrote screenplay)
Cast: David Tomlinson, Peggy Cummins, Ronald Shiner, Brian Reece, Ronald Adam, Alfie Bass, A. E. Matthews.

No Time for Tears (as Sister O'Malley)
Director: Cyril Frankel
Cast: Anna Neagle, Anthony Quayle, Sylvia Syms, Flora Robson, George Baker, Alan White, Daphne Anderson, Michael Hordern, Joan Hickson, Sophie Stewart, Rosalie Crutchley.

The Naked Truth (US: *Your Past is Showing*) (as Ethel Ransom)
Director: Mario Zampi
Cast: Terry-Thomas, Peter Sellers, Peggy Mount, Shirley Eaton, Dennis Price, Georgina Cookson, Miles Malleson, Kenneth Griffith.

1958

The Captain's Table (as Maude Pritchett)
Director: Jack Lee
Cast: John Gregson, Peggy Cummins, Donald Sinden, Nadia Gray,
    Maurice Denham, Richard Wattis, Reginald Beckwith, John Le
    Mesurier, Bill Kerr, Miles Malleson, June Jago.

1959

Passport to Shame (US: *Room 43*) (as Miriam, uncredited)
Director: Alvin Rakoff
Cast: Diana Dors, Herbert Lom, Eddie Constantine, Odile Versois,
    Brenda de Banzie, Jackie Collins, Lana Morris, Margaret Tyzack.

Life in Emergency Ward 10 (as Mrs Pryor)
Director: Robert Day
Cast: Christopher Witty, Rupert Davies, Dorothy Alison, Douglas
    Ives, Charles 'Bud' Tingwell, Wilfrid Hyde-White.

Carry On Nurse (trainee nurse Stella Dawson)
Director: Gerald Thomas
Cast: Kenneth Williams, Charles Hawtrey, Hattie Jacques, Wilfrid
    Hyde-White, Leslie Phillips, June Whitfield, Shirley Eaton,
    Terence Longdon, Kenneth Connor, Joan Hickson, Bill Owen,
    Susan Stephen, Susan Shaw, Ann Firbank, Cyril Chamberlain,
    Bill Oulton, Irene Handl, Hilda Fenemore.

Carry On Teacher (Sarah Allcock)
Director: Gerald Thomas
Cast: Kenneth Williams, Charles Hawtrey, Hattie Jacques, Kenneth
    Connor, Leslie Phillips, Ted Ray, Rosalind Knight, Richard
    O'Sullivan, Carol White, Cyril Chamberlain.

Upstairs and Downstairs (as Blodwen)
Director: Ralph Thomas
Cast: Michael Craig, Anne Heywood, Mylène Demongeot, James
    Robertson Justice, Claudia Cardinale, Sid James, Joan Hickson,
    Daniel Massey, Cyril Chamberlain.

Please Turn Over (as Beryl)
Director: Gerald Thomas
Cast: Ted Ray, Jean Kent, Leslie Phillips, Julia Lockwood, Tim Seeley, Charles Hawtrey, Dilys Laye, Lionel Jeffries, Joan Hickson, June Jago, Victor Maddern.

1960

Carry On Constable (as WPC Gloria Passworthy)
Director: Gerald Thomas
Cast: Sid James, Kenneth Williams, Charles Hawtrey, Hattie Jacques, Kenneth Connor, Leslie Phillips, Eric Barker, Shirley Eaton, Jill Adams, Joan Hickson, Freddie Mills.

Doctor in Love (as Dawn)
Director: Ralph Thomas
Cast: Michael Craig, Virginia Maskell, James Robertson Justice, Ambrosine Phillpotts, Liz Fraser, Irene Handl, Michael Ward, Nicholas Parsons, Fenella Fielding, Ronnie Stevens.

Watch Your Stern (as Ann Foster)
Director: Gerald Thomas
Cast: Leslie Phillips, Kenneth Connor, Eric Barker, Noel Purcell, Hattie Jacques, Spike Milligan, Eric Sykes, Sid James, David Lodge, Ed Devereaux, Robin Ray.

His and Hers (as Hortense)
Director: Brian Desmond Hurst
Cast: Terry-Thomas, Janette Scott, Wilfrid Hyde-White, Kenneth Connor, Kenneth Williams, Nicole Maurey, Joan Hickson, Oliver Reed, Barbara Hicks.

1961

Carry On Regardless (as Lily Duveen)
Director: Gerald Thomas
Cast: Sid James, Kenneth Williams, Charles Hawtrey, Hattie Jacques, Kenneth Connor, Liz Fraser, Esma Cannon, Terence Longdon, Bill Owen, Fenella Fielding.

Mr Topaze (US: *I Like Money*) (as Colette)
Director: Peter Sellers
Cast: Peter Sellers, Nadia Gray, Herbert Lom, Leo McKern, Martita
    Hunt, Michael Gough, Anne Leon, Billie Whitelaw, John
    Neville, John Le Mesurier.

No, My Darling Daughter (as Second Typist)
Director: Ralph Thomas
Cast: Michael Redgrave, Michael Craig, Roger Livesey, James
    Westmoreland, Juliet Mills, Renée Houston, Peter Barkworth,
    David Lodge, Carole Shelley, Terry Scott.

A Pair of Briefs (as Gale Tornado)
Director: Ralph Thomas
Cast: Michael Craig, Mary Peach, Brenda de Banzie, James
    Robertson Justice, Roland Culver, Liz Fraser, Ron Moody, Bill
    Kerr, Amanda Barrie, Judy Carne.

1962

Twice Round the Daffodils (as Harriet Halfpenny)
Director: Gerald Thomas
Cast: Juliet Mills, Donald Sinden, Donald Houston, Kenneth
    Williams, Ronald Lewis, Andrew Ray, Lance Percival, Jill
    Ireland, Sheila Hancock, Nanette Newman.

The Iron Maiden (US: *The Swingin' Maiden*) (as Nellie Carter)
Director: Gerald Thomas
Cast: Michael Craig, Alan Hale Jnr., Jeff Donnell, Cecil Parker, Noel
    Purcell, Roland Culver, Brian Oulton, Judith Furse, Jim Dale.

1963

Nurse on Wheels (as Deborah Walcott)
Director: Gerald Thomas
Cast: Juliet Mills, Ronald Lewis, Noel Purcell, Esma Cannon,
    Raymond Huntley, Athene Seyler, Norman Rossington, Joan
    Hickson, Renée Houston, Jim Dale, Deryck Guyler.

Too Happy A Face

Strictly for the Birds (as Peggy Blessing)
Director: Vernon Sewell
Cast: Tony Tanner, Graham Stark, Jeanne Moody, Valerie Walsh.

1964

Carry On Cleo (as Calpurnia)
Director: Gerald Thomas
Cast: Sid James, Kenneth Williams, Charles Hawtrey, Kenneth
   Connor, Jim Dale, Amanda Barrie, Julie Stevens, Sheila
   Hancock, Jon Pertwee.

1965

The Big Job (as Mildred Gamely)
Director: Gerald Thomas
Cast: Sid James, Sylvia Syms, Dick Emery, Lance Percival, Jim Dale,
   Edina Ronay, Deryck Guyler, Reginald Beckwith, Wanda
   Ventham.

San Ferry Ann (as Mum)
Director: Jeremy Summers
Cast: Wilfrid Brambell, David Lodge, Ron Moody, Graham Stark,
   Ronnie Stevens, Barbara Windsor, Rodney Bewes, Warren
   Mitchell, Lynne Carol.

Carry On Cowboy (as Belle Armitage)
Director: Gerald Thomas
Cast: Sid James, Kenneth Williams, Charles Hawtrey, Jim Dale,
   Peter Butterworth, Bernard Bresslaw, Angela Douglas, Jon
   Pertwee, Peter Gilmore, Percy Herbert, Sydney Bromley, Davy
   Kaye, Edina Ronay.

1966

Doctor in Clover (as Matron Sweet)
Director: Ralph Thomas
Cast: Leslie Phillips, James Robertson Justice, Shirley-Anne Field,
   John Fraser, Arthur Haynes, Fenella Fielding, Jeremy Lloyd,
   Noel Purcell, Eric Barker.

Carry On Screaming (as Emily Bung)
Director: Gerald Thomas
Cast: Harry H. Corbett, Jim Dale, Peter Butterworth, Fenella
  Fielding, Angela Douglas, Charles Hawtrey, Marianne Stone,
  Frank Thornton, Jon Pertwee.

Carry On Don't Lose Your Head (as Désirée Dubarry)
Director: Gerald Thomas
Cast: Sid James, Kenneth Williams, Charles Hawtrey, Jim Dale,
  Dany Robin, Peter Gilmore.

1967

Carry On Follow That Camel (as Zig-Zig)
Director: Gerald Thomas
Cast: Kenneth Williams, Phil Silvers, Charles Hawtrey, Jim Dale,
  Peter Butterworth, Bernard Bresslaw, Angela Douglas, Anita
  Harris, Peter Gilmore.

Carry On Doctor (as Chloe Gibson)
Director: Gerald Thomas
Cast: Kenneth Williams, Sid James, Frankie Howerd, Hattie
  Jacques, Charles Hawtrey, Jim Dale, Bernard Bresslaw, Dilys
  Laye, Peter Butterworth, Anita Harris.

1968

Carry On Up the Khyber (as Lady Ruff-Diamond)
Director: Gerald Thomas
Cast: Sid James, Kenneth Williams, Charles Hawtrey, Bernard
  Bresslaw, Peter Butterworth, Roy Castle, Terry Scott, Angela
  Douglas, Cardew Robinson, Julian Holloway, Peter Gilmore.

1969

Carry On Camping (as Joan Fussey)
Director: Gerald Thomas
Cast: Sid James, Kenneth Williams, Charles Hawtrey, Hattie
  Jacques, Bernard Bresslaw, Peter Butterworth, Barbara
  Windsor, Dilys Laye, Terry Scott, Betty Marsden, Julian
  Holloway, Sandra Caron, Trisha Noble.

Carry On Again Doctor (as Ellen Moore)
Director: Gerald Thomas
Cast: Sid James, Kenneth Williams, Charles Hawtrey, Hattie
    Jacques, Jim Dale, Bernard Bresslaw, Peter Butterworth, Barbara
    Windsor, Patsy Rowlands, Pat Coombs.

1970

Carry On Up the Jungle (as Lady Evelyn Bagley)
Director: Gerald Thomas
Cast: Sid James, Frankie Howerd, Kenneth Connor, Bernard
    Bresslaw, Terry Scott, Jacki Piper, Valerie Leon.

Doctor in Trouble (as Russian Captain)
Director: Ralph Thomas
Cast: Leslie Phillips, Harry Secombe, James Robertson Justice,
    Angela Scoular, Irene Handl, Robert Morley, John Le Mesurier,
    Graham Stark, Freddie Jones, Jacki Piper.

Carry On Loving (as Esme Crowfoot)
Director: Gerald Thomas
Cast: Sid James, Kenneth Williams, Hattie Jacques, Charles
    Hawtrey, Terry Scott, Bernard Bresslaw, Patsy Rowlands,
    Imogen Hassall, Richard O'Callaghan, Jacki Piper, Bill
    Maynard, Peter Butterworth.

Carry On Henry (as Queen Marie)
Director: Gerald Thomas
Cast: Sid James, Kenneth Williams, Charles Hawtrey, Terry Scott,
    Barbara Windsor, Peter Butterworth, Peter Gilmore, Patsy
    Rowlands.

1971

The Magnificent Seven Deadly Sins (as Policewoman)
Director: Graham Stark
Cast: Bruce Forsyth, Bernard Bresslaw, Roy Hudd, Harry Secombe,
    Leslie Phillips, Julie Ege, Harry H. Corbett, Ian Carmichael,
    Alfie Bass, Spike Milligan, Ronald Fraser.

Carry On At Your Convenience (as Chloe Moore)
Director: Gerald Thomas
Cast: Sid James, Kenneth Williams, Charles Hawtrey, Hattie
 Jacques, Bernard Bresslaw, Kenneth Cope, Renée Houston,
 Jacki Piper, Richard O'Callaghan, Bill Maynard, Margaret
 Nolan, Marianne Stone.

1972

Carry On Matron (as Mrs Tidey)
Director: Gerald Thomas
Cast: Sid James, Kenneth Williams, Charles Hawtrey, Hattie
 Jacques, Bernard Bresslaw, Barbara Windsor, Kenneth Cope,
 Terry Scott, Bill Maynard, Valerie Leon, Madeline Smith.

The Alf Garnett Saga (as Gran)
Director: Bob Kellett
Cast: Warren Mitchell, Dandy Nichols, Adrienne Posta, Mike
 Angelis, John Le Mesurier, John Bird, Roy Kinnear.

Carry On Abroad (as Cora Flange)
Director: Gerald Thomas
Cast: Sid James, Kenneth Williams, Charles Hawtrey, Hattie
 Jacques, Peter Butterworth, Bernard Bresslaw, Barbara
 Windsor, Jimmy Logan, Sally Geeson, David Kernan, John
 Clive, Carol Hawkins, Gail Grainger.

Not Now, Darling (as Miss Tipdale)
Director: Ray Cooney
Cast: Leslie Phillips, Ray Cooney, Moira Lister, Julie Ege, Derren
 Nesbitt, Barbara Windsor, Jack Hulbert, Cicely Courtneidge,
 Bill Fraser.

A Christmas Carol (voice only, as Mrs Cratchit)
Director: Richard Williams
Cast: Alastair Sim, Michael Redgrave, Michael Hordern, Diana
 Quick, Melvyn Hayes.

1973

Carry On Girls (as Connie Philpotts)
Director: Gerald Thomas
Cast: Sid James, Barbara Windsor, Peter Butterworth, Bernard
Bresslaw, Jack Douglas, June Whitfield, Robin Askwith, Joan
Hickson, Valerie Leon, Jimmy Logan, David Lodge, Wendy
Richard.

Don't Just Lie There, Say Something! (as Lady 'Birdie' Mainwaring-
Brown)
Director: Bob Kellett
Cast: Brian Rix, Leslie Phillips, Joanna Lumley, Derek Royle, Peter
Bland, Katy Manning, Diane Langton.

The Cobblers of Umbridge (short) (as Lilian Beverly/Carol
Begorrah/Norah Pepper
Director: Ned Sherrin, Ian Wilson
Cast: Roy Kinnear, John Fortune, Lance Percival, John Wells,
William Rushton, Derek Griffiths.

1974

Carry On Dick (as Madame Désirée)
Director: Gerald Thomas
Cast: Sid James, Kenneth Williams, Hattie Jacques, Barbara
Windsor, Kenneth Connor, Bernard Bresslaw, Peter
Butterworth, Jack Douglas, Bill Maynard, Margaret Nolan,
Patsy Rowlands.

1975

Love Among the Ruins (TV) (as Fanny Pratt)
Director: George Cukor
Cast: Katharine Hepburn, Laurence Olivier, Colin Blakely, Richard
Pearson, Leigh Lawson, Gwen Nelson.

Carry On Behind (as Daphne Barnes)
Director: Gerald Thomas
Cast: Kenneth Williams, Elke Sommer, Kenneth Connor, Peter
    Butterworth, Bernard Bresslaw, Patsy Rowlands, Jack Douglas,
    Windsor Davies, David Lodge, Sherrie Hewson, Carol Hawkins,
    Liz Fraser, Marianne Stone.

One of Our Dinosaurs is Missing (as Emily)
Director: Robert Stevenson
Cast: Helen Hayes, Peter Ustinov, Derek Nimmo, Natasha Pyne,
    Bernard Bresslaw, Richard Pearson, Joss Ackland, Amanda
    Barrie, Deryck Guyler, Arthur Howard, Joan Hickson, Jon
    Pertwee, Kathleen Byron, Molly Weir.

1976

Carry On England (as Private Jennifer Ffoukes-Sharpe)
Director: Gerald Thomas
Cast: Kenneth Connor, Windsor Davies, Patrick Mower, Judy
    Geeson, Peter Butterworth, Melvyn Hayes, Diane Langton,
    Peter Jones, David Lodge.

1978

Carry On Emmannuelle (as Mrs Dangle)
Director: Gerald Thomas
Cast: Kenneth Williams, Suzanne Danielle, Kenneth Connor, Peter
    Butterworth, Jack Douglas, Beryl Reid, Larry Dann, Eric Barker,
    Claire Davenport, Victor Maddern.

1985

Deceptions (TV) (as Mrs Thirkell)
Director: Robert Chenault & Melville Shavelson
Cast: Stefanie Powers, Barry Bostwick, Jeremy Brett, James
    Faulkner, Sam Wanamaker, Fabio Testi, John Woodvine,
    Brenda Vaccaro, Fairuza Balk, Gina Lollobrigida.

1990

The Fool (as Lady Daphne)
Director: Christine Edzard
Cast: Derek Jacobi, Cyril Cusack, Michael Hordern, Corin
    Redgrave, Miranda Richardson, Maria Aitken, Paul Brooke,
    Rosalie Crutchley, Patricia Hayes, Stratford Johns, Hugh Lloyd,
    Preston Lockwood, Miriam Margolyes, Jim Carter, Don
    Henderson, Michael Medwin, Jonathan Cecil, Murray Melvin.

1993

One Foot in the Algarve (TV) (as Lady on Plane)
Director: Susan Belbin
Cast: Richard Wilson, Annette Crosbie, Peter Cook, Doreen
    Mantle, Edward de Souza.

Tender Loving Care (TV) (as Daisy Potter)
Director: Dewi Humphreys
Cast: Dawn French, Rosemary Leach, Peter Jones, Robert Pugh,
    Llewellyn Rees.

1995

Arabian Knight (aka: *The Thief and the Cobbler/The Princess and
    the Cobbler*) (voice only as Nurse/Mad Holy Old Witch)
Director: Richard Williams
Cast: Vincent Price, Anthony Quayle, Hilary Pritchard, Sean
    Connery, Kenneth Williams, Stanley Baxter, Donald Pleasence,
    Miriam Margolyes, Josh Ackland, Windsor Davies.

1996

The Canterville Ghost (TV) (as Mrs Umney)
Director: Sydney Macartney
Cast: Patrick Stewart, Neve Campell, Cheri Lunghi, Edward Wiley,
    Donald Sinden, Leslie Phillips, Daniel Betts.

2000

The Last of the Blonde Bombshells (TV) (as Betty)
Director: Gillies MacKinnon
Cast: Judi Dench, Ian Holm, Leslie Caron, Olympia Dukakis, Cleo
    Laine, Billie Whitelaw, June Whitfield, Thelma Ruby.

Television Credits

Include:

1951

Vegetable Village (five episodes)
John of the Fair (as Parlourmaid)

1952

Shop Window (with Hermione Baddeley)
Haul for the Shore (as Maisie)
Shadow Pictures

1953

The Blackbird
Hurrah for Halloween (as Mrs Grouse)

1955

The Makepeace Story Number 4 (as Audrey Fraser)
Curtains for Harry
London Playhouse – 'The General's Mess' (as Daffy Lovell)

1955-56

Here and Now (seven episodes)

1956

The Adventures of Robin Hood (as Nell)
'Theatre' (as Miss Phillips)
Colonel March of Scotland Yard (as Marjorie Dawson)
The Frankie Howerd Show (two episodes)
ITV Play of the Week – 'Traveller's Joy' (as Eva)

1957

The Buccaneers (two episodes, as Abigail)
Space (experimental colour transmission)
The Night Before Christmas
ITV Play of the Week – 'Accolade' (as Phyllis)

1958

On Monday Next (BBC Sunday Theatre)

1959

BBC Sunday Night Theatre: Brian Rix Presents – *Beside the Seaside*
 (as Mrs Pepper)

1960

Our House (series, thirteen episodes, with Hattie Jacques, Charles
 Hawtrey, Bernard Bresslaw and Norman Rossington)
ITV Television Playhouse – 'A Holiday Abroad'

1961

Off Centre (as Mavis Hunter)
BBC Sunday Night Theatre: Brian Rix Presents – *Basinful of Briny*
 (as Daphne Pepper)

Too Happy A Face

1962

Hugh and I (guest appearance, as Elsie)
Dial RIX – Nose to Wheel (two episodes, as Shirley Rix)

1963

The Stanley Baxter Show (series)
A Christmas Night with the Stars
This Is Your Life (Stratford Johns)
Juke Box Jury (panel member)
Don't Say a Word (as herself)

1963-64

The Dick Emery Show (two series, twelve episodes)

1964

The Benny Hill Show (special guest appearance)

1965

Thirty Minute Theatre – 'Love in Triplicate' (as Jill Watson)

1966

Comedy Playhouse – 'Seven Year Hitch' (as Isabel Conway, with
    Harry H. Corbett)
Call My Bluff (with Kenneth Williams)

1967

Sam and Janet (series, six episodes, as Janet)
Before the Fringe (seven guest appearances)
Beechan (produced by Herbert Chappell)
ITV Play of the Week – 'That Old Black Magic' (as Beryl Cockburn)
Till Death Us Do Part (guest appearance, as Gran)

1968

According to Dora (four guest appearances)
Love At Law (produced by Wallace Douglas)
Beryl Reid Says Good Evening
The Eamonn Andrews Show (guest, with Kenneth Williams)
Iolanthe (produced by David Croft)
Till Death Us Do Part (two guest appearances, as Gran)

1969

The Jimmy Logan Show
The Very Merry Widow (as Station Announcer)

1970

The Kenneth Williams Show (series)
The Odd Job (as Kitty Harriman)
Tarbuck's Luck (guest appearance)
Till Death Us Do Part (guest appearance, as Gran)

1971

The Goodies – 'Wicked Waltzing' (as Delia Capone)
Six Dates With Barker (guest appearance, as Kitty Harriman)
Decimal Five (series, voice only)
Father, Dear Father (guest appearance, as Miss Armitage)
A Christmas Carol (voice only, as Mrs Cratchit)

1972

Jackanory Playhouse – 'The Wednesday Wand'
Till Death Us Do Part (four guest appearances, as Gran)
Sykes (guest appearance, as Madge Kettlewell)
Carry On Christmas – Carry On Stuffing

1973

Seven of One (guest appearance, as Mrs Dawkins)
Ooh La La! – 'A Pig in a Poke' (as Amandine)
The Goodies – 'Way Outward Bound' (as Matron)
Sykes (guest appearance, as Madge Kettlewell)
Carry On Christmas

1973-74

Men of Affairs (four episodes, as Lady Mainwaring-Brown)

1974

Till Death Us Do Part (four guest appearances, as Gran)

1975

A Journey to London (as Lady Headpiece)
Carry On Laughing – 'The Prisoner of Spenda' (as Madame Olga),
    'The Baron Outlook' (as Lady Isobel), 'The Sobbing Cavalier' (as
    Lady Kate Houndsbotham), 'One in the Eye for Harold' (as
    Else), 'The Nine Old Cobblers' (as Amelia Forbush), 'The Case
    of the Screaming Winkles' (as Mrs MacFlute), 'The Case of the
    Coughing Parrot' (as Dr Janis Crunbit), 'Under the Round
    Table' (as Lady Guinevere), 'Short Knight, Long Daze' (as Lady
    Guinevere), 'And in My Lady's Chamber' (as Mrs Breeches),
    'Who Needs Kitchener?' (as Mrs Breeches).
This Is Your Life (Peter Butterworth)
Sykes (two guest appearances, as Madge Kettlewell)
Till Death Us Do Part (guest appearance, as Gran)

1976

The Two Ronnies (as Dowager Duchess of Arc)
Cilla (guest appearance)
East Lynne (series, as Joyce)
The Howerd Confessions (three guest appearances)

1977

Lord Tramp (series, six episodes, as Miss Pratt)
It's Your Move (pilot, as wife)

1978

Sykes (guest appearance, as Madge Kettlewell)

1978-80

Born and Bred (two series, eight episodes, as Molly Beglar)

1979

In Loving Memory (guest appearance, as Annie Potter)

1979-80

Worzel Gummidge (eight guest appearances, as Mrs Bloomsbury-
    Barton)

1980

Lady Killers – 'Suffer Little Children' (as Amelia Elizabeth Dyer)
Dick Turpin (guest appearance, as the Countess of Durham)
Virginia Fly is Drowning (as Mrs Rita Thompson) (N.B. Joan
    withdrew from the production after two days' filming following
    the death of Hattie Jacques)

1981

Lady Killers – 'Miss Elmore' (voice only)

1982

Educating Marmalade (guest appearance, as Signora Bandolini)
3-2-1 (Christmas Special)

Too Happy A Face

1983

An Audience with Kenneth Williams
Crown Court (guest appearance as Maureen Vairey)
Waters of the Moon (as Mrs Ashworth)
Hallelujah! (guest appearance, as Ella Scratchitt)

1984

Dramarama – 'Fowl Pest' (as Beryl)
Poor Little Rich Girls (as Madge Henshaw)
Cockles (guest appearance, as Gloria du Bois)
Hay Fever (as Clara)
Tickle on the Tum (guest appearance)
Breakfast Time ('Comedy Map of England', interview)

1985

Agatha Christie's A Murder Is Announced (as Miss Amy
    Murgatroyd)
The Golden Gong (interview)

1986

Movies from the Mansion – 50 Years of Pinewood (documentary
    special)
Doctor Who (guest appearance, four episodes, as Katryca)
In Loving Memory (two guest appearances)

1986-87

Farrington of the F.O. (two series, fourteen episodes, as Miss Annie
    Begley)

1987

Golden Gong – 50 Years of Rank's Films and Stars
Drummonds (guest appearance, as Mrs Fordham)

Super Gran (guest appearance, as Cat Burglar)
And There's More (as herself)
Only Fools and Horses (guest appearance as Auntie Reenie Turpin)

1987-88

Simon and the Witch (two series, thirteen episodes, as Lady Fox
    Custard)

1988

An Audience with Victoria Wood (herself)

1989

Victoria Wood – 'Val De Ree – Ha Ha Ha Ha Ha' (as Susan)
Blankety Blank (as herself)

1990-92

On the Up (three series, nineteen episodes, as Mrs Fiona Wembley)

1990

Cluedo: Christmas special (as Mrs White)

1992

Tonight at 8.30 – 'Fumed Oak' (as Mrs Rockett)
Boys from the Bush (two episodes)

1993

Smokescreen (series, six episodes, as Mrs Nash)
The New Celebrity Squares (as herself)

1994

The New Celebrity Squares (as herself, with Bob Monkhouse, Willie
    Rushton, Wendy Richard and John Inman)
As Time Goes By (two guest appearances, as Madge Hardcastle)
My Good Friend (two guest appearances, as Miss 'Pickles' Byron)
Martin Chuzzlewit (mini-series, as Betsy Prigg)

1995

Pie in the Sky (guest appearance as Harriet Coverly)
Just William (guest appearance as Mrs Miggs)
As Time Goes By (three guest appearances, as Madge Hardcastle)

1996

Hetty Wainthropp Investigates (guest appearance, as Adele
    McCarthy). Cast: Patricia Routledge, Dominic Monaghan
My Good Friend (guest appearance, as Miss 'Pickles' Byron)
As Time Goes By (two guest appearances, as Madge Hardcastle)

1997

As Time Goes By (guest appearance, as Madge Hardcastle)
Spark (guest appearance, as Aunt Hattie)
Noel's House Party (guest appearance as Fairy Queen)
Cluedo (video game, as Mrs White)

1998

What's a Carry On? (documentary/interview)
As Time Goes By (guest appearance, as Madge Hardcastle)

2000

This Morning (interview)
Gloria Hunniford's Open House (interview)

Additional credits include:

Pavlik
Laurier Lister Late Night Revue
As Others See Us
Spring Fling
Living Life Lately (pilot)

Radio Credits

Include:

1952

Rogues' Gallery
Trial and Error

1953

Top of the Town (with Terry-Thomas)
Knock Out

1954

Home and Away
Variety Playhouse
The Jimmy James Programme

1954-55

Ted Ray Time

1955

Calling Miss Courtneidge
Auntie Rides Again
Going Places... Meeting People
Man About Town
Christmas Crackers

1956-57

The Floggits (as Emma Steed, with Kenneth Connor and Elsie and
    Doris Waters)

1957

The Trouble with Today
Follow the Stars

1958

Toast of the Town

1959

Variety Playhouse
It's a Crime

1960

The Michael Medwin Show

1960-61

Something to Shout About (fifty-two episodes, as Mavis Willis)

1961

Roundabout

1962

London Mirror
London Lights

Too Happy A Face

1963

A Touch of the Sun
Star Parade

1964

Play It Cool ('Another Sort of Radio Show', with Ian Carmichael
   and Hugh Paddick)

1965

Who's Your Father (pilot)

1966

Today in Scotland (interview)

1966-68

Sam and Janet (as Janet)

1967

Late Night Extra (interview)
Roundabout (interview)

1968

A Bannister Called Freda (with Kenneth Williams)

1969

Open House

1969-70

Stop Messing About (with Kenneth Williams)

1970

Keeping Amy Kettle off the Road

1971

Open House
Rita Bollard's Favourite Programme

1972

Open House
Brothers in Law

1973

Late Night Extra (interview)

1976

Open House (interview)
The Story of Revue

1989

The Life of Kenneth Connor

1995

Today's The Day (BBC Radio 2, with Leslie Phillips, Ian Lavender
    and Barry Cryer)
Paradise Unbalanced (pilot)

1996

101 Dalmatians
England's Glory
Two Sisters
Passport to Pimlico

Too Happy A Face

1997

Miss Marple: 4.50 From Paddington (as Elspeth McGillicuddy)

1999

Bristow (series, with Liz Fraser)

2000

Dogged Persistence (with Elizabeth Spriggs)

Additional credits:

London Lights
Pigs Have Wings
Sixth Sense
Early Morning
Uncle Silas

Singles

Hurry Up Gran (1963)
Oh Not Again Ken (1963)
Spring Song (1963)
Men (1963)
The Lass With the Delicate Hair (1967) (directed by Johnny Harris,
    produced by Alan A. Freeman)
Sweet Lovely Whatsisname (1967)

Appendix A

Joan's performances during her time at RADA:

1st Term 1948:

The Shrew (as 1st Player, Tranis, Philip)
Dear Brutus (as Mrs Coade)

2nd Term 1949:

Secrets (as Susan, Mrs Eustace, Mainwaring)

3rd Term 1949:

After the Dance (as Julia Brown)
Romeo and Juliet (as Lady Capulet)

4th Term 1949:

His House in Order (as Millie Thorne)
Peace in Our Time (as Nora Shattock, Maudie)

5th Term 1950:

Cock a doodle Dandy (as Marion, ASM)
Fortunato (as Atamanta the Invincible)
Pavane for King Henry (as Katherine Howard)

6th Term 1950:

Dark Hours (as Old Woman)
King of Nowhere (as Sally Rimmer)

Finals 1950:

Giaconda Smile (as Doris Mead)
And So to Bed (as Mrs Pepys, Doll)

Appendix B

A small selection of items featured in the inventory of Joan's flat following her death.

The Entrance Hall

A late 19th century mahogany inlaid occasional table
A small late 19th century mahogany Sheraton revival display cabinet
A silver christening tankard engraved JS 1930
A baby's chewing ring and rattle with mother-of-pearl handle and silver repousse detail
A picture of a Mediterranean town roofscape and five assorted framed pictures

The Reception Room

An Edwardian walnut music cabinet
An antique pine corner cabinet
A circular mahogany tripod table and smoker's tripod table
An Edwardian mahogany and satinwood banded square revolving bookcase on a stand with four cabriole supports
A semi-circular Georgian mahogany fold-over games table with baize lined interior
An Edwardian rectangular overmantel glass in a gilt frame with shell cresting
An adjustable swivel chair in green leather-style cover and matching stool
A large two-seat sofa in cream cover, a matching armchair and draw stool
An oval Japanese Imari shallow dish and a pair of circular Imari plates with scalloped edges
A Coalport white and gilt part dessert set (12 items)

A cut-glass decanter with silver collar, a pair of cut-glass decanters, a claret jug and two further decanters

A green Chinese vase lamp, an alabaster vase lamp and sundry smokers' items

10 assorted framed pictures

Miss Sims' Bedroom

A 19th century Georgian style mahogany dressing chest

A Georgian mahogany circular tip-up occasional table

Four framed Vogue posters, a modern painting of Paris and sundry framed works

The inventory also included items in the guest bedroom (most notably an Edwardian occasional table), the kitchen and store room (where amongst other things were an ebonised display cabinet with bowed centre, a late 19th century walnut centre table and two oval bevelled looking-glasses).

Bibliography

Bright, Morris & Ross, Robert, *Mr Carry On – The Life and Work of Peter Rogers*, BBC, 2000.

Davies, Russell (editor), *The Kenneth Williams Diaries*, HarperCollins Publishers, 1993.

Davies, Russell (editor), *The Kenneth Williams Letters*, HarperCollins Publishers, 1995.

Fazan, Eleanor, *Fiz and Some Theatre Giants*, Friesen Press, 2013.

Hewson, Sherrie, *Sherrie – Behind the Laughter*, HarperCollins Publishers, 2011.

Lewis, Roger, *The Man Who Was Private Widdle*, Faber & Faber, 2001.

Lewisohn, Mark, *Radio Times Guide to TV Comedy*, BBC, 1998.

Merriman, Andy, *Hattie – The Authorised Biography of Hattie Jacques*, Aurum, 2007.

Parsons, Nicholas, *The Straight Man*, Orion, 1994.

Perry, Jimmy, *A Stupid Boy*, Century, 2002.

Phillips, Leslie, *Hello*, Orion Books, 2006.

Ross, Robert, *The Carry On Companion*, B.T. Batsford Ltd, 1996.

Sims, Joan, *High Spirits*, Partridge, 2000.

Stevens, Christopher, *Born Brilliant – The Life of Kenneth Williams*, John Murray (Publishers), 2010.

Waterman, Dennis, *ReMinder*, Hutchinson, 2000.

Whitfield, June, *…And June Whitfield*, Bantam Press, 2000.

Williams, Kenneth, *Back Drops*, Futura Publications, 1984.

Windsor, Barbara, *Barbara: The Laughter and Tears of a Cockney Sparrow*, Arrow Books, 1991.

Windsor, Barbara, *All of Me*, Headline Book Publishing, 2000.

Notes on the Chapters

Chapter 1

1   Joan Sims, *High Spirits*, Partridge, 2000, p. 2.
2   1911 Census records.
3   Yvonne Doyle, interview with the author, 2013.
4   Joan Sims, *High Spirits*, Partridge, 2000, p. 4.
5   1901 Census Records.
6   Yvonne Doyle, interview with the author, 2013. Joan never knew her paternal grandparents both of whom died in 1928.
7   The exact origins of the nickname are something of a mystery. Yvonne Doyle suspects her mother would have been called Richard if she had been a boy.
8   Letter from Joan Sims to her parents, courtesy of the estate of the late Joan Sims.
9   The children of George and Sarah Ladbrook: Noel (1923-1943), Geoffrey (1925-2005), Patrick (1928-2002) and Audrey Levenson (1929-2005).
10   *Express*, 24th December 1936.
11   *TV-AM*, Joan Sims interview, 1987.
12   *Breakfast Television*, 'Comedy Map of Britain', Joan Sims TV interview, 1984.
13   Eleanor Fazan OBE, interview with the author, 2011.
14   *Daily Mail*, 26th December 1998.
15   Joan Sims, *High Spirits*, Partridge, 2000, p. 12.
16   Joan Sims, *High Spirits*, Partridge, 2000, p. 19.
17   Joan's pianoforte reports from 1940 and 1941 survive to this day and showed that she passed her elementary and preparatory grades, gaining 79% and 72% respectively. Although Joan did not continue lessons for very long her early skills never left her and she was confident enough to

'tinkle the ivories' in her final role as Betty in *The Last of the Blonde Bombshells*.

18 *Basildon Standard*, 15ᵗʰ February 1964.

19 Athene Seyler CBE (1889-1990), a distinguished and long-lived stage and film actress who won the Gold Medal at RADA in 1908. Her stage career spanned over fifty years. Her character name in *Breath of Spring* was repeated in the feature film *Make Mine Mink* (1960), in which she starred with Terry-Thomas, Hattie Jacques, Elspeth Duxbury and Billie Whitelaw. Following RADA, Joan would later work on stage and screen with Miss Seyler. She died in 1990, aged 101.

20 One advantage to becoming a star actress before the age of thirty was that in later years Joan did not have to go through the ordeal of auditions to secure work in the profession.

21 *My Weekly*, 23ʳᵈ September 2000.

22 Joan's RADA reports, courtesy of the estate of the late Joan Sims.

23 Sir Kenneth Barnes (1878-1957), Director of the Royal Academy of Dramatic Art, 1909-1955. He was knighted in 1938.

24 Jimmy Perry, *A Stupid Boy*, Century, 2002. Jimmy would see Joan again fifty years later at Ronnie Barker's party and wrote, '… time had not been kind to her. Sadly she hardly recognised me', pp. 278-279.

25 Pat Clayfield, interview with the author, 2012.

26 Pat Clayfield, interview with the author, 2012.

27 *The Stage*, 30ᵗʰ March 1950.

28 Pat Clayfield, interview with the author, 2013.

29 Letter sent on behalf of Sir Kenneth Barnes, 1ˢᵗ May 1950, courtesy of the estate of the late Joan Sims.

30 This is the date given in Joan's autobiography. RADA's archives list Joan's last day at the Academy as 26ᵗʰ July 1950. Six receipts from the Autumn of 1948 to the Summer of 1950 were posted to Joan's father from RADA showing Joan's tuition fees of £21.00 per term (the equivalent of approximately £650 in 2013).

31 Joan Sims, *High Spirits*, Partridge, 2000, p. 31.

32 Joan's final RADA report, summer, 1950, courtesy of the estate of the late Joan Sims.

33 When told about the prize she received upon graduating Kenneth Williams would famously comment that it was ironic that Joan had subsequently spent most of her career 'falling on her arse'.

34 Letter to Joan from Dorothy Maher, 4th April 1950, courtesy of the estate of the late Joan Sims.

35 Joan wrote to the BBC to inform them that she was solely represented by Peter Eade on 12th July 1950, source BBC Written Archives.

36 Pat Clayfield, interview with the author, 2013.

Chapter 2

37 Pat Clayfield, interview with the author, 2012.

38 Bruce Copp, interview with the author, 2012.

39 Four years younger than Joan, Dilys Laye began her career on stage in 1948 and made her film debut in *Trottie True* in the following year. Pretty, dark haired and petite, Dilys was a natural extrovert and by 1954 had made her New York stage debut in *The Boy Friend* with Dame Julie Andrews. Dilys would later appear in four *Carry On* films, notably and aptly playing Joan's best friend in *Carry On Camping*. Her career on stage, screen and television lasted until her death from lung cancer at the age of seventy-four in 2009.

40 *The Sketch*, 13th January 1954.

41 *The Stage*, 1954.

42 Eleanor Fazan OBE, interview with the author, 2011.

43 Ron Moody, letter to the author, 2013.

44 Thelma Ruby, letter to the author, February 2012.

45 Fenella Fielding, interview with the author, 2012.

46 Pat Clayfield, interview with the author, 2012.

47 Eleanor Fazan OBE, letter to the author, 2014.

48 Pat Clayfield, interview with the author, 2012.

49 Pat Clayfield, interview with the author, 2012.

50 Anthony Asquith (1902-1968), film director whose credits included *Pygmalion* (1938), *The Winslow Boy* (1948), *The Way to the Stars* (1945) and *The Importance of Being Earnest* (1952). Joan had an uncredited role in his 1954 film, *The Young Lovers*.

51 Letter to Mr J. H. Sims from The Railways Executive London Midland Region, 3rd September 1952, courtesy of the estate of the late Joan Sims.

52 Pat Clayfield, interview with the author, 2012.

53 Joan Sims, *High Spirits*, Partridge, 2000, p. 56.

54 Joan Sims, *High Spirits*, Partridge, 2000, p. 53.

55 Fenella Fielding, interview with the author, 2012.

56   William Westwood, 2nd Baron Westwood (1907-1991).

57   Pat Clayfield, interview with the author, 2012.

58   Pat Clayfield, interview with the author, 2012.

59   Pat Clayfield, interview with the author, 2013.

60   Pat Clayfield, interview with the author, 2013.

61   Thelma Ruby, email to the author, 2014.

62   Deborah Ann Minardos died in 2006, aged seventy-four. Her son, Tyrone Power Junior, went on to become a film actor with appearances including *Cocoon* (1985), *Soulmates* (1992) and *Elvis in Paradise* (2005).

63   Courtesy of the estate of the late Joan Sims.

64   Bob Grant (1932-2003) perhaps best known as Jack Harper in the long-running comedy series, *On the Buses*. He committed suicide at the age of seventy-one.

65   Joan Sims, *High Spirits*, Partridge, 2000, p. 115.

66   *The Stage*, 6th August 1964.

67   Don McCorkindale, born 1940, the son of 'Big' Don McCorkindale, the South African heavyweight boxing champion, and the stepson of boxer and actor Freddie Mills (1919-1965). Don appeared in minor roles in *Carry On Sergeant* and *Carry On Cabby*.

68   Don McCorkindale, email to the author, 2013.

69   Joan Sims, *High Spirits*, Partridge, 2000, p. 116.

70   Pat Clayfield, interview with the author, 2012.

71   *Croydon Times*, 21st August 1964.

72   *The Stage*, 6th August 1964.

73   Patsy Rowlands (1931-2005) made her *Carry On* debut as Miss Fosdick in *Carry On Again Doctor* in 1969 and went on to appear in eight more *Carry On* films and an episode of *Carry On Laughing* (TV, 1975).

74   Nicholas Parsons CBE, interview with the author, 2013.

75   Nicholas Parsons, *The Straight Man,* Orion, 1994.

76   Nicholas Parsons CBE, interview with the author, 2013.

77   Patricia Franklin would go on to appear in a total of seven *Carry On* films, from *Carry On Camping* in 1968 to *Carry On England* in 1976. More recently she featured in *Shaun of the Dead* (2004) and *Hot Fuzz* (2007).

78   Lord Rix, letter to the author, 2013.

79   At the end of her life Joan refused to be photographed with a cigarette in case it would influence young fans to take up the habit. 'Terrible

habit. I smell like a road digger,' she admitted to journalist Deborah Ross (*Independent*, 29th May 2000).

[80] *The Stage*, 26th October 1967.

[81] Eunice Gayson (1928-), British leading actress perhaps best remembered as Sylvia Trench in the first two Bond films, *Dr No* and *From Russia with Love*. Eunice had worked with Joan in rep in 1954.

[82] Tim Goodchild, email to the author, 2013.

[83] Nicholas Ferguson, interview with the author, 2013.

[84] Paul Chapman, letter to the author, 2012.

[85] *The Stage*, 1971. Among the additional cast members of *Good Time Johnny* were Eric Flynn (1939-2002), the father of actors Daniel and Jerome Flynn, and the future *Doctor Who* star, Mary Tamm (1950-2012).

[86] *The Stage*, 2nd June 1977.

[87] Sir John Betjeman, Poet Laureate (1906-1984), Spike Milligan, English comedian, writer, musician and poet (1918-2002), Sir Tim Rice (1944-), the multi award-winning lyricist well known for his work with Andrew Lloyd Webber (Baron Lloyd Webber), and Aubrey Woods, English actor (1928-2013).

[88] *The Observer*, 19th August 1977.

[89] *TV-AM*, Joan Sims interview, 1987.

[90] *Photoplay Film Monthly*, July 1975.

[91] Pat Clayfield, interview with the author, 2012.

[92] Peter Jones (1920-2000), a well-known character actor who had also worked on *Carry On Doctor* and *Carry On England* after gaining fame on television as Mr Fenner in four series of *The Rag Trade* (1961-63 & 1977).

[93] Barry Evans (1943-1997) shot to fame on television in *Doctor in the House* and *Mind Your Language* in the 1970s. In later years he struggled to find acting work and was working as a taxi driver at the time of his mysterious death aged fifty-three.

[94] *New Straits Times*, 27th February 1988.

[95] *Gulf News*, 21st January 1988.

[96] Arnold Ridley OBE (1896-1984), writer of *The Ghost Train* and a well-known character actor. He made a cameo appearance in *Carry On Girls* in 1973 and starred in seven series of *Dad's Army* (1967-77).

Chapter 3

[97] Pat Clayfield, interview with the author, 2012.

[98] Eleanor Fazan OBE, interview with the author, 2011.

[99] Pat Clayfield, interview with the author, 2012.

[100] Eleanor Fazan OBE, interview with the author, 2011.

[101] David Kernan, email to the author, 2013.

[102] Michael Codron CBE, British film and theatre producer, born 1930. He was the original stage producer of *Not Now Darling*. Joan starred in the 1973 film version of the production.

[103] Cyril Chamberlain (1909-1974), a well-known character actor who appeared in more than a hundred feature films including seven *Carry On* films (*Sergeant, Nurse, Teacher, Constable, Regardless, Cruising* and *Cabby*) before his retirement in 1963.

[104] *The Stage*, 8th May 1958.

[105] *The Stage*, 17th November 1960.

[106] *Twice Round the Daffodils* (1962) was another such comedy, in which Joan featured in an effective supporting role opposite Kenneth Williams.

[107] Joan Sims, *High Spirits*, Partridge, 2000, p. 111.

[108] Pat Clayfield, interview with the author, 2012.

[109] The pair later worked together in *A Murder Is Announced*. In later years Sylvia Syms took on a variety of character roles, notably playing Queen Elizabeth, The Queen Mother in the 2006 Dame Helen Mirren film, *The Queen*. She received a belated OBE in 2007.

[110] Barbara Windsor MBE, interview with the author, 2012.

Chapter 4

[111] Pat Clayfield, interview with the author, 2012.

[112] Pat Clayfield, interview with the author, 2012.

[113] Following a serious illness in 1957, when she became paralysed and was not expecting to live, Pat Clayfield left the world of acting. She made a full recovery from her dramatic illness and in later years she worked for Collins Publishers in London.

[114] Pat Clayfield, interview with the author, 2012.

[115] Pat Clayfield, interview with the author, 2012

[116] Some sources spell Antony's name Anthony. Joan always referred to him as 'Tony'.

117 Joan Sims, *High Spirits*, Partridge, 2000, p. 81.
118 Nicholas Parsons CBE, interview with the author, 2013.
119 Patricia Baird died in June 1997 but as of October 2012 all of Antony's children were still alive, reference http://www.rootschat.com/forum/index.php?topic=69408.0.
120 Joan Sims, *High Spirits*, Partridge, 2000, p. 80.
121 Eleanor Fazan OBE, interview with the author, 2011.
122 *My Weekly*, 23rd September 2000.
123 Joan Sims, *High Spirits*, Partridge, 2000, p. 83.
124 Joan Sims, *High Spirits*, Partridge, 2000, p. 84.
125 Yvonne Doyle, interview with the author, 2013.
126 Pat Clayfield, interview with the author, 2012.
127 Eleanor Fazan, interview with the author, 2011.
128 *Daily Mail*, 26th December 1998.
129 Nicholas Parsons CBE, interview with the author, 2013.
130 Antony's death certificate gives his date of birth as 1st January 1919 and place of birth as 'U.K.' It seems likely that he was born in Glasgow, Scotland. His name is given as Anthony (rather than Antony) and no occupation was listed on the certificate. He died from lung cancer and chronic obstructive airways disease.
131 Pat Clayfield, interview with the author, 2012.
132 Joan Sims, *High Spirits*, Partridge, 2000, p. 174.
133 Pat Clayfield, interview with the author, 2012.
134 Pat Clayfield, interview with the author, 2012.
135 Pat Clayfield, interview with the author, 2012.
136 Joan Sims, *High Spirits*, Partridge, 2000, p. 85.
137 *Manchester Weekly News*, 4th July 1964.
138 Pat Clayfield, interview with the author, 2012.
139 Undated newspaper clipping from Joan's private collection, titled 'Unfashionable', courtesy of the estate of the late Joan Sims.
140 http://www.zoopla.co.uk/property/38-hurlingham-road/london/sw6-3rq/23172711
141 *Manchester Weekly News*, 4th July 1964.
142 *Basildon Standard*, 15th February 1964.
143 Sir Tom Courtenay, leading British actor born in 1937 and best known for his starring roles in films such as *Billy Liar* (1963) and *Doctor Zhivago* (1965). He was knighted in 2001.
144 Sir Tom Courtenay, interview with the author, 2013.

145 Noel Harrison (1934-2013), the actor/singer/athlete son of actor Sir Rex Harrison (1908-1990), best known for his 1968 hit recording of the song *The Windmills of Your Mind*.

146 *Basildon Standard*, 15th February 1964.

147 *Gravesend & Dartford Reporter*, 8th November 1963.

148 Nicholas Ferguson, interview with the author, 2013.

149 Christopher Stevens, *Born Brilliant – The Life of Kenneth Williams*, John Murray (Publishers), 2010, p. 260.

150 Barbara Windsor, *Barbara: The Laughter and Tears of a Cockney Sparrow*, Arrow Books, 1991, p. 77.

151 Joan Sims, *High Spirits*, Partridge, 2000, p. 136.

152 A version of Kenneth's proposal to Joan was featured in the television drama *Kenneth Williams: Fantabulosa* in 2006, with the character of Joan played by Beatie Edney. Here the pair was seen walking through the corridors of Pinewood Studios when Kenneth suddenly proposes, with the character of Joan turning him down.

153 Nicholas Ferguson, interview with the author, 2013.

154 Nicholas Parsons CBE, interview with the author, 2013.

155 Joe Grossi, email to the author, 2013.

156 Bruce Copp, interview with the author, 2012.

157 Pat Clayfield, interview with the author, 2012.

158 Pat Clayfield, interview with the author, 2013.

159 Sir Tom Courtenay, interview with the author, 2013.

160 Private information.

161 Deborah Ross, *The Independent*, 29th May 2000.

162 Pat Clayfield, interview with the author, 2012.

163 Pat Clayfield, interview with the author, 2012.

164 *Daily Mail* , 26th December 1998.

165 Nicholas Ferguson, interview with the author, 2013.

166 Joan Le Mesurier, interview with the author, 2012.

167 Fenella Fielding, interview with the author, 2012.

168 Pat Clayfield, interview with the author, 2012.

169 Nicholas Parsons CBE, interview with the author, 2012.

170 *Gulf News*, 21st January 1988.

171 Dilys Laye married secondly Alan Downer in 1972 and they had one son, theatrical agent Andrew Downer. Alan died in 1995. Barbara Windsor found lasting happiness when she married her third husband, actor Scott Mitchell, in 1999.

[172] Eleanor Fazan OBE, interview with the author, 2011.

[173] Eleanor Fazan OBE, interview with the author, 2011.

[174] *Manchester Weekly News*, 4th July 1964.

[175] Courtesy of the estate of the late Joan Sims.

[176] *TV Times*, 20-26th June 1987.

Chapter 5

[177] Christine Ozanne , letter to the author, 1998.

[178] Leslie Phillips, *Hello*, Orion Books, 2006, p. 204.

[179] Rosalind Knight, born 1933, the daughter of leading actor Esmond Knight (1906-1987) and stepdaughter of actress Nora Swinburne (1902-2000). She appeared in *Carry On Nurse* and *Carry On Teacher* and has since enjoyed a busy career on stage, screen and television.

[180] Joan had already worked with Ted Ray several years earlier on his radio series. She was a great fan of his work and the pair became good friends up until his death in 1977.

[181] Bright, Morris & Ross, Robert, *Mr Carry On - The Life and Work of Peter Rogers*, BBC, 2000, p. 92.

[182] Mark Lewisohn, *Radio Times Guide to TV Comedy*, BBC, 1998.

[183] Ernest Maxin, interview with the author, 2012.

[184] *Hampstead and Highgate Express*. Ernest Maxin and Leigh Madison enjoyed a long and blissfully happy marriage until her death at the age of seventy-four on 8th January 2009. They had one son, Paul. In addition to *Our House*, Leigh also appeared in minor roles in *Carry On Sergeant* and *Carry On Nurse*.

[185] *East London Advertiser*.

[186] Joan Sims, *Movie Mansions* interview, 1986.

[187] Nicholas Parsons CBE, interview with the author, 2013.

[188] Source: Bright, Morris & Ross, Robert, *Mr Carry On - The Life and Work of Peter Rogers*, BBC, 2000.

[189] Julie Harris, letter to the author, 2000.

[190] Information courtesy of the estate of the late Joan Sims.

[191] Pat Clayfield, interview with the author, 2012.

[192] Joan Sims, *High Spirits*, Partridge, 2000, p. 56, and Eleanor Fazan interview with the author, 2013.

[193] *Manchester Weekly News*, 4th July 1964.

[194] *Basildon Standard*, 15th February 1964.

195 *TV Mirror*, 21st February 1959.

196 Following this visit Joan received a letter from an employee of the Health Farm who had obviously warmed to her. Part of the letter reads: 'I don't want to appear to be rude but did you lose the amount of weight you wanted to loose, [sic] and do you feel better after your rest.' Private letter, February 1959, courtesy of the estate of the late Joan Sims.

197 Fenella Fielding, interview with the author, 2012.

198 *Basildon Standard*, 15th February 1964.

199 *Manchester Weekly News*, 4th July 1964.

200 *Photoplay Film Monthly*, July 1975.

201 Angela Douglas, letter to the author, 2013.

202 Fenella Fielding, interview with the author, 2012.

203 Joan had been asked by Arthur Haynes to appear in his highly successful television show. Sadly the appearance never came about since Haynes died suddenly on 19th November 1966, aged fifty-two.

204 Undated newspaper article from the archives of the late Joan Sims.

205 *El Espectador*, from the estate of the late Joan Sims.

206 Leon Greene, letter to the author, 1999.

207 Vincent Ball, letter to the author, 1998.

208 Joan Sims, *High Spirits*, Partridge, 2000, p. 148.

209 Joan Sims, *High Spirits*, Partridge, 2000, p. 126.

210 BBC Archives, reference 35/EKW. Joan's role in *The Night Before Christmas* earned her £66 in 1957 and her work in *Hurrah for Halloween* in October 1953 earned her £21.

211 *Hugh and I*, in which she played Elsie in July 1962, BBC Archives, ref. 35/DA.

212 *Sykes*, as Maude, 7th October 1973, paid £300, BBC Archives, Ref. 35/JW

213 Singer and actress Mary Millar (1936-1998) would find fame in later life as Rose in the popular sitcom *Keeping Up Appearances* (1991-95).

214 Mark Lewisohn, *Radio Times Guide to TV Comedy*, BBC, 1998.

215 *Radio Times*, 12th January 1966.

216 *The Stage*, 9th February 1967.

217 *Iolanthe* earned Joan £735 (BBC Archives, ref. 35/JDW) while *Love At Law* brought her a fee of £572 (BBC Archives, ref. 35/JM).

218 BBC Written Archives, Ref. 35/BH.

219 Joan was always a welcome guest of Frankie's – but sometimes an expensive one. After recording an episode of the 1976 series *The Howerd Confessions*, Frankie invited Joan to join him and his manager for a meal. Joan said she wasn't particularly hungry so opted for an omelette. The bill came to £45 for the three of them, causing Frankie to gasp, 'You said you weren't hungry. Heaven knows what would have happened if you'd been peckish!' Source: *The Sun*, 24th August 1976.

220 Anita Harris, conversation with the author, 2013.

221 Joan rarely played opposite Barbara Windsor in the *Carry On* films, although they did briefly cross swords in *Carry On Girls*. Likewise, Joan was only occasionally required to shoot scenes with Hattie Jacques. *Carry On* Christmas specials on television would see the three leading ladies of the series share more on-screen time, and Joan would also work with Hattie in episodes of *Sykes* on television in the 1970s.

222 Barbara Windsor MBE, interview with the author, 2012.

223 Sandra Caron, letter to the author, 1997.

224 Dilys Laye, letter to the author, 2001.

225 Russell Davies (Ed.), *The Kenneth Williams Diaries*, HarperCollins Publishers, 1994, p. 325.

226 Various versions of this story have been told and published.

227 Joan Sims, *High Spirits*, Partridge, p. 136.

228 Russell Davies (ed.), *The Kenneth Williams Diaries*, HarperCollins Publishers, 1994, p. 330.

229 Russell Davies (ed.), *The Kenneth Williams Diaries*, HarperCollins Publishers, 1994, p. 348.

230 Joan Sims, *High Spirits*, Partridge, 2000, p. 136.

231 Pat Clayfield, interview with the author, 2013.

232 Christopher Stevens, *Born Brilliant – The Life of Kenneth Williams*, John Murray (Publishers), 2010, p. 261.

233 Christopher Stevens, *Born Brilliant – The Life of Kenneth Williams*, John Murray (Publishers), 2010, p. 261.

234 Eleanor Fazan OBE, interview with the author, 2011.

235 Nicholas Ferguson, interview with the author, 2013.

236 Barbara Windsor MBE, interview with the author, 2012.

237 Letter courtesy of the estate of the late Joan Sims.

238 Source: Deborah Ross, *The Independent*, 29th May 2000.

239 Jacki Piper, born 1946, appeared in four *Carry On* films: *Carry On Up the Jungle, Loving, At Your Convenience* and *Matron*.

240 Jacki Piper, interview with the author, 2001.

241 *Radio Times*, 19th February 1970.

242 Anna Karen, conversation with the author, 2013.

243 Ray Brooks, email to the author, 2013.

244 Jimmy Logan OBE, letter to the author, 1999. Jimmy Logan died from cancer on 13th April 2001 aged seventy-three.

245 David Kernan, email to author, 2013.

246 *Gulf News*, 21st January 1988.

247 *The Stage*, 30th March 1967.

248 Joan would appear in several *Carry On* small-screen spin-offs, including eleven episodes of *Carry On Laughing* in 1975.

249 *The Stage*, 7th December 1972. Joan was paid £150 for her work on *Jackanory* in July 1972. BBC Archives Ref. MJR/ND. Her accident involved a glitter-covered metal star swinging towards her face and hitting her left eye. No treatment was necessary but the event was officially recorded on a BBC Accident and Industrial Disease Report Form, and Norman Rutherford subsequently wrote a note to Joan on 25th July 1972 to check on her well-being.

250 Barbara Windsor MBE, interview with the author, 2012.

251 *TV-AM*, Joan Sims interview, 1987.

252 *Daily Express*, November 1993.

253 *Daily Express*, 21st March 1974.

254 After the production wrapped Joan and Helen Hayes continued to exchange Christmas cards up until the latter's death at the age of ninety-two in 1993, and among Joan's possessions was a 1974 newspaper interview of Helen Hayes. In her autobiography Joan wrote that Helen Hayes even invited her to stay at her home in Mexico – a trip Joan never had the courage to take. (Norah Holland also became friends with Miss Hayes, and acted as her stand-in for *Hawaii Five-O*.)

255 Joan Sims, *High Spirits*, Partridge, 2000, p. 168.

256 Bruce Copp, interview with the author, 2012.

257 *Guardian*, April 1975.

258 Sherrie Hewson, *Sherrie – Behind the Laughter*, HarperCollins Publishers, 2011, p. 89-90.

259 Undated interview from Joan's private collection, circa 1973, titled 'Carry On stargazing with Roger Elliott', courtesy of the estate of the late Joan Sims.

Chapter 6

[260] David Kernan, email to the author, 2013.

[261] Bruce Copp, interview with the author, 2013.

[262] Joan Le Mesurier, interview with the author, 2012.

[263] Sir Tom Courtenay, interview with the author, 2013.

[264] Nicholas Ferguson, interview with the author, 2013.

[265] Sir Tom Courtenay, interview with the author, 2013.

[266] Eleanor Fazan OBE, interview with the author, 2011.

[267] Joan Le Mesurier, interview with the author, 2012.

[268] Sherrie Hewson, *Sherrie – Behind the Laughter*, HarperCollins Publishers, 2011, p. 90.

[269] Pat Clayfield, interview with the author, 2012.

[270] Pat Clayfield, interview with the author, 2012.

[271] The code to reach Joan via telephone was ring three times, ring off, ring three times, ring off, ring three times.

[272] Pat Clayfield, interview with the author, 2012.

[273] Eleanor Fazan OBE, interview with the author, 2011.

[274] Nicholas Ferguson, interview with the author, 2013.

[275] Lord Rix, letter to the author, 2013.

[276] Peter Quince, letter to the author, 2003.

[277] *The Sun*, 24th August 1976.

[278] *The Sun*, 24th August 1976.

[279] Joan Sims, *High Spirits*, Partridge, 2000, p. 154.

[280] Pat Clayfield, interview with the author, 2012.

[281] Fenella Fielding, interview with the author, 2012.

[282] *The Stage*, 16th December 1976.

[283] Until her appearance as Lady Daphne in the star-studded costume drama *The Fool* in 1990.

[284] http://news.bbc.co.uk/1/hi/entertainment/880386.stm.

[285] Source: *The Unforgettable Joan Sims*, 2002.

[286] David Kernan, email to the author, 2013.

[287] Pat Clayfield, interview with the author, 2012.

[288] Nicholas Ferguson, interview with the author, 2013.

[289] Pat Clayfield, interview with the author, 2012.

[290] Eleanor Fazan OBE, interview with the author, 2011.

[291] Deborah Ross, *The Independent*, 29th May 2000.

[292] Joan Sims, *High Spirits*, Partridge, 2000, p. 165.

[293] Pieter Rogers (1928-2006), not to be confused with *Carry On* producer Peter Rogers.

[294] Baby farm: a term given to the unregulated trade involving babies who were taken in, fostered or 'adopted' for a lump-sum payment, paid by the mother of the baby to another woman. Generally speaking a mother's decision to 'farm' her baby out was viewed with a great deal of stigma. A number of women became baby farmers simply to make money and failed to care properly for the children (leading to the early death of the child) or simply murdered them outright in order to 'farm' more children. Amelia Dyer ultimately pleaded guilty to just one murder (that of four-month-old Doris Marmon).

[295] Nicholas Ferguson, interview with the author, 2013.

[296] *TV Times,* 20-26th June 1987.

[297] *Gulf News,* 21st January 1988.

[298] Joan Le Mesurier, interview with the author, 2012.

[299] Pat Clayfield, interview with the author, 2012.

[300] *Basildon Standard,* 15th February 1964.

[301] *Manchester Weekly News,* 4th July 1964.

[302] Mary Jacques had telephoned Hattie complaining of feeling unwell. Hattie arrived at her mother's home just in time – Mary collapsed and died in her daughter's arms having suffered a pulmonary embolism. Source: *Hattie – The Authorised Biography*, by Andy Merriman, Aurum, 2007, p. 202.

[303] Andy Merriman, *Hattie – The Authorised Biography*, Aurum, 2007, p. 204

[304] Andy Merriman, *Hattie – The Authorised Biography*, Aurum, 2007, p. 205.

[305] Joan Le Mesurier, interview with the author, 2012.

[306] Joan Le Mesurier, interview with the author, 2012.

[307] Bruce Copp, interview with the author, 2012.

[308] Andy Merriman, *Hattie – The Authorised Biography*, Aurum, 2007, p. 210.

[309] Joan Le Mesurier, interview with the author, 2012.

[310] Joan Le Mesurier, interview with the author, 2012.

[311] At the time of Hattie's death Joan was contracted to play Mrs Rita Thompson in a television adaptation of *Virginia Fly is Drowning*. After completing six days' rehearsal and two days' filming Joan withdrew

from the project. BBC records show her contract was cancelled due to the artist being 'unwell'.

[312] *My Weekly*, 23rd September 2000.

[313] Pat Clayfield, interview with the author, 2012.

[314] Gladys's death, which occurred at St John's Nursing Home, 129 Haling Park Road, South Croydon, was registered by her brother-in-law, Malcolm John Mumford. Her date of birth was erroneously recorded on her death certificate as 1898, instead of 1896. She died from 'Bilateral Gangrene of Legs and Generalised Arteriosclerosis'. Source: Gladys Marie Sims, death certificate, 26th January 1981.

[315] Pat Clayfield, interview with the author, 2012.

[316] Kenneth Williams, *Back Drops*, Futura, 1983, p. 36.

[317] Yvonne Doyle, interview with the author, 2013.

[318] Joan Le Mesurier, interview with the author, 2012.

[319] Bruce Copp, interview with the author, 2012.

[320] Bruce Copp, interview with the author, 2012.

[321] Eleanor Fazan OBE, interview with the author, 2013.

[322] Pat Clayfield, interview with the author, 2012.

[323] Letter courtesy of the estate of the late Joan Sims.

[324] Joan Sims, *High Spirits*, Partridge, 2000, p. 174.

[325] Joan Le Mesurier, interview with the author, 2012.

[326] Eleanor Fazan OBE, interview with the author, 2011.

[327] Deborah Ross, *The Independent*, 29th May 2000.

[328] Pat Clayfield, interview with the author, 2012.

[329] Joan Sims, *High Spirits*, Partridge, 2000, pp. 174-175.

[330] Joan Sims, *High Spirits*, Partridge, 2000, p. 175.

[331] Pat Clayfield, interview with the author, 2013.

[332] Barbara Windsor MBE, interview with the author, 2012.

[333] Barbara Windsor MBE, interview with the author, 2012.

[334] Una Stubbs, letter to the author, 2012.

[335] Her one piece of television work in 1981 appears to have been providing the voice of 'Belle Elmore' in an episode of *Lady Killers*.

[336] Joan Sims, *High Spirits*, Partridge, 2000, p. 176.

[337] The Falklands War, 2nd April – 14th June 1982.

[338] Pat Clayfield, interview with the author, 2012.

[339] *Gulf News*, 21st January 1988.

[340] Eleanor Fazan OBE, interview with the author, 2011.

[341] Joan Le Mesurier, interview with the author, 2012.

342 Barbara Windsor MBE, interview with the author, 2012.

343 Nicholas Parsons CBE, interview with the author, 2013.

344 Bob Larbey, letter to the author, 2012.

345 Joe Grossi, email to the author, 2013.

346 Pat Clayfield, interview with the author, 2012.

347 Sylvia Syms OBE, interview with the author, 2012.

348 *Electronic Telegraph*, 28th August 2000.

349 Hattie Jacques notably declined an OBE for services to charity in 1976. Source: *Hattie – The Authorised Biography* by Andy Merriman, Aurum, 2007.

350 Pat Clayfield, interview with the author, 2012.

351 Vincent Graff, 1993.

352 The exceptions are *The Unforgettable Joan Sims*, a television documentary released in 2002, and the rather unflatteringly titled *Always the Bridesmaid*, a 2004 radio special about Joan and Pat Coombs, which included interviews with Liz Fraser, June Whitfield and Sir Norman Wisdom.

353 Elizabeth Spriggs' final role was in the Michael Caine film *Is Anybody There?* She died following surgery on 2nd July 2008 aged seventy-eight before the film had been released.

354 *Basildon Standard*, 15th February 1964.

355 Eleanor Fazan OBE, interview with the author, 2011.

356 Joan Sims, *High Spirits*, Partridge, 2000, pp. 200-201.

Chapter 7

357 Geoffrey Palmer OBE, interview with the author, 2013.

358 Sheila Steafel, email to the author, 2013.

359 Renée Asherson, letter to the author, 1998.

360 Sylvia Syms OBE, email to the author, 2012.

361 Paola Dionisotti, email to the author, 2012.

362 Paola Dionisotti, email to the author, 2012.

363 Stefanie Powers, letter to the author, 2012.

364 Garfield Morgan: English character actor, born 1931, well known on stage, screen and television. He was the second husband of Dilys Laye, and died ten months after her in 2009.

365 Joan was referring to seeing Leslie Phillips, Kenneth Williams, Kenneth Connor and Charles Hawtrey semi-nude as they ran from the showers

naked in one of their scenes. Posterior shots were seen in the final film release.

366 http://www.denofgeek.com/dvd-bluray/7761/doctor-who-trial-of-a-time-lord-dvd-pt1#ixzz2RDn27ioi

367 Joan Sims, *High Spirits*, Partridge, 2000, p. 180.

368 Mark Lewisohn, *Radio Times Guide to TV Comedy*, BBC, 1998.

369 Angela Thorne, letter to the author, 1997.

370 Angela Thorne, letter to the author, 2013.

371 John Quayle, letter to the author, 2012.

372 *TV Times*, 13-19th June 1987.

373 Gyles Brandreth, email to the author, 2013.

374 Deborah Ross, independent.co.uk website on 29th May, 2000.

375 *TV-AM,* Joan Sims interview, 1987.

376 David Kernan, email to the author, 2013.

377 David Kernan, email to the author, 2013.

378 Joan Le Mesurier, interview with the author, 2012.

379 Joan Le Mesurier, interview with the author, 2012.

380 Bruce Copp, interview with the author, 2012.

381 Nicholas Ferguson, interview with the author, 2013.

382 *Gulf News*, 21st January 1988.

383 *Daily Mail*, 26th December 1998.

384 Pat Clayfield, interview with the author, 2012.

385 *Daily Mail,* 26th December 1998.

386 Geoffrey Palmer OBE, interview with the author, 2013.

387 Fenella Fielding, interview with the author, 2012.

388 Pat Clayfield, interview with the author, 2012.

389 Russell Davies (ed.), *The Kenneth Williams Diaries,* HarperCollins Publishers, 1994, p. 440.

390 Yvonne Doyle, interview with the author, 2013.

391 Joe Grossi, email to the author, 2013.

392 Letter to Joan Sims from Francis Pan, Catering Manager, Shangri-La Hotel, Singapore, 29th February 1988, courtesy of the estate of the late Joan Sims.

393 Joan Sims' credit card receipt, courtesy of the estate of the late Joan Sims.

394 Joe Grossi, email to the author, 2013.

395 *TV-AM,* Joan Sims interview, 1987.

396 Joan Sims, *High Spirits*, Partridge, 2000, p. 181.

[397]   Barbara Windsor, *All of Me*, Headline Book Publishing, 2000, p. 233.

[398]   Joan Sims, *High Spirits*, Partridge, 2000, p. 181.

[399]   Kenneth Williams would later write about the 1984 fire and Charles Hawtrey's boyfriend languishing in the bedroom. Source: Russell Davies (ed.), *The Kenneth Williams Letters,* HarperCollins Publishers, 1995, p. 278.

[400]   Joan would also make a guest appearance in the second series of *Super Gran*, playing Cat Burglar, in 1987.

[401]   Gudrun Ure, letter to the author, 2003.

[402]   Barbara Windsor, *All of Me*, Headline Book Publishing, 2000, p. 395.

[403]   Source: Roger Lewis, *The Man Who Was Private Widdle*, Faber & Faber, 2001.

[404]   Barbara Windsor MBE, interview with the author, 2012.

[405]   The budget for *Carry On Cleo* was £194,323 with Gerald Thomas and Peter Rogers receiving £7,500 each. Sid James and Kenneth Williams received £5,000 each and Charles Hawtrey £4,000. Rather than her usual fee of £2,500 Joan received a basic rate of £125 per day for the film. Source: Robert Ross, *The Carry On Companion*, B. T. Batsford Ltd., 1996.

[406]   Nicholas Ferguson, interview with the author, 2013.

[407]   Joe Grossi, email to the author, 2013.

[408]   Joan Sims, *High Spirits*, Partridge, 2000, p. 150.

[409]   Nicholas Ferguson, interview with the author, 2013.

[410]   Eleanor Fazan OBE, interview with the author, 2011.

[411]   Receipt from The English Design Partnership, 20th May 1993, courtesy of the estate of the late Joan Sims.

[412]   Victoria Wood OBE, letter to the author, 2012.

[413]   *Gulf News*, 21st January 1988.

[414]   Dora Bryan OBE (1923-2014), leading British star character actress who appeared in *Carry On Sergeant* (1958) and *A Taste of Honey* (1961) for which she received a BAFTA Award. She appeared in two episodes of *On the Up* (playing Tony's mum) in 1990 and continued acting on stage, screen and television until 2006. She was often mistaken by members of the general public for Joan Sims (and vice versa).

[415]   Dennis Waterman, *ReMinder*, Hutchinson, 2000, p. 244.

[416]   Judy Buxton, conversation with the author, 2004.

[417] Judy Buxton, email to the author, 2013. Since her role in *On the Up* Judy Buxton has worked consistently in the theatre, often touring with her husband, actor Jeffrey Holland (best known as Spike in the long-running sitcom, *Hi-de-Hi!*, 1980-1988).

[418] Frankie Howerd OBE, died on 19th April 1992 aged seventy-five, just days before *Carry On Columbus* went into production.

[419] Barbara's last appearance in a *Carry On* film had been in 1974 although she had co-hosted *What A Carry On* in 1978 with Kenneth Williams and had featured in several television spin-offs in the early 1980s.

[420] Barbara Windsor, *All of Me*, Headline Book Publishing, 2000.

[421] In 2000 Bernard Cribbins would admit his memory of '*Carry On Columbus* has faded almost completely now – thank God!' Source: Bernard Cribbins OBE, letter to the author, 2000.

[422] Barbara Windsor MBE, interview with the author, 2012.

[423] Barbara Windsor, *All of Me*, Headline Book Publishing, 2000.

Chapter 8

[424] Betty Box, the wife of Peter Rogers, died from cancer on 15th January 1999, aged eighty-three. Her funeral in Amersham on 23rd January was one of the few Joan ever attended. Joan was seen to 'lock walking sticks' with director Ralph Thomas (1915-2001). Source: *Mr Carry On – The Life and Work of Peter Rogers* by Morris Bright and Robert Ross, BBC, 2000.

[425] Dame Judi Dench, letter to the author, 1997.

[426] Dame Judi Dench, email to the author, 2013.

[427] Geoffrey Palmer OBE, interview with the author, 2013.

[428] Pat Clayfield, interview with the author, 2012.

[429] Private letter, 13th July 1995, courtesy of the estate of the late Joan Sims.

[430] Letter from Bruce Douglas Mann, Douglas-Mann & Co., to Joan Sims, 30th August, 1996, courtesy of the estate of the late Joan Sims.

[431] Elizabeth Spriggs, letter to the author, 1997.

[432] Gulf News, 21st January 1988.

[433] Joan Sims, *High Spirits*, Partridge, 2000, p. 190.

[434] Joan Sims, *High Spirits*, Partridge, 2000, p. 190.

[435] Barbara Windsor MBE, interview with the author, 2012. Joan also encountered the same remark in her latter years – usually from taxi drivers.

[436] George Cole OBE, letter to the author, 2012.

[437] Cast Insurance Medical Certificate, 15th September 1994, courtesy of the estate of the late Joan Sims.

[438] Geoffrey Palmer OBE, interview with the author, 2013.

[439] Joan Le Mesurier, interview with the author, 2013.

[440] Sir Donald Sinden, interview with the author, 2013.

[441] Leslie Phillips, *Hello*, 2006.

[442] Following Peter Eade's death in 1979 Joan was represented by London Management and from 1986 until 1996 by Mahoney Gretton Associates.

[443] Joan Sims, *High Spirits*, Partridge, 2000, p. 190.

[444] Bob Larbey, letter to the author, 2012.

[445] Frank Middlemass, conversation with the author, 2004.

[446] Richard Griffiths OBE, letter to the author, 2012.

[447] *The Stage*, 15th August 1996.

[448] Leslie Phillips CBE, letter to the author, 1997.

[449] Pat Clayfield, interview with the author, 2013.

[450] Pat Clayfield, interview with the author, 2012.

[451] Alan Curtis, interview with the author, 1998.

[452] Guests at the *Carry On* 40th Anniversary celebrations at Pinewood Studios included Barbara Windsor, June Whitfield, Leslie Phillips, Jack Douglas, Fenella Fielding, Dilys Laye, Shirley Eaton, Bernard Cribbins, Norman Rossington, Brian Rawlinson, Betty Marsden, Anita Harris, Valerie Leon, Jacki Piper, Richard O'Callaghan, John Clive, Bill Pertwee, Alan Curtis, Norman Mitchell, Burt Kwouk, Liz Fraser, Alan Hume, Norman Hudis, Angela Grant, Marianne Stone, Suzanne Danielle and Frank Thornton.

[453] Peter Rogers, letter to the author, 1997.

[454] *My Weekly*, 23rd September 2000.

[455] Geoffrey Palmer OBE, interview with the author, 2013.

[456] Pat Clayfield, interview with the author, 2012.

[457] Pat Clayfield, interview with the author, 2013.

[458] *Daily Mail*, 26th December 1998.

[459] For many of her early starring roles on screen Miss Syms has never received royalties. It is worth noting that *Ice Cold in Alex* is still constantly repeated on television.

[460] Sylvia Syms OBE, interview with the author, 2012.

[461] Eleanor Fazan OBE, interview with the author, 2011.

[462] Source: Pat Clayfield, interview with the author, Joan Sims interviews and *High Spirits*, Partridge, 2000. Generally Joan preferred to drink tea rather than coffee and it was only in her latter years that she took to drinking large amounts of soft drinks.

[463] Nicholas Ferguson, interview with the author, 2013.

[464] Eleanor Fazan OBE, interview with the author, 2011.

[465] Pat Clayfield, interview with the author, 2012.

[466] Eleanor Fazan OBE, interview with the author, 2011.

[467] By this stage in her life Joan had given up driving and sold her car, something she debated about for a long time. Her car had become a nuisance, since parking was an issue, and she was reliant on friends and neighbours to occasionally start it for her.

[468] Jimmy Perry, *A Stupid Boy*, Century, 2002, pp. 278-279.

[469] Thelma Ruby featured in a minor role as Vera, a dementia patient, in *The Last of the Blonde Bombshells*.

[470] Jennifer Gosney, the first wife of actor Barrie Gosney (1926-2008). Jennifer's brother, Tony Walton, was the first husband (1959-67) of Dame Julie Andrews.

[471] Thelma Ruby, letter to the author, 2012.

[472] Thelma Ruby, letter to the author, 2012.

[473] Deborah Ross, *The Independent*, 29th May 2000.

[474] Undated interview from Joan's private collection, circa 1973, titled 'Carry On stargazing with Roger Elliott', courtesy of the estate of the late Joan Sims.

[475] Eleanor Fazan OBE, interview with the author, 2011.

[476] Nicholas Parsons CBE, interview with the author, 2013.

[477] Joan Sims, *High Spirits*, Partridge, 2000, p. 195.

[478] Television interview, *Open House with Gloria Hunniford*, broadcast 16th June 2000.

[479] Some correspondence did survive Joan's 'cull' – see Chapter 8.

[480] *Electronic Telegraph*, 28th August 2000.

[481] June Whitfield, *And June Whitfield*, Bantam Press, 2000.

[482] June Whitfield CBE, letter to the author, 2012.

[483] The same stick can be seen behind Joan when she lunched with Thelma Ruby in February 2000. She also used a foldable black walking stick and was photographed with this during a rare outing in September 1999 when she attended a party to celebrate the British Film Industry's Top 100 Film poll results.

484 In addition to the BAFTA and Golden Globe Awards, Dame Judi
     Dench received an Emmy Award Nomination for Outstanding Lead
     Actress (Miniseries or a Movie), a Screen Actors Guild Award
     Nomination (for Outstanding Performance by a Female Actor in a
     Miniseries or Television Movie) and an American Comedy Award
     Nomination for Funniest Female Performer in a TV Special. Sir Ian
     Holm received an Emmy Award Nomination for Outstanding
     Supporting Actor (Miniseries or a Movie). There were further Emmy
     Nominations for Outstanding Costume and Hairstyling.

485 *Electronic Telegraph*, 28th August 2000.

486 Annanova News Service (UK).

487 *Electronic Telegraph*, 28th August 2000.

488 Peter Rogers chose to cast Hattie Jacques in *Carry On Dick* in 1974,
     despite the fact that she was by that time deemed uninsurable for film
     work due to heart problems and high blood pressure.

489 Pat Coombs, letter to the author, 8th August 1999. Pat Coombs suffered
     from osteoporosis from 1998 although she continued to work on radio,
     notably with June Whitfield and Roy Hudd, until shortly before her
     death on 25th May 2002, aged seventy-five.

490 Joan Sims, *High Spirits*, Partridge, 2000, p. 199.

491 Private Health Care Membership Statement, courtesy of the estate of
     the late Joan Sims.

492 Barbara Windsor MBE, interview with the author, 2012.

493 Eleanor Fazan OBE, interview with the author, 2013.

494 Letter from Alison Barrow to Joan Sims, 16th June 1999, courtesy of the
     estate of the late Joan Sims.

495 Letter from Alison Barrow to Joan Sims, 20th September 1999, courtesy
     of the estate of the late Joan Sims.

496 Pat Clayfield, interview with the author, 2012.

497 Roger Lewis, born 1960, British writer whose biography of Charles
     Hawtrey *The Man Who Was Private Widdle* was released in 2002.

498 *Daily Telegraph*, 3rd June 2000.

499 Pat Clayfield, interview with the author, 2012.

500 Geoffrey Hutchings (1939-2010), now best known for his role as Mel
     Harvey in the ITV sitcom *Benidorm*, Samantha Spiro (1968-), an
     award-winning actress most recently familiar in television's *Grandma's
     House* (2010-12) and Chrissie Cotterill (1955-) perhaps still best

remembered as Debbie Burgess in television's *May to December* (1989-94).

[501] *Electronic Telegraph*, 28th August 2000.

[502] *Daily Star*, 26th April 1998. Interestingly the article featuring Jack Douglas's interview, titled 'Cor Slimey!', was kept by Joan and was among her personal papers following her death.

[503] Pat Clayfield, interview with the author, 2012.

[504] Valerie James and her family made a formal complaint to the Independent Television Commission (ITC) saying that 'the on-air promotion for Terry Johnson's play was misleading'. It was later ruled the programme should not have been described as a true story (*The Stage*, 21st September 2000).

[505] Pat Clayfield, interview with the author, 2012.

[506] Joan Sims, *High Spirits*, Partridge, 2000, p. 155.

[507] *The Stage*, August 2000.

[508] *Daily Telegraph*, 17th August 2000.

[509] Joan Sims, *High Spirits*, Partridge, 2000, p. 115.

[510] Barbara Windsor MBE, interview with the author, 2012.

[511] *Electronic Telegraph*, 28th August 2000.

[512] Barbara Windsor MBE, interview with the author, 2012.

[513] Barbara Windsor MBE, interview with the author, 2012. As far as is known Joan never bought a wig since only weeks later she was admitted to hospital.

[514] *My Weekly*, 23rd September 2000.

[515] Yvonne Doyle, interview with the author, 2013.

[516] Pat Clayfield, interview with the author, 2012.

[517] Eleanor Fazan OBE, interview with the author, 2011.

[518] Pat Clayfield, interview with the author, 2012.

[519] Eleanor Fazan OBE, interview with the author, 2011.

[520] Yvonne Doyle, interview with the author, 2013.

[521] Elizabeth Hatton, conversation with the author, 2013.

[522] Pat Clayfield, interview with the author, 2012.

[523] Source: Probate Grant, The District Probate Registry at Brighton, 23rd July 2001.

[524] Pat Clayfield, interview with the author, 2012.

[525] Pat Clayfield, interview with the author, 2012.

[526] Norah Holland died from pneumonia following a stroke at Wycombe Hospital, High Wycombe, on 8th January 2003. She was eighty-two years old.

[527] Yvonne Doyle, interview with the author, 2013.

[528] Joan's death certificate stated the primary cause of her death to be liver failure and diverticular disease. She was also suffering from diabetes mellitus and chronic obstructive airways disease. Most sources state that Joan died on 28th June 2001. This is erroneous and is merely the day her death was announced to the media by Richard Hatton.

[529] A former actor, Richard Hatton became one of Britain's leading theatrical agents, creating Richard Hatton Ltd in 1954. He discovered Sean Connery and among his other clients were Robert Shaw and writer Lukas Heller. He died on 18th September 2007.

[530] Dave Freeman (1922-2005), a prolific scriptwriter who worked on countless television and radio programmes from the 1950s. He also wrote the scripts for episodes of *Carry On Laughing* (TV, 1975), *Carry On Behind* (1975) and *Carry On Columbus* (1992). Source: letter to the author, 2001.

[531] Private letter from Peter Rogers to Richard Hatton, 28th June 2001, and private letter from Audrey Skinner to Richard Hatton, 4th July 2001.

[532] Gillies MacKinnon, email to the author, 2013.

[533] Geoffrey Palmer OBE, interview with the author, 2013.

[534] From Philippians IV 4-9. Revised Standard Version.

[535] Pat Clayfield, interview with the author, 2012.

[536] Joan's ashes were later scattered at Putney Vale Crematorium.

[537] Private information. Norah Holland was, however, present at Joan's Thanksgiving Service in October 2001.

[538] Gerald Kaufman, *Daily Mail*, 29th June 2001.

[539] *Daily Mail*, 2nd July 2001.

[540] Gerald Kaufman, *Daily Mail*, 29th June 2001.

[541] *Weekend*, 23rd February 2002.

[542] Margaret Nolan, letter to the author, 1998.

[543] This was confirmed to the author by Pat Clayfield with whom Joan discussed the matter and has also been written about by Joan's contemporaries.

[544] Thelma Ruby, letter to the author, February 2012.

[545] Andrew Young, *Mail Online*, 14th August 2009.

[546] Mr Sykes was contacted in connection with this book in May 2012 at which time he had suffered a fall and was unable to offer any assistance to the author. He died, aged eighty-nine, on 4th July 2012.

[547] Jaz Fox had also entertained guests at the Pinewood Studios tribute to Joan in October 2004.

[548] Darren Carey, conversation with the author, 2013.

[549] Angela Thorne, letter to the author, 2013.

Index